GUIDE TO

FLORIDA

FRUIT AND VEGETABLE GARDENING

First published in 2009 by Cool Springs Press, an imprint of the Quayside Publishing Group, 400 First Avenue North, Suite 400, Minneapolis, MN 55401 USA

Cool Springs Press titles are also available at discounts in bulk quantity for industrial or sales-promotional use. For details write to Special Sales Manager at Quayside Publishing Group, 400 First Avenue North, Suite 400, Minneapolis, MN 55401 USA.

To find out more about our books, visit us online at www.coolspringspress.com.

ISBN-13: 978-1-59186-464-6

Managing Editor: Cindy Games
Copyeditor: Billie Brownell
Design: Bill Kersey, KerseyGraphics

Photography
Chestnut Hill Tree Farm: 183, 185
Thomas Eltzroth: 113, 123, 147, 155
iStockphoto: 40, 57, 58, 66, 78, 89, 91, 95, 99, 100, 103, 107, 109, 115, 117, 134, 141, 143, 145, 163, 167, 168, 173, 187, 189, 191, 202, 205, 207, 209, 211, 215, 217, 230, 231
Jupiter Images: 8, 10, 11, 12, 15, 16, 19, 24, 34, 41, 43, 44, 47, 48, 50, 60, 61, 65, 62, 68, 69, 70, 71, 72, 73, 74, 75, 81, 85, 87, 89, 91, 95, 97, 98, 103, 105, 107, 109, 111, 115, 117, 129, 131, 137, 139, 141, 143, 145, 151, 153, 163, 165, 167, 171, 173, 175, 218, 187, 189, 191, 197, 199, 218, 221, 222, 225, 226, 227, 228, 229, 234
Joe Lamp'l: 29
Leu Gardens, City of Orlando: 17, 18, 20, 23, 27, 31, 41, 43, 44, 45, 47, 77, 83, 85, 87, 93, 97, 101, 105, 119, 120, 121, 125, 127, 133, 135, 148, 157, 159, 160, 171, 179, 180, 185, 193, 195, 197, 201, 207, 213, 223, 224, 232, 233, 236 238, 240, 241, 242, 245
Eric Schmidt: 177, 215
Neil Soderstrom: 52, 53, 55, 58

Printed in China
10 9 8 7 6

GUIDE TO

FLORIDA

FRUIT AND VEGETABLE GARDENING

ROBERT BOWDEN

Cool
Springs
Press

Growing Successful Gardeners™
www.coolspringspress.com
MINNEAPOLIS, MINNESOTA

DEDICATION

To my thoughtful and loving wife, Gailann

CONTENTS

Beans	Mustard
Beet	Okra
Broccoli	Onion
Brussels Sprouts	Parsley
Cabbage	Peanut
Cantaloupe	Pepper
Carrot	Potato
Cauliflower	Pumpkin
Celery	Radish
Collards	Rutabaga
Corn	Spinach
Cucumber	Squash
Eggplant	Strawberry
Endive	Summer Pea
English Pea	Sweet Potato
Garlic	Swiss chard
Kale	Tomato
Kohlrabi	Turnip
Leek	Watermelon
Lettuce	

WELCOME TO GARDENING IN FLORIDA

Growing plants in Florida can be a most rewarding experience.
No, let me rephrase that, it's lots of fun. As gardeners, we can
till the soil year-round, and the seemingly endless days of
sunshine and pleasant weather are the envy of our northern
gardening comrades. Plant roots enjoy the warm soil
throughout the year and their leaves enjoy bountiful rain in all
but a few months in late winter. For those interested in growing
vegetables and fruits, Florida is paradise. Cool mornings,
balmy days, rainy afternoons—what more could one ask for?

North Florida (the area from Pensacola to Jacksonville
south to Ocala) experiences a true change of seasons when fall
approaches, unlike the peninsula. Leaves turn brilliant shades
of red, yellow, and orange, and nighttime temperatures have

been known to reach single digits on occasion. The soil is often characterized as a sandy loam with clay in some places, and long-leaf pines and magnificent centurion live oaks dot the landscape. For those moving from more northern climes, areas of North Florida are the most like their former locations. Cold winters, cool springs, balmy summers, and pleasant autumns are the norm. The schedules of vegetable planting and harvesting are most like northern states, and pests and diseases are diminished as a result of winter's cold temperatures. Because of the soil's ability to retain moisture and nutrients, gardeners in North Florida can water less and apply fertilizer less often and in smaller amounts than their neighbors in Central and South Florida.

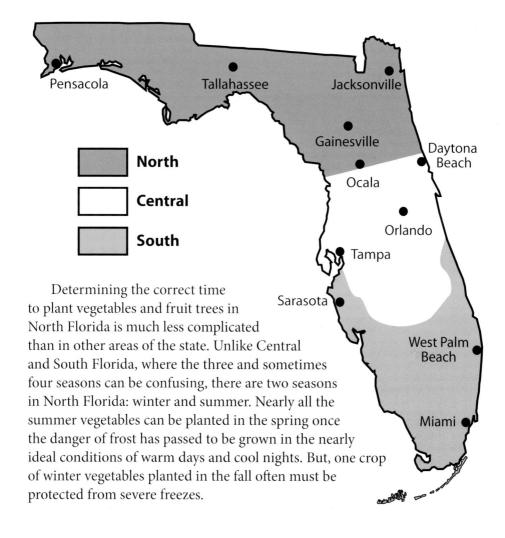

Determining the correct time to plant vegetables and fruit trees in North Florida is much less complicated than in other areas of the state. Unlike Central and South Florida, where the three and sometimes four seasons can be confusing, there are two seasons in North Florida: winter and summer. Nearly all the summer vegetables can be planted in the spring once the danger of frost has passed to be grown in the nearly ideal conditions of warm days and cool nights. But, one crop of winter vegetables planted in the fall often must be protected from severe freezes.

Central Florida (the area from Ocala to Lake Wales) has the best features of both North and South Florida. The soils, although low in nutrients, are sandy and drain well. (There are pockets of muck soils, which are highly organic but poorly drained, but they are the exception.) In the summer, from May to October, daytime temperatures get very hot (95°F) every day and nighttime temperatures rarely drop below 75°F. Autumn is of short duration, from November through December; winter includes January and February; and spring in Central Florida consists of March and April. If you have moved here from a more northern climate, scheduling the planting and harvesting of vegetables will be very confusing. As an example, tomatoes can be planted in the fall and the spring, but they will succumb

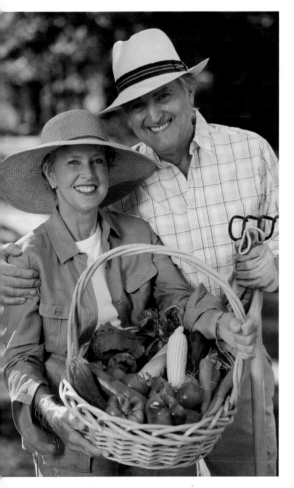

to winter cold and cannot grow in summer given our extreme summer heat. If you plant tomatoes too late in the fall, the occasional cold snap will kill them. If you plant too late in the spring, the summer heat will make them wish they were dead. That's why the planting table on pages 36–39 is so valuable. It takes all the guesswork out of the what, where, and when to plant.

The most difficult thing to get used to in Central Florida is the realization that you can't work outside all day like you can in North Florida. The older one gets, the less time one wants spend in the summer heat. In the summer, don't be surprised if you can't work past 11:00 a.m. I find that I often go outside after dinner to do a little gardening after the day has cooled just a bit. Wide brim straw hats are essential and you must have copious amounts of water close at hand whenever you are outside performing your gardening chores in Central Florida.

Because the sandy soil in Central Florida drains so well there is nothing to keep organic matter, water, and fertilizer from percolating right through the root zones of plants. While in North Florida a regular fertilization program may require two applications, in Central Florida four or five fertilizer applications are not uncommon. A small amount of fertilizer applied often to the plants is the norm. Applying water, however, is a different story. If you water often in small amounts, the roots tend to migrate close to the surface, and with the onset of hot weather the roots will likely die or be injured because of the heat. It's important to water *infrequently but deeply*. By watering for longer periods, the sheer weight of additional water will force it deep into the soil. Plant roots will follow the water and, in turn, will grow deeper into the cooler soil. When hot weather returns, the roots will be growing in deep, cool soil—just the way they like it. I often see homeowners merely sprinkling their landscape plants and lawn with a water hose and the tip of a finger; then they wonder why their plants die when hot weather comes along. Water deep for the best plant growth and leave the fingertip water sprinkling for washing the car.

The first time I added good, rich compost to my untouched vegetable garden soil, I thought I was finished. Later that season, most of the compost had either burned away in the hot sun or seeped deep into the soil, far away from the roots of my vegetables and fruits. Given that I have added four to five inches of compost to my garden every year for decades, the best I can figure is that my gardening counterparts in China must have some really good soil by now. The point is, you must add compost or organic matter to the soil every year or, even better, several times a year. Adding compost to the garden is not a onetime deal. The more you add the better the soil's ability to retain water and the less fertilizer you will have to add. An added benefit of a good, organic, rich soil is that you will have fewer numbers of nematodes (see page 57 for "Nematode Nemesis"). The sandy soils of Central Florida can be enriched with landfill compost (available free in most counties), homemade compost, oak leaves, peat moss—just about any natural material that will further decompose. In February and March, when the oak trees lose their leaves, I gather literally hundreds of bags from my neighboring street curbs and spread the contents over my entire garden. In the shrub borders I just let the leaves lay there as mulch; eventually, they will break down and add organic matter to the soil. In the vegetable garden I use them as mulch to hold the weed barrier down. Later, I turn them into the soil with a rototiller or shovel after the growing season is over.

I have one last thing to share about growing veggies and fruits in Central Florida: *everything* you have heard about the bugs is true. They are everywhere and they come in nearly every shape, size, and color you can imagine. Some bite, most suck, and many chew, but they all enjoy the little seedlings and seeds you thoughtfully place in the ground for them to eat. Because Central Florida doesn't get much cold weather compared to North Florida, pests can be a real problem. But, as you will read in this book, bugs rarely adversely affect healthy plants. Keep the plants healthy—well fed, well watered, and grown in adequate sunlight—and most will fare very well. There might be a need for an occasional "intervention" from time to time, but as long as the plants are growing well, bugs should not be a problem. Critters, such as slugs and nematodes, can be troublesome but they can be managed, also.

If there is a heaven on earth it's South Florida (which includes the tip of the peninsula and the coastal areas to Cocoa Beach on the east coast and to Tampa on the west coast). The greatest thing about living in South Florida is that, with minor exceptions, you can grow fruit and vegetables year-round. Due to South Florida's moderate temperatures (Key West has never had frost), growing tropical fruit trees is a passion of many gardeners there. Many of the tropical fruits that most of the civilized world only dreams about, such as mango, lychee, and avocado, all grow in backyards like apples grow in upstate New York. Do you need a banana for your corn flakes or orange juice for breakfast? Go into your backyard and pick some fresh fruit! Do you need a little snack after dinner? Well, go pick a cluster of longans, and eat them as you watch a colorful sunset on the horizon. Mango and papaya

Impress your neighbors! When cucumbers are still small, place a narrow-mouthed jar over the fruit and let the cucumber grow inside the jar. When the jar is filled, harvest the fruit (by cutting the cucumber off the vine), pour a little vinegar in the jar to cover the cucumber, and watch your neighbors try and figure out how you did that!

smoothies are minutes away. Your fresh star fruit salad will be a big hit at the next plant society's potluck.

The soil is variable in these areas and commonly ranges from sand to organically rich muck to limestone-rich "marl." Sandy soil is great for gardens provided you enrich it with compost. Marl, though, is another story all together. Marl is made of clay and calcium carbonate and as such is extremely difficult to work with. As you read the fruit tree sections in this book, you will notice that in many cases, the planting instructions indicate to place a tree *on top* of the marl and place a large bed of composted soil around the rootball in a ten- to twelve-foot diameter, to a depth of two feet. The tree's roots will never penetrate the marl; they'll simply grow in the prepared soil above the native soil. I remember when I lived in the Florida Keys contractors building houses would have to use dynamite to create a home's foundation; the backhoes couldn't budge the rock an inch. Of course, if you live in the muck-rich Homestead area, growing fruits and vegetables couldn't be easier.

The best use of the carwashing nozzle in a garden is to wash aphids off any new growth. For bad infestations, blast them twice a day.

That's the good news. If you thought bugs in North and Central Florida were bad, then take pity on the gardeners in South Florida. It rarely gets cold—we were looking for winter parkas when temperatures got down into the mid-sixties in the Keys. Apparently, bugs and diseases enjoy the mild temperatures, too. Diseases of all kinds are common because of the daily 3:00 p.m. rainstorms. You can drench or spray with copper or sulfur only to have it wash off the next day in the rain. The same goes for insecticides. There are cultural practices that can be utilized to alleviate some of the troubles such as planting resistant selections, choosing appropriate planting dates, and so forth. But, my recommendation is to simply know what you are getting into. If you haven't grown vegetables or fruit trees before, start small—one or two trees and a small garden plot is fine. As you become more proficient and you know what performs well and what doesn't, your garden can become larger and more trees can be planted. Gardening in South Florida is not a onetime activity—it's a journey.

GROWING YOUR OWN: THE GARDEN

Planning, planting, and harvesting vegetables are some of the rewarding life experiences that everyone should encounter. The satisfaction of being outside in the garden in the cool early morning while the dew still clings to the tomato leaves, the pleasure of digging in freshly tilled soil with its earthy scent, and the taste of eating a fresh-picked strawberry that you planted yourself just months ago are all pleasures everyone needs to feel once in this lifetime. In the garden you can listen to the neighborhood wake up in morning, and spend time with family at dusk. In your vegetable garden you can proudly share your bounty of green peppers with neighbors, and donate newly dug potatoes to the local food bank.

Library shelves are filled with books on how to raise vegetables, and one would think by the sheer number of pages that it is a complicated and difficult task to master. Let's just say it can be as complicated or as easy as you want it to be.

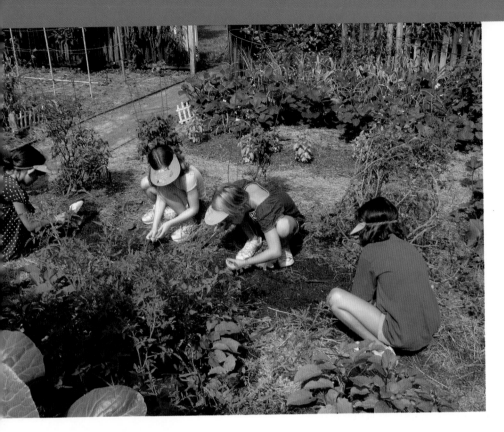

HOW TO GET STARTED

Why Grow Your Own?

There are many reasons to grow your own, but simply put, vegetables and fruit fresh out of the garden just taste better. If you have ever eaten an orange right off the tree, or munched on fresh snow peas right off the vine, you know what I mean. If you have never grown a garden before, well, you are in for a real treat.

Let's talk a bit about growing food for the first time. The home food gardening trend has become very popular but for the first-timer it may all seem more than a little overwhelming. Where should I place the garden? Do I even have enough sun? What about my dirt; is it okay, and if it's not, what do I do about it? What do I grow? When do I grow it? When do I pick it? For the "newbies"—relax. It's *okay* to make mistakes, and, boy oh boy, will you make them over the next few years! I still laugh at *my* slip-ups that I made decades ago. That's one thing we will all have in common; we'll share successes and failures. Gardening should always be fun and enjoyable. The minute it gets to be work, stop, and buy your food at a store.

For us old-timers, growing food is just what you're supposed to do. Our grandparents and parents did, and that's what we do, too. I must say, though, despite my years growing things, every year I learn something new—a new growing technique, a new harvesting sign, a new variety of "something," or a new tool. Reading a seed catalog that came in the mail is like reading a good book for the first time and not knowing the ending. Certainly with vegetables and fruit you know how it's *supposed* to end, but with plants, and weather, and the revolving cast of pest

characters, one never really knows how it will turn out until the very last chapter. Every season there are more than a few surprises, a twist in the plot.

Gardening creates memories. Someone in my office recently planted her very first vegetable garden. She invited her daughter and nearly two-year-old granddaughter to join her, and together they planted tomatoes and beans. It may not seem like much now but all of them will remember sharing that experience for a long time. Some of my best memories of my father are of him and me planting and later eating carrots and beans in the garden. My brother and I would occasionally have a ripe tomato fight in the kitchen (we'd spend days cleaning *those* messes), and my mother and I would can leftover vegetables for people in town who couldn't afford to buy any. I learned my ABCs by reading the plant descriptions in a Burpee Seed Company catalog, and I learned to write by oh, so, carefully printing my seed wish list on the order form. Life has become much more complicated since then, but the cycle of life in the garden remains the same. (I should text that to my almost-grown children.)

Especially now, growing your own fruit and vegetables is the right thing to do. Ever since I read Rachel Carson's book *Silent Spring*, I have believed we should all be on a never-ending quest to make the planet we live on a better place, one small step at a time. We can all do something to help the cause, and growing food without using harmful chemicals is my own way of effecting change. I'll be very honest: I have and still do, on occasion, use chemicals to slay a bug or disease, but I do everything else possible first and use them only as a last resort. There are some cultural growing techniques that will deter pests and diseases, and one of the purposes of this book is to share a few of those methods so that you will use them first and reach for the bug spray last. We can all play a part. The famous anthropologist Margaret Mead said, "Never underestimate the power of a few committed people to change the world. Indeed, it is the only thing that ever has."

When you grow vegetables and fruit you are sustaining yourself, if only partly, and for that reason growing food is a very personal thing as well. Certainly, as you increase your know-how, you'll feel more comfortable growing things, and the more you grow, the more you learn.

Getting Started

If you are new to gardening it can seem a bit daunting at first. After all, there are countless Internet pages dedicated to the subject, thousands of books discuss the topic ad infinitum (or is that ad nauseum), and home improvement stores dedicate entire departments to gardening. Where do you start?

Whether you are a seasoned gardener or new to the whole idea of digging in the dirt, remember that a small, well-maintained garden is better than a large, unkempt one. Even those of us who have been gardening for decades forget that, and we often plant more than we can care for, or even use or share. By season's end, believe me, you'll be cussin' that 20-foot row of yellow banana peppers. Small is better.

Remember, it's okay to make mistakes; just make certain you learn from them. That's where a garden journal comes into the scene. It doesn't have to be expensive or fancy; it can be a spiral-bound notebook. The important goal is find ways to make your garden better year after year. For instance, if you planted tomatoes in November only to see them killed by an early frost, write that down in your journal. Next year as you plan you'll know to plant the tomatoes sooner. Maybe one fertilizer works better than another. You will find that certain varieties of vegetables work better than others in your garden. The journal will help you remember the varieties that work best and the ones that didn't perform as well. I know many gardeners who actually staple an empty seed pack or two into the book to help jog their memories. Don't forget to review your notes from time to time, too. One of the trickiest parts of growing plants in Florida is knowing *when* to plant. If you have moved here from somewhere else or have never grown a food garden before, your journal will become your best friend and will remind you not only *what* to plant, but *when*.

Your neighbors and fellow gardeners are an invaluable source of information. If I have noticed one thing about gardeners, it's that they all are willing to share their experiences. Just mention the word, and they will help you any way they

> Place a birdbath in the garden to encourage birds to visit. Birds love to eat bugs and can help as automatic bug-eating machines.

can. Watch the newspapers and the Internet for notices about classes at garden centers or local botanical gardens. Most often taught by seasoned gardeners in the area, the speakers are invaluable to experienced and novice gardeners alike. Growing fruits and vegetables are always popular topics so be sure to sign up early. Classes will often be separated into beginner and expert levels, so there's no reason to be intimidated thinking that the class will be over your head. One more thing—because growing food is so popular, many botanical gardens have display gardens that demonstrate how and when to grow vegetables and fruit trees. Track down a gardener close by and ask questions—after all, that's what they get paid for.

Planning the Garden
Site Placement

You have heard people say that in real estate it's all about location, location, location. The same is true for growing fruits and vegetables. One of the biggest mistakes new gardeners make is to squeeze a vegetable garden or plant a fruit tree into a space where the microclimate isn't conducive to growing. A good example is the amount of sunlight a site receives; any amount over eight hours is fine, but don't think that six hours will be enough—it won't be. Plants grown in too little sun will grow long and "stretched." Because they are not receiving enough sun, they won't be able to produce an adequate amount of fruit. In just about every book I have read about gardening there is a chart that describes those vegetables and fruit trees that can grow in less than ideal sunlight. Don't fall for it. Planting where seeds or transplants don't get enough sun is asking for trouble. Because they don't get enough light, they will begin to suffer from stress and inevitably diseases and insects will move in. You will spend the rest of the plant's life trying to keep it bug free when, had it been planted in the right spot to begin with, it wouldn't have a problem.

The same advice works for drainage. Have you ever heard the phrase "You can't make a silk purse from a sow's ear"? If the site you're contemplating is soggy and wet most of the year, you need to think about building raised gardens. Unless the site has a slight slope to it or can be drained, you will be fighting a lost cause. On the other hand, if you have clay, be thankful that you will fertilize and water less than those of us growing in sand. Adding compost and/or sand to the planting location will aid the drainage.

Another thing to keep in mind—don't plant fruits and vegetables where there is competition for water and nutrients. Rototilling or using a shovel to turn the soil over is virtually impossible if nearby tree roots have extended into the place you have selected to plant your food garden. If you think annuals and perennials are hungry wait to see how much water a tree can suck up out of the ground. Not long after you have watered your veggie garden soil, it will be bone dry because the tree has thirstier (and more) roots than the squash. Likewise, fertilizer is absorbed by neighboring tree roots, so although the tree will be happy, the vegetables and fruit trees might not get enough "groceries" despite your best efforts.

Remember that many of the fruit trees described in this book can grow very large. Mangoes, for instance, can grow to 30 feet tall and 30 feet wide. Plant them where they have a chance to grow without being heavily pruned. Many of the small trees such as plums, nectarines, and peaches can be planted fewer than 15 feet away from a house or other structure, while others such as loquat and avocado are going to need some room. The more you have to prune, the fewer fruits you will have; so give them room to spread their branches.

Size Does Matter!

If you are new to growing vegetables, it may be difficult to judge how large or small your garden should be. Not to worry: Start small and adjust as needed. I discovered that as my family situation changed (departures, new arrivals, marriages), the garden changed, too. One of my children absolutely loved snow peas; in fact, he would come home after school and dash out into the garden to see if there were any to eat. Now that he is

married, no one else in the house likes them, so we don't grow them anymore. And that is how it should be. Simply jot down in your garden journal the veggies that everyone likes and grow those. Take my word for it, there is nothing more frustrating than to grow the "perfect 10" broccoli if no one eats it. That's wasted space that could have grown something someone would have enjoyed.

This is not to say that you shouldn't experiment with a new vegetable or two every season. Just like Picasso and his blue period, one year I had my "purple period" and the new veggies were all purple—purple cauliflower, purple kale, and purple mustard! Who knew if anyone would eat them, but they sure looked pretty out there in the Florida sun.

A small, well-maintained garden is better than a large, unkempt one. Even experienced gardeners need to be reminded of that. There is no shame in growing *one* tomato plant or *one* cucumber plant. Try your luck, see how they taste, see if they are easy or difficult to grow on your site, and see if anyone eats them. Remember, the next season isn't that far away in Florida; you can adjust then. Unlike our northern gardening friends, if the one tomato plant worked well this fall, next spring when you plant the spring tomato crop you can grow more. That's the great thing about living in Florida: something is always growing in the garden.

What to Grow?

Grow what you and your family will eat. If you're not sure about a crop, talk to you neighbors who grow food and ask them what grows best for them. Attend same classes at your local botanical garden and see what others are growing. If you have a small garden or are just starting out, you may want to postpone growing things like watermelon and cantaloupe because they require so much space. Some plants perform better than others depending on where you live in Florida. Many fruit trees, for instance, have been hybridized so heat tolerance is built into their genetic make-up. Others, like mangoes and lychees, simply can't take cold weather and should only be planted where it stays warm most of the time. The plant profiles in this book describe different climate ranges and my recommended varieties. Unfortunately, there are some things that just won't grow in Florida. Although many have tried, we can't grow good, big, full, crunchy apples here. Yes, there are a few varieties that will survive, but *surviving* and *thriving* are two different things. We can't grow cherries here, either. There is a long, long list of fruit trees and veggies that just won't take the heat and humidity. On the other hand, you just can't grow a good banana in Cleveland. Rather than obsess over the things you *can't* grow, think of all the amazing things you *can* grow here, and be thankful you don't have to shovel that white stuff anymore.

> The Top Ten vegetables grown by gardeners are, in order of preference: tomato, bean, corn, cucumber, peas, lettuce, radish, summer squash, melon, and beet.

Plan It On Paper

You don't need to be a landscape designer, but creating a garden on paper is a good thing. Prepare the plan by including dimensions of your garden plot, the list of veggies you want to grow, and the spacing needs of each. If you fly by the seat of your pants on this one you may plant a tomato in the front instead of the back where it would get the proper amount of water. Or, you might plant the broccoli on 12-inch centers instead of 36-inch centers. Prepare the plan with all the information you can gather and then set it aside for a day or two. After a few days, look at it again, make any adjustments, and just do it. Just remember a few things:

- ➤ Plant in full sun (at least 8 hours).
- ➤ Site the garden where water is readily available.
- ➤ Plant away from tree roots.
- ➤ Think small.
- ➤ Rotate crops. Do not plant the same vegetables in the same spots every year.

Do you want to start a discussion with other gardeners? Ask them this seemingly simple question: "Should I plant my rows north to south or east to west?" It's like asking about foreign policy or political affiliation. Go on the Internet to read what the research there states. It seems everyone has an opinion and the "data" to back it up; however, the truth is, *it really doesn't matter*. Just be smart about it. Clearly, if you plant in an east-to-west orientation, you don't want to place taller plants on the south side of the garden because the tall plants will shade the smaller plants behind them. If you are planting east to west, plant the tall stuff in the back or on the north side of the garden. If you're planting in a north-to-south orientation, just make sure you plant the taller plants together and graduate to smaller plants on either side of them. Tall plants can be planted at either end or in the middle, provided less tall plants are planted on either side and less tall plants next to them and so on. If you use an overhead irrigation system, be certain that it either is tall enough to spray the water out over the tall stuff to the smaller ones or locate the tall plants the farthest away from the sprinklers.

> Do you usually have too much zucchini maturing at one time? Plant one hill or one plant in a row and, when that plant begins to bear fruit, plant another to spread out the harvest.

It's okay to make mistakes, so don't fret about the small stuff. All of this should be fun and enjoyable. There are no plant police watching your every move. One of the great things about gardening is sharing your horror stories with other gardeners, and believe me, there are some show stoppers out there. Once the garden is ripped up after the harvest, you can laugh about your bloopers and move on.

Growing More in Less Space
Cluster Gardening

For the life of me I have never been able to figure out why gardeners plant vegetables in single rows. Maybe it's the photos of corn in their long rows that we have seen in photographs, or maybe it's because "we have always done it that way." The plain truth is that planting in single rows is inefficient. I've used the term "cluster gardening" for many years to describe various methods of gardening that best describes whatever space is available to grow food. It maximizes yields of a given planting area over the entire growing season. Cluster gardening has many advantages, such as:

> When vegetables are grown close together, weed seeds don't have the necessary light to germinate, and weeding is reduced to almost nothing. Weeds simply cannot compete with the vegetables.

> Because you reach in from the edges of a wide bed to plant seeds and harvest the fruit, the soil won't become compacted by anyone stepping on it. The soil in the bed will stay nice and "relaxed," just like you want it.

- You'll use less water because of the small amount of space being used.
- Although the total number of fruit harvested from individual plants may be less, because of the increase in the number of plants, the total yield will be higher than single-row plantings.
- Less mulch is needed. With cluster gardening, the rows are often wider and only the walking paths need mulch, instead of the entire garden.
- Heavy rain is less likely to splash dirt on your growing vegetables. If you have ever eaten grit-laden spinach that has been grown in straight rows, this advantage will really appeal to you.
- Even the most inhospitable of sites can be used to create areas that can produce food.
- Harvesting is easier; you can pick more vegetables from a single location.
- Less fertilizer is needed because all of the soil that has been prepared is used.

A combination of several techniques is often used for the best advantage in the vegetable garden. Even in small urban plots where space is limited, cluster gardening will yield more in less space per square foot than traditional methods.

Square Foot Gardening

One of the best-known forms of cluster gardening is the square foot gardening method created by Mel Bartholomew. The method uses soil plots, which are 4 feet x 4 feet square, and each plot is further subdivided into 1-foot squares using twine or string. It's a really ingenious method of positioning plants close together as needed by the individual plants. Seeds are carefully placed into the soil with very exacting measurements as determined by the needs of the person or family that is growing the plants. Because the plots are small and can be reached from all sides, maintenance is less overwhelming even for first-time gardeners. The number of individual plants depends on how many people will be eating the vegetables. For more information, refer to Mr. Bartholomew's book *All New Square Foot Gardening* (Cool Springs Press 2006).

Raised Beds

Raised bed gardening is another form of cluster gardening. Because the prepared soil literally sits atop the native soil, raised beds offer a number of advantages:

> - Even in areas where the soil is soggy from a high water table, you can grow food in raised beds.
> - In urban areas, raised beds can be placed on top of old or abandoned pieces of property, such as old home sites that have since been torn down, old parking lots, and so forth.
> - Even on rooftops, raised beds (containing a "light" soil) can be utilized to grow food.

Raised beds are traditionally made of 2-inch x 10-inch or 2-inch x 12-inch boards, 4 feet wide, and as long as the space will permit. I have seen raised beds that are 30 feet long. That's a bit too long for me—it takes time to walk all the way around to the other

side if you need something; but 20 feet long is not uncommon. Items other than boards can be used, too. Raised beds can be made of steppingstones, interlocking concrete wall stones, Florida limestone rock—anything that will keep the improved soil from spilling out will work. I have seen some pretty inventive ideas in urban gardens all over the country.

There are other good things about raised bed gardens. In cooler areas of the state, the soil in raised beds warms up faster than the surrounding native soil, and plants can be planted into the soil earlier than usual. Because you only want to place "good" soil in the bed, the new soil should have better drainage than the soil beneath the bed. Given that the raised bed is just that, the elevated planting, cultivating, and harvesting is easier on the back. This makes it a good choice to use in gardens designed for the physically impaired or older gardeners who have a difficult time bending over. The raised bed can be as high as you make it; I have seen a raised bed in an assisted living facility that was three feet high and was maintained by seniors who were 85 years old—and older!

Wide Row Planting

Second only to square foot gardening, wide row planting is the most popular alternative form of cluster farming. It is best suited to small plants including lettuce, spinach, onions, carrots, beets, radishes, turnips, and bush beans. Instead of single rows of plants a seedbed ranging from 24 to 48 inches wide is prepared for planting. The seeds of the chosen vegetable are then thinly sprinkled over the entire seedbed and tamped gently to provide good soil-seed contact. As the seedlings emerge from the soil they must be thinned to the distance recommended on the seed package.

Walking on soil after it has been cultivated will compact it. Place a 2- x 8-inch plank between the rows and stand on it when planting.

Wide row planting is a very effective way to increase vegetable yields per square foot. You simply lean across the bed to pull weeds or harvest. Because of the beds and the corresponding lack of walking paths, wide row gardening yields four to six times greater yield per square foot than traditional methods. Not all vegetables lend themselves to wide row planting, however; corn and tomatoes, for instance, need plenty of space and sun to grow properly. Larger plants *can* be planted using the wide row method: they just need more space between each plant. Think of it this way; instead of planting a single row of beans, plant three to four rows of beans next to each other in a wide row (with proper spacing) and the yield increases exponentially over single row plantings. This works with cabbage, peppers, and English peas, too.

My first experience in wide row planting happened purely by accident. I was determined to plant my vegetable garden one year despite twenty-mile-per-hour winds. As I sprinkled the seeds over the seedbed, the wind gusted and, well, the rest is history. I had inadvertently spread seeds 2 to 3 feet wide, but as it turned out, the carrots grew quite well and I have been practicing wide row planting ever since.

Grow Up, Not Out

It seems that most yards that accompany new homes are
getting smaller and smaller as the price of real estate soars.
Gardeners need to be more creative regarding ways to
grow plants in small spaces. (There are bush forms of some
traditional vegetables that I will talk about later.) Clearly,
growing cantaloupe and watermelon in small gardens are out
of the question, given their needs for space. Impossible, that is,
unless you grow *up*. Growing plants on trellises, teepees, cages,
stakes, strings, or fences has many advantages over growing
them on the ground. Cucumbers, cantaloupe, winter squash,
and small gourmet watermelons can be grown vertically. The
advantages are many: the fruit remains cleaner and virtually
free of slugs and other ground-dwelling critters, the fruit can
be seen more easily for harvesting, and during harvest you
won't step on the vines, causing injury that promotes diseases.
If you have limited space, look for vining varieties of the
standard vegetables. Pole beans versus bush beans, for instance,
will produce higher yields than bush forms. For large-fruited
vegetables (melons, squash, and so forth), extra support will
be needed to prevent the fruit from pulling the vine off the
support structure. Companies make expandable plastic mesh,
but recycled women's nylon stockings work very well.

Just make sure that whatever you use, a tall structure

should be placed at the *north side* of the garden so the structure will not shade out the vegetables behind it.

Interplanting

Interplanting is another way of maximizing yield in limited spaces, and many gardeners think that by placing certain vegetables together they seem to grow better (although there is no hard data to support it). Interplanting involves planting two or more different crops together in the same wide row or single row without overfilling the space. When young peppers are planted in the garden, there are lots of spaces between the individual plants until they grow larger. By interplanting other vegetables that mature at a faster rate (and are harvested earlier than the peppers), the space is better utilized and the "quick" crops are gone before the peppers reach their full size. Quick crops in this case could include radishes, lettuce, or even spinach.

I have seen gardeners interplant flowers and herbs with vegetables. They swear it reduces the number of pests in the garden, but even if that weren't the case, it sure makes a dull, ordinary vegetable garden look impressive.

Varieties That Save Space: Dwarf Plants

Although technically not a form of cluster gardening, planting bush forms of vegetables that normally take up lots of space is particularly valuable to gardeners who have small gardens. Not everyone has lots of space to grow vegetables. Growing up is one alternative; the other is to grow special varieties of vegetables that have been hybridized to grow fully formed fruit on smaller or bush-type plants. Even if you only have a patio or terrace, dwarf varieties can be easily grown in large containers. For example, bush forms of cucumbers grow fully formed 6- to 7-inch cukes but on plants that only grow 2 feet long instead of the normal vining 7 to 8 feet. Vining forms of beans instead of bush forms are fun to grow, and even various melons have been bred to grow smaller vines and full-sized fruit. It may take some hunting but they are out there. Even corn has a dwarf cultivar, midget 'Golden Bantam'. It only grows 3 feet tall but produces ears of corn that are 4 to 5 inches long.

OTHER VARIETIES OF DWARF PLANTS

Bean, French	'Safari'
Beet	'Baby Canning', 'Pablo F1'
Cabbage	'Pixie', 'Minicole F1', 'Redcap F1', 'Shelta F1'
Carrot	'Baby Spike', 'Short and Sweet'
Cauliflower	'Idol'
Cucumber	'Salad Bush', 'Spacemaster', 'Bush Champion'
Eggplant	'Morden Midget', 'Bambino'
Kale	'Dwarf Blue Curled'
Lettuce	'Tom Thumb', 'Little Gem', 'Saladin'
Pak choy	'Extra Dwarf', 'Joi Choy', 'Black Summer'
Pea, English	'Little Marvel', 'Half Pint'
Pumpkin	'Jack Be Little', 'Small Sugar', 'Baby Boo'
Swiss chard	'Bright Lights', 'Rhubarb'
Tomato	'Patio', 'Small Fry', 'Tiny Tim'

Container Growing

No discussion about growing fruit trees or vegetables would be complete without talking about growing them in containers. Those with large yards can spread out and grow lots of fun things. Despite the perception, those with smaller yards or no yards living in apartments, condos, and zero lot lines *can* grow lots of fruit and vegetables even though they may not have any land at all. It just takes a little ingenuity.

All of the guidelines to growing vegetables and fruit trees in the ground is true for those growing in containers. You need full sun (at least eight hours), plenty of water, and good soil. Growing in containers has the advantage over growing in the ground—the modification or addition of soil amendments is much easier in containers because of the size of the container. It's one thing to change the mix of garden soil; it's much easier to do the same in containers. Are you tired of the soil in the eggplant pot? Just throw it in the compost pile and start fresh! Do you need to change the pH? Just add a tiny bit if sulfur and you're done. This isn't so in a bigger garden.

I enjoy gardening in containers because they are mobile. If you're like me, you like to change things up a bit, and what better way to do that than to move pots around. Today I like the arrangement that way, tomorrow I may not. Learn to play with textures, heights, and colors of the fruits and vegetables for unique combinations. You can even plant vegetables and fruits with annual and perennial flowers in very attractive combinations.

The containers themselves are a fun part of container growing experience. You are only limited by your imagination. I have seen the theme parks use horse troughs, galvanized trash cans, and even metal pails hung from chains to grow

vegetables. It seems everyone has gotten the container bug because everywhere I go, I see someone selling pots. Not only do they have beautiful colors, they also have incredible shapes. The materials have changed a great deal over the last several years. We used to be able to get pots in terracotta clay. That was it. Now, of course, they come in plastic, urethane foam, and fiberglass. Hauling heavy clay pots from place to place is a thing of the past. I use plastic or foam pots almost exclusively nowadays because in the Florida heat, a clay container pulls any available water out of the potting soil through evaporation, and as a result we may have to water every day or twice a day depending on the location. Many of the plastic and foam pots are so well designed you can't tell the clay from the foam, anyway. An expensive clay pot can crack and break apart while the foam and plastic will seemingly last a lifetime. For containers larger than 24 inches in diameter, you might want to think about putting the pot on casters to make moving easier.

Timing

They say timing is everything, and that's especially true in Florida gardening. With fruit trees, the plants are usually grown in plastic nursery containers and can be planted anytime. I like fall planting best, however, because although the air begins to cool down in the fall, the soil is still warm, and the roots continue to grow until the soil cools down. When spring arrives, the roots have established themselves and are ready to supply the leaves and branches with all the water and nutrients they need as the air warms up. If trees are planted in the spring, or worse yet, in the heat of the summer, the roots are asked to perform a Herculean task with just the roots they came with. It's not uncommon to see fruit trees die because of a lack of water several months after they have been planted.

With vegetables it's a different story. Because many of the things we grow are sensitive either to heat or cold, they have to be planted at the time of the year that they grow best. If you plant a tomato too late in fall, just as the tomato plant begins to produce nice red fruits, a frost will hit and there goes the tomato plant. If you plant too late in spring, just as the tomato begins to set fruit, hot weather arrives and the plant will die because of the heat and humidity. That's why timing is so important. The planting chart found on pages 36–39 may become your second-best gardening friend (after your garden journal). The correct planting season is absolutely critical to Florida gardening. Even after planting vegetables in all three growing zones for twenty-five years, I still get it wrong. During the growing season it's best to stagger the planting of some crops to harvest at the peak of nutrition and flavor. Vegetables like beans, radishes, and lettuce should be planted in small quantities every two to three weeks to harvest them when they taste best. Others, like carrots and potatoes, can be harvested at various stages in their development and you will still get the same nutritional value.

Pay special attention to the insect and disease charts in the appendices of this book. You will notice a few descriptions caution against the use of pesticides when the flowers are in bloom. Do not spray insecticides on fruit trees and vegetables while flowers are in bloom. For vegetable applications, it's hard not to apply pesticides when they not in bloom because they are in bloom most of the time during the growing season. In this case, it's best to apply pesticides during the late morning or early afternoon hours when the pollinators are less active.

RECOMMENDED VARIETIES

Vegetable	North Zone	Central Zone	South Zone	Recommended Varieties	Plant Spacing (inches)	Row Spacing (inches)	Direct Sow or Transplant	Planting Depth (inches)
Bean								
Bush	Mar-Nov	Oct-Apr	Oct-Apr	Bush Blue Lake 274, Commodore Improved, Contender, Greencrop, Tendergreen Improved, White Half Runner, Royal Burgundy Purple Pod, Improved Golden Wax, Cherokee Wax	6	18	D	1
French	Mar-Nov	Oct-Apr	Oct-Apr	Soleil, Fortex, Maxibel, Nickel, Petite Filet, Delinel	6	18	D	1
Italian	Mar-Nov	Oct-Apr	Oct-Apr	Roma II, Venice, Baroma	6	18	D	1
Lima	Mar-Nov	Oct-Apr	Oct-Apr	Dixie Buttterpea Speckled, Jackson Wonder, Fordhook 242, Speckled Calico, Henderson, Christmas Pole, Burpee Improved, Eastland, Big Mama (lima)	6	18	D	1
Pole	Mar-Nov	Oct-Apr	Oct-Apr	Kentucky Wonder, Blue Lake, Kentucky Blue, Kentucky Wonder Wax Pole, Asparagus Yard Long, Half White Runner, Purple Podded, Romano, Big Mama (pole)	6	18	D	1
Shell					6	18	D	1
Beet	Sep-Mar	Oct-Mar	Oct-Mar	Detroit Dark Red, Chioggia, Burpee's Golden, Cylindrica, Early Wonder, Green Top Bunching, Piatta D'Egitto, Yellow Detroit	2-3	12-18	D	½
Broccoli	Sep-Jan	Sep-Jan	Sep-Jan	Packman, High Dividend, Green Comet, Green Goliath	24	24	D/T	½-1
Brussels sprouts	Sep-Jan	Sep-Jan	Sep-Jan	Jade Cross, Long Island Improved	24	24	D/T	½-1
Cabbage	Sep-Jan	Sep-Jan	Sep-Jan	New Jersey Wakefield, Copenhagen Market, Bonnies, Hybrid, Mammoth Red Rock, Savoy Chieftain	18	24	D/T	¼
Cantaloupe	Mar-Apr	Feb-Apr	Aug-Sep & Feb-Mar	Ambrosia, Bush Star, Honey Rock, Planter's Jumbo	24	48	D/T	½-1
Carrot	Sep-Mar	Oct-Mar	Oct-Feb	Nantes Half Long, Chatenay Royal, Imperator 58, Tendersweet, Cosmic Purple, Snow White	2	12-18	D	1/16

RECOMMENDED VARIETIES

Vegetable	North Zone	Central Zone	South Zone	Recommended Varieties	Plant Spacing (inches)	Row Spacing (inches)	Direct Sow or Transplant	Planting Depth (inches)
Cauliflower	Sep-Jan	Sep-Jan	Sep-Jan	Snowball, Brocoverde, Cheddar, Violet Queen	18	18	D/T	¼-½
Celery	Jul- Sep	Jul- Sep	Jul- Sep	Giant Pascal, Stoke's Golden Plume, Golden Self Branching	6	24	T	$1/16$
Collards	Jan-Dec	Jan-Dec	Jan-Dec	Yates Strain, Georgian Southern	36	36	T	
Corn	Feb-Apr	Jan-Apr	Oct-Mar	Golden Cross Bantam, Early Sunglow, Sweet Riser, Kandy King, Silver Queen, How Sweet It Is, Sweet Ice, Peaches and Cream, Seneca Dancer	8	30	D	1
Cucumber								
Fall Garden	Aug-Sep	Sep	Sep-Oct	**Garden Straight:** Eight, Dasher II, Cherokee	10	36-48	D/T	½
Winter Garden	too cold	too cold	Nov-Dec	**Pickling:** Ohio MR 17, Pixie **Bush:** Burpee's Bushmaster **Greenhouse:** Toska, Fabulous,				
Spring Garden	Feb-Apr	Jan-Mar	Jan-Mar	Sweet Success				
Summer	too hot	too hot	too hot					
Eggplant	Jun-Sep	Jun-Sep	Jun-Sep	Black Beauty, Cloud Nine, Calliope, Casper, Green Goddess, Machiaw, Rosa Biancha, Apple Green	30	30-36	T	
Endive	Sep-Apr	Dec-Mar	Dec-Feb		6	18-24	D/T	¼
Kale	Sep-Mar	Sep-Mar	Sep-Mar	Dwarf Blue Curled Scotch, Red Russian, Yates Blue Curled, Nero de Toscana	18	24	D/T	½
Kohlrabi	Sep- Mar	Sep-Mar	Sep-Mar	Early White Vienna, Kolibri, Grand Duke, Early Purple Vienna, Kosak and Superschmelz	6	18	D	½
Lettuce	Sep-Oct & Feb-Mar	Sep-Mar	Sep-Jan	**Crisphead:** Iceberg, Ithaca, Great Lakes, Hanson Improved **Romaine:** Freckles, Cimmaron Red, Parris Island, Dark Green Bibb, Big Boston **Buttercrunch:** May Queen, White Boston, Merveille des Quartre Saisons, Baby Star **Leaf:** Black Seeded Simpson, Red Sails, Oak Leaf, Ruby Red, Salad Bowl, Tango, Deer Tongue	6	12-18	D/T	½

RECOMMENDED VARIETIES

Vegetable	North Zone	Central Zone	South Zone	Recommended Varieties	Plant Spacing (inches)	Row Spacing (inches)	Direct Sow or Transplant	Planting Depth (inches)
Mustard	Sep-May	Sep-Mar	Sep-Mar	Florida Broad Leaf, Southern Giant Curled, Big Red, Misuna, Tatsoi	8	18-24	D	½
Okra	Mar-Aug	Mar-Aug	Aug-Sep	Clemson Spineless, Alabama Red, Baby Bubba, Cow Horn, Evertender, Little Lucy, Red Burgundy, White Velvet	24	36	D/T	½
Onion	Sep-Mar	Sep-Mar	Sep-Mar	Crystal Wax Bermuda, Excel, Red Creole, Granex White, Granex Yellow, White Lisbon Bunching, Crimson Forest, Barletta, Matador (shallots)	4	18-24	D/T	½
Pea, English	Jan- Mar	Sep- Feb	Sep- Feb	Little Marvel, Sugar Snap, Wando, Oregon Sugarpod II, Green Arrow	2	30	D	1
Pea, Southern	Mar-Aug	Mar-Aug	Aug-Apr	Brown Crowder, California Blackeye, Knucklehull Purplehull, Mississippi Silverskin, White Acre, Zipper Cream	4	30	D	1-2
Peanut	Jun	Jul	Aug	Valencia	8	24	D	1 ½
Pepper	Feb-Mar & July-Sep	Feb-Mar & July-Sep	Aug-Sep	**Standard Sweet:** Yolo Wonder, Cubanelle, Sweet Banana, Early Calwonder, Keystone Resistant Giant, Purple Beauty, Pimento **Hybrid Sweet:** Big Bertha, Gypsy **Standard Hot:** Caribbean Red, Chili Jalapeño, Habenero, Hungarian Yellow Wax, Long Thin Cayenne, Tampiquero, Scotch Bonnet **Hybrid Hot:** Super Chili	18	24	T	$1/8$
Potato	Jan-Mar	Jan-Mar	Sep-Jan	Kennebec, Yukon Gold, Red Pontiac, French Fingerling, Adirondack Red, Adirondack Blue, Russian Banana	8	36	D	6
Spinach	Oct-Nov	Oct-Nov	Oct-Jan		6	24	D/T	½

RECOMMENDED VARIETIES

Vegetable	North Zone	Central Zone	South Zone	Recommended Varieties	Plant Spacing (inches)	Row Spacing (inches)	Direct Sow or Transplant	Planting Depth (inches)
Squash	Mar-Apr & Aug-Sep	Feb-Mar & Aug-Sep	Jan -Feb & Sep	**Summer Squash:** Prolific Straightneck, Summer Crookneck, Peter Pan, Early White Scallop **Winter Squash:** Spaghetti, Table King, Table Queen, Table Ace, Waltham, Early Butternut **Zucchini:** Cocozelle, Spineless Beauty, Black Beauty, Gold Rush, Eightball and Caserta **Unique forms:** Ambercup, Bonbon, Bush Delicata, Calabraza, Golden Hubbard	36	36-48	D/T	
Sweet potato	Mar-Jun	Feb-Jun	Dec-Sep	Beauregard, Hernandez, Picadito (boniato)	12	48	T	
Swiss chard	Sep-Mar	Oct-Mar	Oct-Mar	Bright Lights, Erbette, Monstruoso, Fordhook Giant, Italian White Ribbed, Ruby Red	12	18-24	D/T	½
Tomato	Feb-Mar & Aug	Mar 1 & Aug 1	Aug-Mar	**Indeterminate (large fruit):** Better Boy, Bonnie Best, Bragger **Indeterminate (small fruit):** Red Cherry, Sweet 100, Sweet Chelsea, Husky Cherry **Determinate (large fruit):** Walter, Sun Coast, Floramerica, Flora-dade, Duke, Sunny and Celebrity. **Determinate (small fruit):** Floragold, Florida Petite, Patio, Micro-Tom	36	30-36	T	½
Turnip	Jan-Apr & Aug-Oct	Jan-Mar & Sep-Nov	Oct-Feb	Purple Top White Globe **Greens only:** Seven Top, Southern Green, heroin and Topper. **Roots only:** Golden Ball, Just Right, Lunga Bianca A Colletto Bianca, Tokyo Cross, White Lady	3	12-18	D	½
Watermelon	Mar-Apr & Jul-Aug	Jan-Mar & Aug	Jan-Mar & Aug-Sep	Jubilee (Florida Giant), Crimson Sweet and Charleston Grey 133, Sugar Baby, Mickeylee	36	84	D/T	1 ½

STARTING AT THE BEGINNING WITH SEEDS

It's a fact that starting vegetables from seed is more cost effective than buying plants from a garden center. Depending on the vegetable variety, a packet of fifty or so seeds will cost anywhere from $1.25 to $2.50. When I went to the garden center recently, I noticed that garden-ready vegetable plants in large peat pots cost from $2.50 to $3.50 each. If you were planting for a family you would need to take out a small loan to buy enough plants to make a garden worthwhile. Another thing I noticed was there were not many varieties available on the shelf. Perhaps you don't want to grow the standard zucchini squash, but instead, want the golden-yellow variety. You would be hard pressed to find anyone in a nursery growing that one for commercial sale. However, over in the seed section of the store you might find that variety, or if you spend even five minutes on the Internet you'll probably locate ten sources.

If you grow your own plants and later collect seeds from those plants, you know how they have been grown. Nearly everyone would agree that growing food without the use of chemicals is a good idea, but if you buy seedlings from a store you really don't know if they have been sprayed with chemicals at the nursery. I'm a firm believer in the "less is better" theory, and I want to know that the food I feed my family is safe. In that regard, there is a great deal of satisfaction to be found growing plants from seed. You have taken the time to select the right container, the correct soil, planted the seed at the correct depth, and watered the seeds carefully for proper germination. When the little seedlings push their way up out of the soil, it is a proud moment. And when you harvest in a few months, you will know that you really accomplished something.

Direct Sow vs. Transplants

In the vegetable charts (pp. 36–39), there is acolumns titled "Direct Sow or Transplant" to guide your planting efforts. For the most part, when possible, planting directly into the soil is better than planting transplants because the plant roots are not disturbed during the transplanting procedure. When seeds come up through the soil their roots and stems are at the correct height and they seem to grow better than transplants. There are some plants, including beans, peas, and squash, for instance, that just don't like to be moved once they're planted. If you must plant seedlings, grow them in peat cups and plant them gently into the garden when it's time.

To prepare your garden for planting, follow these tips. For single row planting, after lifting and turning the soil with a lifting fork or rototiller, rake the seedbed smooth, especially when small seeds are being planted. Straight rows are important later to distinguish the weed seedlings from the vegetable seedlings. To prevent compacting the soil, start at one end of the garden and work toward the other end. Many people place a board between the rows to help distribute the gardener's weight and to avoid leaving deep footprints in the rows. Others simply cultivate the pathways after the planting is completed. Both methods work fine. Pound a stake or stick into the ground at either end of the seedbed and stretch a string between the two stakes. Make a slight impression, also referred to as "drill," into the seedbed using the entire handle of a hoe or rake laid down in the loamy soil. Sow the seeds according to the recommendations on their packages. Larger seeds such as squash, beans, and peas need to be planted deep; the sharp edge of a hoe can be used to make a deep furrow (1 to 2 inches deep) for the larger seeds. Gently tap the seeds out of the package—not too many—or place fine seeds in your hand and gently sow the seeds into the drill using a rubbing motion between your thumb and index finger. Don't worry whether the seeds are right side up or not. They will figure that out themselves and make any corrections needed. Go back over the slight soil impression to make certain there are no gaps; always leave a few seeds in the package to sow a week or so later to fill in the gaps where the seeds didn't germinate. Gently cover the seeds with your hands or feet and tamp the seeds to obtain a good seed-soil contact. Immediately mark the rows by placing a stick or plant label at the end of each; plastic labels available at garden centers work fine but the wooden ones deteriorate too quickly. Use a china marker or grease pencil to write the name and variety of the seed planted. Water gently every day using a watering can until the seeds sprout.

If you want to start seeds in egg cartons, be sure to use the styrofoam type, *not* the paper type. By the time the seeds are large enough to transplant, a paper carton will have fallen apart.

Others vegetables, such as broccoli, cabbage, and tomatoes, can easily be grown as transplants in peat cups or recycled cell-packs, and moved to the garden later. (Usually, transplants are moved when the seedling has three to four pairs of "true" leaves.) Just be very careful when pulling them out of the cell packs to make sure you get all of the roots. One of the biggest problems concerning seedlings is planting them too deep. Plant them a little higher or at the same depth they were growing in the container. Especially with members of the Brassica family of crops—cabbage, cauliflower, broccoli—stem rot is very common if they are planted too deep.

Root crops, including potatoes, carrots, and rutabagas, have to be planted directly into the garden. Onions can vary in their planting requirements. For example, Lisbon bunching onions are best planted directly into the soil from seed. Others, such as the variety 'Granex' and shallots, should be planted into the garden as sets (or individual bulbs) so that one-half of the onion bulb can be seen above the soil. Check the seed packages or plant marker for planting specifics.

Sowing Seeds Indoors: Getting a Head Start

Nearly all vegetable seeds can be planted directly into the garden, sometimes referred to as "direct sown," and many can be planted earlier indoors to get a head start. Because of their fleshy taproots, a few vegetables cannot tolerate being transplanted. (Refer to the chart on pages 36–39 for a list of those that must be direct sown.) Many gardeners plant seeds in some type of container with good potting soil several weeks before they are to be planted out into the garden to get that jump on the season (maybe we're impatient). If you don't have the inclination or simply don't have room to start seeds indoors, don't fret; just wait until the temperature is right and plant them in the ground at the right time.

If you want to get a head start, though, the good news is that you don't need fancy equipment or greenhouses to grow plants from seeds. A container, some potting soil, water, and sun are all you need. Generally, you will plant seeds indoors several weeks before they are to be planted into the garden. In many areas of Florida if you plant seedlings outside too soon, they could be killed by frost. Likewise, in the fall if you plant

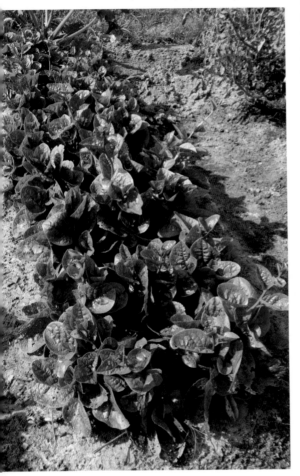

them outside too soon, they could shrivel up and die due to the heat. Every vegetable has a different length of time to maturity, so study the chart on pages 36–39 before you get started. Once you spend a few minutes with it, you'll have a better sense of when to plant.

Once you have selected the seed, it's time to plant (assuming you're in the right season). Begin by tapping the packet, forcing the seeds to the *top*. Carefully open the seed packet by tearing the *bottom* of the package. Gently sprinkle the seeds over the soil leaving a few seeds in the packet. In case all of the seeds don't germinate, you will have extra seeds to fill in the seed tray or complete a row in the garden so there won't be gaps. The seed package can be folded tightly from the bottom, held closed with a paper clip, with the full variety name intact at the top. Store in an airtight container in the refrigerator. Many seeds (beans, corn, broccoli, and cucumbers, for instance) can be stored this way for several years. I find it's helpful to mark the opening date on each packet with an indelible marker for quick reference.

Let's talk dirt. When seedlings are small and just beginning to grow, they are very vulnerable to a variety of maladies such as root rots, stem rots, leaf spots, and so forth. For that reason it is important to get the seeds off to a good start by growing them in soil that is free of diseases. You can dig some soil out of your yard and sow the seeds in it, but you would be amazed to know of all the bad things in there: fungi, bacteria, viruses, microscopic worms—the list is endless. It's a wonder that anything can grow in it. Because growing seeds indoors is a modification of a seed's normal outdoor environment with its good air circulation, predatory insects, and such, it's important that the transplant potting soil be as critter free as possible. Yes, you can sterilize garden soil in small amounts by heating it to 180°F for one hour. I tried it once in the kitchen oven using my wife's roasting pan but the odor was pretty bad. Later, I tried the barbeque grill and it worked okay, but I find that it's much easier to buy proper potting soil at a garden center instead. (By the way, ever since I used that roasting pan, the Thanksgiving turkey has never been quite the same.) Potting soil in bags is usually clean enough to start seeds without any worry.

Selecting the right container to grow the seeds in couldn't be easier provided you remember a few things. First, the soil needs to have good drainage. Anything less than "good" and the seeds will become waterlogged and die. Water them from the top or bottom using a saucer, it doesn't make any difference as long as the seeds are not washed away with a heavy stream of water when they are watered. When I can find them, I like to use peat cups or expandable peat pellets to start seeds. Peat cups can be filled with potting soil and the seeds planted as usual. The peat pellets need to be expanded first (hot water works well to hasten this process), and then the seed is inserted at the proper depth into the sterile medium. When the seedlings are ready and the planting time is right, the peat pot or peat pellet can be planted directly into the garden. Just about anything else can be used, too. Egg cartons, the bottoms of milk cartons, and even newspaper folded into cups

> When transplanting seedlings grown in peat pots, remove the upper 1 inch of the cup. If this is left, the remaining peat pot "rim" will act like a wick to draw water out of the ground causing the soil in the peat pot to dry out more quickly.

will work. Reusing old plastic trays from last season's annuals work very well and it beats throwing them into the landfill.

Seeds may also be broadcast over a seed tray or "flat," and covered with the correct amount of soil. Unlike seeds grown in individual containers, the seedlings must be gently lifted from a tray and later placed into individual containers for planting into the garden. Lifting or "pricking out" the seeds can be done once the seedlings have produced two to three sets of leaves that look like the plant's mature leaves. An old dinner fork (or a new one, if your spouse isn't looking) works fine for this purpose. Just stick the fork into the soil, *gently* lift the seedling and its roots from the tray, and place the seedling into its new pot of sterile potting soil. Water gently and grow as you would other plants until the seedling is ready to plant outdoors. When sowing seeds in trays, be careful not to plant the seeds too closely together. If there is limited air circulation, seedlings often succumb to diseases.

Cut seed potatoes three or four days before planting, dust liberally with sulfur, and allow them to air dry before planting.

When sowing seed read the instructions on the packet, or, if you buy in bulk from a feed store, ask the salesperson how deep the seeds should be planted. As a general rule, seeds are usually planted twice as deep as their diameter. Place the soil into the container, plant the seeds at their proper depth, and water gently. Once a seed has been watered, it's important to keep watering often until the seedling emerges from the soil. As long as the soil is well drained, watering every day will be sufficient. Once a dry, newly planted seed becomes wet, it begins to expand and it is at this stage when a seed is most vulnerable. Be careful not to let the soil dry out.

Planting seed directly into the garden soil is some of the most fun you will have in the garden. You will need a rake, the seeds, and some stakes and string. Rake out the seedbed so it is nice and fine and free of dirt clumps. Measure a foot or so in from the edge of the garden and stretch the string across the garden between the stakes. For single row planting, a hoe handle lightly pressed into the soil makes a nice indentation or furrow for small seeds; larger seeds will need a furrow 1 to 2 inches deep, which can be made using the edge of a hoe.

One more thing: plants grown too closely together will not grow properly. The carrots will be tiny, the cauliflower won't grow a curd, and the tomatoes will be small. This is true for transplants and those grown directly in the ground. Once the seeds begin to emerge from the soil you will see that you planted too many. The tendency is to sow seeds too closely because when the seeds are small it is almost impossible to sow them evenly. It happens to everyone, so don't feel bad. Unfortunately, the seedlings must be grown at their proper spacing, so any excess seedlings must be removed or "thinned." Seedlings grown in individual containers or those grown in the garden need to be thinned and spaced according to the chart on pages 36–39 or by the instructions found on the seed packet. Trust me on this: you must thin seedlings to get good production. Thinning should be done in either of two ways. Using scissors, snip off all but one seedling per container at the soil level, selecting the largest and sturdiest to remain. To thin in the garden, this means getting "up close and personal" (on your hands and knees) and clipping all but the best at the correct distance apart. Seedlings can also be removed by pulling the seedling to the side when the soil is moist. This method lessens the damage to those plant roots remaining in the ground. Once the process is completed, water the remaining seedlings with a gentle spray.

Finally, once the seeds have been sown in a pot or flat, place the seeds in a warm location. Until the seedlings emerge from the soil, sunlight is not necessary. Once the seeds sprout move them to a sunny location, and water as needed to keep the soil moist. After a few weeks, check the holes in the bottom of the pot for evidence of root growth. Once the roots have become well established in the pot (every plant will grow at different rates), it's time to plant them out into the garden.

Moving Outdoors

Once indoor-grown seedlings have emerged from the soil, it's important that they be acclimated to the outdoors gradually. Otherwise, they will resemble a Yankee on a Florida beach in August. Plants, especially seedlings, can get sunburned, too. After the seedlings emerge, they need to be toughened up. Take them outside for an hour or so every day, increasing the length of exposure until they can be in the sun all day. This process is called "hardening off." If the transplants are being planted in a cooler time of the year, be careful of freezing temperatures, and protect the new plants with row cloth available at most garden centers or with lightweight, old blankets.

Saving Seeds

One of the questions most asked of gardeners is, "Can I save the seed from my vegetables and fruit trees and grow new plants?" As you would expect, the answer is "yes" and "no"— nothing is easy in this line of work. I am not a geneticist, but let me explain the best I can.

First, the question begs to be asked, why bother? After all, it's much easier to simply go to the local feed store, garden center, or nursery and buy them either in bulk or in seed packs right off the shelf. But there are some good reasons. It's important to remember that when seed companies collect seed to sell the following year, they collect *all* the seed of a given plant on their farm. That includes both the very largest and the runts of the pack, and the seeds are mixed together. When you collect seeds in your garden you will collect seeds from only the largest and healthiest of the crop. Assuming Mendel was right about genetics, many of the positive traits that you selected the seeds for—resistance to disease, vigor, height, and so forth—will pass down to most of the next generation in the seed. True, not all will be the best and the greatest, but hopefully many will be. With some plants, saving seed will take some sacrifice. After all, let's say you have selected a specific plant because of certain qualities; maybe it's spineless or has good insect or disease resistance. To collect the seed from a plant with unique characteristics means you will have to let that plant go to seed, and that means you won't be able to eat it. It will be difficult to watch a perfectly good plant go to seed and not be able to taste it, but that's the name of the game.

Lifelike rubber snakes and lizards work very well to keep birds away from your bean and squash seed as the seedlings emerge.

I save seeds for one simple reason: I know what has been sprayed on the parents. Many commercial companies' seeds are sprayed with insecticides and/or fungicides to prevent pests from eating them or to prevent them from going bad during storage. If you collect your seeds from your plants that have not been sprayed and then store them in your refrigerator, you're safe on both counts.

One more thing about saving seeds: You can save a ton of money. I bought several packages of vegetable seeds recently. Not only were there very few seeds in each package (there seem to be fewer and fewer every year) but a small package of seed cost more than $1.50. If you multiply that cost times the number of different vegetables on your planting list, you'll see that you will spend a small fortune. Even worse, most fruit trees are not sold as seed but as fairly expensive saplings that must be purchased in nursery containers. Granted, many must be grafted onto hardy, resistant rootstock, but for those that can be grown from seed, the savings can be tremendous. (Of course, what you trade is the time already spent growing the tree to sapling stage; sometimes, it's worth the investment to obtain a plant that's already started.)

One common mistake many gardeners make is collecting the seed too soon. The fruit of vegetables and fruit trees should be mature, maybe even a little past ripeness. Collect the seed from the fruit, gently wash the seeds with plain water to remove any pulp or flesh, and air dry the seeds in a cool, dry location. A shady spot, using newspaper as the drying material, in a well-ventilated space works best. In Central and South Florida where the humidity is very high, gardeners can also dry seeds by placing them in silica gel for a period of time (small seeds take only four to five days while large seeds can take up to ten days). Tomatoes are the exception to the rule. I usually mash the fruit and let it ferment for a few days outside until it starts to look nasty. The fermented pulp, often two to three days old, is then placed in a glass or jar filled with water. After stirring the fruit pulp for a few minutes I let the entire concoction rest. The seeds that sink to the bottom are viable and those that float on top can be thrown out with the pulp. Dry the "good" seeds like other seeds described and store in a location that has low humidity and cool temperatures.

Remember that seeds are living things and need to be treated as such. First, to prevent mold on stored seeds make sure they are dried thoroughly before they are stored. Often it looks like the seed is dry but it may not be. Change the drying papers often during the process and turn the seeds over a few times to make certain that all sides are dried equally. The storage containers can make a difference, too. Metal-capped glass jars work well, but they are clumsy to work with if you only have a few seeds. Old 35mm plastic film containers work fine, provided you don't have many seeds. My favorite is a simple plastic sandwich bag with a top that can be sealed. With the clear plastic bag, the seeds can be observed often and moldy seeds can be removed quickly. Bags store flat and many can be stored together. Make sure you label any storage container well with an indelible marker or inexpensive labeling machine available from the local office supply store. A grease pencil or china marker works equally well.

Seeds need to be stored in a cool, dark place to arrest the diseases and bacteria that could harm them and to keep the seeds in a suspended state until they are asked to sprout in the garden. There are lots of photographs in books that show handsome garden sheds with jars of seeds on a shelf just waiting to be planted. Nothing could be worse for seed. My shed is always twenty degrees warmer than it is outside and as for air circulation, well, there is none. That's where the refrigerator comes in. Claim a vegetable crisper drawer as *your* space. Just take it, and don't relinquish it to anyone. It fulfills all the requirements: good air circulation, cool temperatures, and low humidity. Seeds stored in this environment can last for several years. Finally, don't share the space with any ripening fruit, especially apples. The ethylene gas that apples emit could have a negative impact on the viability of the seeds.

When you get ready to use the seeds, spread ten or so evenly on a damp paper towel. Cover the seeds with another damp paper towel or simply roll the single thickness up into a roll. Place the seeds in a warm location, and check them periodically over the next several days to see if the seeds have germinated. If many seeds have sprouted, fewer seeds will be needed to grow the fruit. If just a few have sprouted, you know that more seeds will have to be sown to get the same number of plants from the same given space.

CREATING THE PERFECT SOIL

If you live in an area of Florida with good, rich soil, thank your lucky stars because you have a leg up on everyone else. Throughout the Sunshine State many of our soils consist of those with high clay content, sandy loam, deep sugar sand, muck, peat, or limestone rock covered by marl or sand. The "soil" in which we are expected to grow plants often needs work, and lots of it.

If you look at sandy soil under a microscope you will see what appear to be small rocks. There is nothing there that retains water, there are no nutrients. In some areas of the state there is a red clay that requires a pick-axe to plant anything, and in other areas you'd need dynamite to blast a planting hole. It's a crazy place to try to grow anything, let alone food for your family. Make no mistake, however, everyone who lives here *can* grow fruits and vegetables; it just may be a little harder in some places than others. But first, let's talk a bit about what makes a great garden soil.

Loose is Best

When someone describes soil as "loose," what they mean is that it crumbles in the hand. That's the ideal, but few people have loose soil naturally. If you do not, loose soil can be attained by adding organic matter (leaves, peat moss, and compost) to both sandy and clay soils. With clay soil, the soil sticks together in the hand, and, of course, sandy soil flows through the fingers like . . . sand. There are variations throughout the entire spectrum but the bottom line is that vegetables and fruits like soil that allows their roots to travel outward from their centers without difficulty and that is free of obstructions. Imagine tiny, tender roots as they meander through the soil in search of nutrients and water. Clay or rocky soil impedes the fragile root hairs from rambling their way through the dirt. Clay is made up of very tiny soil particles held together very closely by chemical bonds. As a result, water has a tough time draining through clay soil, and it becomes waterlogged. In clay soils, the presence of organic matter "breaks" up the soil to allow water and nutrients to move around and down.

In sandy soils, organic matter absorbs and "grips" water and nutrients to keep them around for the plant to use. Otherwise, in sandy soils, plant roots would have to grab what they can as any water passes by.

And another thing: raise your right hand and promise me that you will never, ever, try to till, dig, or otherwise "work" the soil while it's wet. Have you ever seen a farmer on a tractor plowing the soil when it's wet? Soil has a specific structure that develops over centuries. There are certain structural bonds that you and I cannot see that keep soil loose, which is just the way we like it. But, add a little water and then try to plow or till it. You'll watch all of Mother Nature's work go right down the drain. Big clods will form, the soil won't drain properly, and plants don't grow properly. If you work wet soil *even once* it will take years and years of backbreaking labor to get it right again. So, the next time it begins to rain, have enough sense to come inside, and leave the dirt alone until the water drains away.

Well Drained Is the Goal

Roots, like people, need air to breathe, and in waterlogged soils the tiny pockets of air a plant's roots need to breathe are filled with water. Ultimately, the plant will die because it is drowning. In areas whose typical soil is deep clay or where limestone rock is close to the surface, getting soil to drain well may be difficult. Mechanical means, such as installing plastic drain lines like those used in septic tanks, may be the only alternative. If the clay in your proposed garden spot isn't too deep, organic matter and *coarse* sand thoroughly mixed in over a period of many years may alleviate poor drainage. In other locations where the clay is never-ending or where the rock is just below the surface as it is in South Florida, raised bed gardening or container gardening may be the only answer. For fruit trees, a large bed (the size depends a great deal on the strength of your back) several feet in diameter and 18 inches deep of good soil brought in from elsewhere will create an artificial, aboveground bed into which the tree's roots can grow. For vegetable gardens, smaller beds 4 feet wide work best. You should be able to reach into the center of the bed to plant seeds and pull weeds without stepping onto the soil and compacting it. The length depends on how strong your back is and how much soil you want to haul. The longer the bed, the more soil you will need. Raised beds can be made of any number of things, including 2- x 10-inch boards nailed together, rocks, and even concrete blocks or seawall stones. Anything that will hold the soil in the bed without releasing toxic chemicals will work fine. I have seen people plant vegetables in old tires, but I am not convinced that the stuff tires are made of is safe to use to grow food.

To improve fruit set on tomatoes, shake the tomato stake or hit the top of the stake a few times. Attaching an electric toothbrush to the stake and allowing it to vibrate for a few minutes works even better!

Good Ol' Dirt

When a gardener speaks of the soil being "neutral," they're not referring to its political affiliations. Instead, they are talking about the relative acidity or alkalinity of the soil. As a general rule, the soils far west of the Mississippi River are on the alkaline side and, to the east, are acidic. What that means is that certain plants grow better (or worse) depending on the alkalinity or acidity of your soil. You may also have heard of "pH" and that figure refers to how soil registers acidity or alkalinity on a scale from 1 to 14, with 7 being neutral (neither acid nor alkaline). For instance, lemon juice and battery acid are acidic and fall in the 0 to 7 range; whereas seawater and bleach are alkaline and fall in the 7 to 14 pH range. Pure water is neutral, or 7 on the pH scale. The pH of soil is important because the soil carries nutrients such as nitrogen, phosphorus, and potassium that allow the plant to grow and fight off diseases. As the pH increases or decreases, certain nutrients become more or less available for the plant's use.

The soil in a garden should be periodically tested and

decisions made how to adjust it for optimum performance. A simple pH test kit, available at any garden center, is used to see how the existing garden soil compares to the scale. The kit will also have a color-coded chart for comparison to the indications provided by the garden soil. The instructions in the kit will give details of what to add to get the results you want. You can also test the soil by using litmus papers, available at many local drug stores. Mix a little of the soil with distilled water, and let it settle for a few minutes. Dip the litmus paper in the water and let it rest for one minute. The chart that comes with the litmus papers can be compared to the test paper, and the correct pH can be determined.

Rather than use hay or straw as a mulch around your veggies, use oak leaves instead. Apparently slugs don't like the bitter taste of the leaves and will stay away.

Most vegetables and fruit trees like soil to be slightly acidic from 6.0 to 7.0. To make the soil more alkaline, add dolomitic lime; to make the soil more acidic, add sulfur. Remember to change the pH only one point at a time. Changing pH should be considered a long-term project, so alterations to the soil pH should occur little by little. If the soil is too alkaline, consider creating a raised bed with good garden soil instead.

The Roots Run Deep

Good, deep garden soil is the ideal to strive for. Often, just below the surface a layer of clay or rock is lurking, making it difficult for roots, nutrients, and water to move easily. Many vegetables require deep soils for their roots to develop properly. Potatoes and carrots, due to their nature as root crops, require good, deep loamy soil to form properly. Other plants such as fruit trees depend on deep soils to anchor themselves in the soil to avoid being blown over in the wind. Having deep garden soil encourages the roots to search deeply for available water. If ever water is in short supply the roots will be deep enough they can obtain moisture and avoid being dried out and scorched by the sun. If you have clay or rock hardpan, achieving deep soil may take many *years* to accomplish, but don't give up hope. Even if raised beds are an option, bringing up a little of the native soil every time you prepare for the next crop will help create deep soil over time.

The Nematode Nemesis

Organic matter is a gardener's best friend. It loosens the soil, it helps sandy soils retain water, and it helps clay soils drain better. It also does many other good things.

For instance, throughout the warm areas of the world, microscopic parasitic worms lurk in the soil looking for tender little roots to bite. They live on the plant sap inside the roots and by feeding on the roots they prevent the plant from getting all the nutrients and water it needs to flourish. Now, mind you, we are not talking one or two worms. In one cubic foot of soil, there could be hundreds of thousands of these worms called "nematodes." There is not just one type of worm, but there are *many* different types, all creating havoc for the plant. As a defensive mechanism a plant's roots will begin to grow around each nematode as the plant tries to create

a scab to fend off the invader. The roots become knobby in appearance, and after awhile there aren't enough viable roots to absorb water and nutrients. Finally, the plant simply gets tired and dies. No matter how much water you give, no matter how much fertilizer you add, no matter how much you talk to it, the plant will die.

We are not absolutely certain how organic matter works, although there are many theories, but one theory is that the more organic matter there is in the soil, the fewer nematodes you will have. Many think that it has to do with the decay of organic matter and the creation of something called "humus." Humus is a combination of leftover dead plant material and microorganisms including bacteria and fungi. Humus allows the plant to cling to water and nutrients and the end result is a healthier plant. It's been my experience that by adding fallen, disease-free leaves, compost, and green cover crops (also called "green manures") over time, the nematode population will dwindle.

Feed the Soil

Last year when talking to a fellow gardener, I heard him say that he was going home to put some "groceries" on his garden. After that visual faded, the more I thought about what he had said, the more sense it made. As you plan the garden, think about feeding the hungry plants and their needs. Some people place fertilizer *around* the plants after they are planted; others place fertilizer *in* the soil and turn it under before planting. Either makes sense, but in either case the soil needs to be checked first to see what nutrients are present to start with. Apply fertilizer to fruit trees only two months after they have been planted. Any garden center has soil-testing kits of test tubes and color charts that can be used to check the fertility and pH of the soil. Every kit is different, but usually a little soil is placed into the test tube, the tube is then filled with water, and a capsule of powder is opened and placed in the tube. The whole thing is shaken for a few seconds and allowed to rest for an hour or so. In that time the soil will settle to the bottom and the water will change color. The colored water is then compared to the color charts in the accompanying booklet that came with the kit. Depending on the color, the booklet will provide recommendations on how much of specific fertilizers to apply for optimum plant growth. It's so simple my eight-year-old daughter has used it.

Fertilizers *can* get a little complicated; just go to a nursery and try to figure out all those numbers on the different fertilizer bags. But, with a little knowledge, it's very actually simple. Once the soil tests are complete, apply the recommended amount to the entire garden area. Later as the plants grow you can add fertilizers in the amounts recommended in each of the plant profiles. If you want to be very specific, individual types and amounts of fertilizer can be added by applying the fertilizer alongside of each plant, called sidedressing, and scratched into the soil.

Whether you apply synthetic fertilizer or organic fertilizer is up to you. Add no more than the recommended amount and water it in well after application. If you add more than the recommended amount, then all your hard work would be for naught when the plants die from too much fertilizer. Plus, excess fertilizer will wash into and accumulate in bodies of water and even the aquifer, polluting them.

The next thing is to add organic matter. We know for certain that the addition of organic matter, regardless of the soil type, helps plants grow better. Any amount is better than none, but a 3- to 4-inch layer of compost spread over the entire space and turned into the soil either by a shovel or rototiller will work just fine.

When fertilizing fruit trees, make sure you put the fertilizer where the roots are. I've seen people in my neighborhood toss a coffee can or two full of fertilizer around the base of a tree. Unfortunately, that's not where the roots are. Fertilizer is wasted, or worse it causes damage to the trunk of the tree. Think of the fertilized area around the tree as a doughnut. Measure from the trunk of the tree halfway to the very edge of the foliage (called the "drip line"), add that measurement

> Most vegetables don't like deep cultivation because it breaks off their tender roots. Instead, cultivate to a depth of 1 inch to prevent bringing weed seeds to the surface.

to the drip line circle, and fertilize that area. For example, let's say the distance from a tree trunk to the drip line is six feet. Beginning from a three-foot circle away from the trunk, add the recommended amount of fertilizer to an additional three feet beyond the drip line of the tree. Granted, there are many more roots growing beyond the drip line, but the tree will utilize what is applied in the doughnut area.

Fruit trees should be fertilized according to the advice given in each of the plant profiles found in this book.

Many years ago when I was growing vegetables in a community garden at Florida A&M University, the gardener next to me had a garden spot that produced more vegetables and fruits than any garden I have seen since. My garden, on the other hand, produced what I thought was a pitiful amount. He started working in the garden at the same time that I did, and he even used the same varieties. One day I asked him how he did it, and his response was simple: "Take care of the soil and the plants will take care of themselves." I listened to what he had to say, but quite frankly I didn't believe it. Surely nothing could be that simple. But over the years, as I added compost and oak leaves, my garden began to improve. It never has looked as good as his (after all, he had a good head start), but I always remember what he had to say and I've taken his advice to heart. What I learned more than thirty years ago still holds true today, and with every wheelbarrow full of compost I add to the soil I remember his words. Don't expect wonders overnight, but with the more good things you add to bare ground, the better it will be for growing food.

WATERING THE GARDEN

Water is Florida's most precious resource and it's important that we use it to full advantage and not waste it. When providing water for a thriving vegetable garden or flourishing fruit trees, there are many ways to make the best use of it.

Watering 1–2–3

Grow plants in the correct season. Squash grown in the heat of summer will always be asking for more water; it's just the wrong season to try to grow it. Plant summer vegetables when it's hot and plant cool-weather crops when the air begins to cool down. It may seem obvious, but many gardeners try to "stretch" a season and the end result can be troublesome.

Make use of mulch. In addition to suppressing weeds and eventually adding organic matter to the soil as it breaks down, mulch does a great job of moderating soil temperatures and reducing evaporation. Mulch applied at a depth of 2 to 3 inches does a fine job, but too much may prevent water from reaching the soil. Oak leaves or straw will work just fine. A 2- to 3-foot circle of mulch around the base of a fruit tree will not only conserve water, it will prevent lawn mower damage to the bottom of the trunk.

Watch indicator plants in the garden. Because fruit trees have deep roots it is sometimes difficult to tell when they need water. In the vegetable garden, it's hard to tell when plants need water until it's too late. There are, however, always one or two plants in the garden that display signs of water distress (wilting) before any other. Those plants can be your "indicator plants"; just hold off on the watering until your indicator plants begin to droop. When they begin to wilt, water everything in the garden nice and deep. Using indicator plants will allow you to water only when needed, which will force the plant roots to grow deep into the soil.

Maximizing Water Efficiency

Vegetable plants and fruit trees need three things to grow properly: water, sunlight, and nutritionally rich soil. Of the three, we have plenty of sunlight, and soil can be fairly easily amended to "create" the desired soil. Water, however, is quickly becoming *the* issue at hand. Unfortunately, water in Florida is in high demand and its availability in quantities we have utilized in the past is becoming smaller. North Florida gardeners are lucky to have some clay in their soil, which holds onto both water and nutrients. It's Central and South Florida where watering the garden often equates to real work. All three zones can need vast amounts of water in drought conditions; it's just that water in North Florida tends to hang around a bit longer. In the other two zones, water slips through the sandy soil like a sieve, and more frequent watering may be necessary to grow trouble-free vegetables and fruit. Unfortunately, the most-often used method of water application, aboveground sprinklers, is the most inefficient. In some studies it was discovered that more than 40 percent of the water applied using this method evaporates before it even hits the ground. We all need to learn how to use water in a more ecologically prudent manner.

Let's talk about the water itself and where it comes from. Most of the water used by Florida homeowners comes from under the ground. It's pumped up from layers of water in the ground called "aquifers." It's from these aquifers that we obtain most of the water we drink and the water we use to irrigate our plants. Because so many people seem to like our weather and have moved here, demand has exceeded available resources; some water now comes from desalination plants along either coast. In some areas of the state there is talk of pumping water from local rivers. Whether you get your water from municipally owned water agencies or from wells on your own property, many think there is not enough water to go around. Reclaimed water (treated water from wastewater treatment plants, also called "grey water"), is being introduced to communities throughout the Sunshine State, and it is being used to irrigate landscaped areas but it is *not* recommended for food crops.

> Submerge pots with a hole in the bottom adjacent to squash and melons to serve as a water reservoir. Fill the pots with water often to prevent the melons and squash from drying out in the sun.

Whether you agree or disagree about whether there is enough water to go around (some people think there may be enough water but that it just isn't being distributed properly), I think everyone will agree that water conservation is in everyone's best interest. The secret to watering a garden that produces food is to use whatever water you have available—municipal water, well water, rain barrels, and so forth—at its highest efficiency. Not only is it wise to save water but it's wise to save money; the water coming out of your faucet is only going to get more expensive in the years ahead.

Rain Barrels, Drip Irrigation, and You

The simplest method to watering plants is to collect rainwater in a rain barrel. A rain barrel can be used to save water for plants during dry periods. Rain barrels can also be set up to slowly release the collected rain to areas that can soak up the water, reducing storm water runoff and increasing groundwater recharge. That means, of course, that the water must be removed from the barrel and distributed to the plants. Water collected in a rain barrel that comes off the roof or into gutters and downspouts is not considered drinkable or "potable," however. Birds and animals have been on the roof, so water from the roof can contain bacteria and other disease-causing organisms. How you use this water in your garden and the type of plants you use it on is an important consideration. Rain barrel water is fine if it's used to water non-edible plants such as flowers or lawns. Water from a rain barrel can be used only in the same way that other nonpotable water is used.

When you use rain barrel water, avoid using overhead irrigation. It is best to use this type of stored water for drip or trickle irrigation. This prevents contamination of edible aboveground plant parts that are hard to clean, especially leafy greens. The vegetable is not safe to eat unless it is thoroughly washed using potable water first. Rain barrel water should not be used close to harvest time to water the vegetable garden and should *never* be used to wash fruits or vegetables from the garden prior to consumption.

All thoughts of diseases aside, the way I did it as a child was to simply dip a watering can into the barrel and water plants with the watering can. That's fine if you're ten years old. The older you get, however, the fewer trips you can make to the barrel to dip out water. Remember, a 2½-gallon watering can filled to the top with water weighs in at a whopping twenty pounds. On a hot summer day, my trips to the rain barrel have been getting fewer and fewer. But, many rain barrels have faucets located near the bottom so the water can be retrieved more easily, especially if the barrel is elevated a foot or so. I have seen pump systems advertised on the Internet that connect to a drip irrigation system to supply water to specific plants, but that gets complicated.

In overhead irrigation, water is applied to a garden via a variety of sprinklers. It is a very inefficient system, and any water lingering on the plants creates a great habitat for the growth of disease organisms. If you must use overhead irrigation make certain that you water deeply and as infrequently as possible while still maintaining adequate soil moisture for fruit production. It is generally accepted that watering in the morning before 10 a.m. works best; this gives the plants a chance to dry off during the day, reducing the chance of diseases. While overhead irrigation is easy (all you need is a hose and sprinkler), it is clearly the most ineffective way to disperse water.

The best system would be a system that doesn't get the foliage and stems wet, and distributes water at the root zone 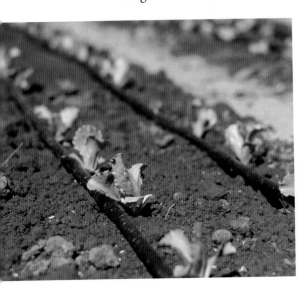 rather than letting it evaporate before it hits the plants. Such systems include drip systems, micro jet irrigation, and soaker hoses. Drip and micro jet irrigation systems utilize a series of supply hoses, generally ½ to ⅝ inch in diameter under low pressure, with many smaller tubes emanating from the supply tube to individual plants. All three types of "soakers" can be placed above or below newspaper mulch, and they should be placed beneath the black plastic mulch when growing melons and pumpkins. Both drip systems need a valve to control the dispensing of water at the proper time and a back flow preventer to prevent irrigation water from backing up into the drinking water system. Battery-operated control valves or electrically operated solenoids turn the water on and off to individual areas of the garden or individual trees. Trees need more emitters than an individual cabbage plant, which in turn needs more water than a head of lettuce. Your system can be engineered to fit the specific needs of your vegetable garden or the number and size of the trees you are growing. Older trees have more roots than young ones and consequently need more emitters as time goes on. If you have sandy soil, the emitters will have to be closer together because water doesn't travel far horizontally in sand. If you have clay soil the emitters can be spaced farther apart. All three systems reduce soil erosion and nutrient leaching.

As its name implies, the drip method utilizes a small head that *slowly* drips a predetermined amount of water into the soil around the plants' roots below. Drippers can be purchased that distribute different amounts of water depending on your specific needs. Clearly, lettuce requires less water than a tomato plant and the drip heads can be adjusted to water only what's needed, in the right amount, to the right plant, to the right place (the root zone). That's downright efficient.

Micro jets also utilize the same large and small supply tubes, but rather than emitting a drip of water, it utilizes a small spray head. The head sprays a predetermined amount of water to a wide area of the root zone (unlike the drip method, which delivers water to a smaller area and works primarily through capillary action). Both systems work extremely well but are initially more expensive than a simple hose and sprinkler set. Depending on the design of the garden each year, the supply lines may have to be replaced to utilize proper spacing. Although it takes more time initially to set up, both the drip and the micro jets are the most efficient systems on the market today.

One last thought about watering. Soaker hoses work very well and provide water to the immediate root zone where it's needed. Many are very inexpensive and many brand names of hoses are recycled from old tires. A soaker hose connects to a standard garden hose, is very economical, and puts the water where it's required; that sounds like a pretty good system to me for someone just starting out. Included in the soaker category are emitter tubes that work like a soaker hose—only better. They water evenly from beginning to end. They won't clog, and connect easily to a faucet, garden hose, or existing underground sprinkler head. Netafim™ is a good example of an emitter tube, and it is readily available at garden centers and home improvement stores (www.Netafim.com). Emitter tubes can be placed on top of or below the soil surface and can be purchased with variable spacing and water amounts.

Garden Tools

Entire books have been written about gardening tools. If you visit any home improvement store, you will see rows of tools of every description and for every purpose. The reality is you don't need that many.

Tools are most often advertised as a help to make gardening easier. Who doesn't want a little help? Gardening of any kind in Florida, whether it's growing roses or fruit trees, is hard work. If I remember one thing my father said about gardening, it's that there are no short cuts to growing plants. You have to put in the work to get anything worthwhile in return. By 10 a.m. the sun is beating down on your head, and the humidity from the previous afternoon's rain is oppressive. That's why many gardeners will hang up their gloves until after dinner when temperatures return to a bearable level. But to get started, these are all the tools you will need:

Hats

Let's start with the basics. Dorky as they may be, if you don't want sunburn (and the health problems that come from getting too much sun) you'll need a straw hat with a wide brim. I've seen a few in mail order catalogs that would require a small loan to buy them. *Save your money.* An eight dollar hat works just as well as a thirty dollar hat. They all will get wet from sweat, sprinklers, and rain. The straw will give way when an errant tree branch hits your head (better the hat than your head). You may even have to replace it midseason, but it's only going to cost another $8 instead of $30. Remember, one of the reasons to grow your own food is to save money. Your neighbors may think the hat looks funny but it may save you a trip to the dermatologist down the road. Cloth hats with wide brims are equally as good and can be washed often. You'll pay more, but they will last a long time.

Gloves

A good pair of gloves is another basic tool. But, confession time, it may be a guy thing, but I have never been a fan of gloves (primarily because I can never keep track of them). If you decide to wear them, gloves are something you should not try to save money on. Inexpensive gloves won't last as long as those that cost a little more, and the cheap gloves aren't designed as well; sometimes, a cheap glove will give you a blister before a hoe handle does. Good gloves will prevent blisters, dirty fingernails and hands, and will protect your hands from scratches. Good goatskin gloves are worth their weight in gold and are tough enough to prevent most prickles from gouging your hand.

Shovels

Picking the right shovel is critical. Like selecting a watering can, you need to take time to decide which type is best for you. Remember, your shovel will be your best gardening friend for a long time (perhaps even decades) and selecting the right one is a significant decision. It may seem I am giving the selection of a tool too much weight but a shovel can make you or break you when it comes to the garden. Really, it can determine whether you have a pleasant experience or one that's, let's say, not so pleasant.

Shovels come in two basic types: one has a somewhat rounded steel blade (round shovel) and the other has a flat blade (spade). Each one works well but you will need to decide which performs best for you. Both are used to dig holes and turn soil over in preparation for planting. Likewise, shovel handles come in two "varieties" as well; one is a straight handle and the other has a T- or D-shaped handle. Both a round shovel and a spade can be manufactured with either a straight or a T-shaped handle. The straight-handled round shovel is the most commonplace. However, the spade with a T- or D-shaped handle is the most versatile. This type of handle gives the shovel some turning leverage and can be used for longer periods with less hand strain.

Again, don't try to save money on a shovel. Buy a good shovel. Either type of shovel should have two heavy "lips" at the very top of the blade on either side of the handle. These lips will permit you to place greater force on the blade when you step on it without hurting the arch in your foot. The bigger the lip, the greater the force that can be applied to the shovel blade.

The manufacturers in the United Kingdom *really* know how to make a worthwhile shovel and the expense is certainly worth it; after all, you will have it for a long time. Several good dealers of steel T- or D-shaped handled spades can be found on the Internet and at local specialty stores. And remember, shiny, stainless steel shovels aren't necessarily better than standard steel models.

A few things about shovel maintenance are important to know. First, make certain the shovel blade is sharpened regularly. There is nothing more discouraging than trying to cut through sod or a root with a dull blade. An inexpensive steel file can sharpen the blade before you place it back into the garden shed ready for use next time. This brings up the next point: clean the blade and handle before you put it away. A light spray of WD-40® on the blade before you hang the shovel up will help keep the shovel in good shape for a long time. When you need it, it will be ready to go. And one last thing—an old-time gardener taught me this fact about shovels many years ago. As he was watching me replace a broken shovel handle, he simply said, "A broken shovel handle is a sign of a lazy man." It made me pause. Sure enough, I had forced the shovel handle down with most of my weight while trying to remove a tree root. Had I spent more time digging and less time trying the force the shovel to do something it wasn't designed to do, I would still have that shovel with its original handle today.

Trowels

A trowel is basically a small shovel. I can say with great certainty that I have spent more money buying trowels to replace broken ones than I have for any other tool. Most trowels on the market have wooden handles with a bar attached to a blade with rivets. When you apply any pressure at all, the rivets break off, making the tool unusable. Ask any professional gardener and they will tell you, hands down, the best trowels are made from one piece of aluminum and have a comfortable foam handle. A $4 trowel is worth just that. Get the good kind.

Hoes

Pick up a hoe and you know hard work is just around the corner. Hoes are used to remove weeds around cultivated plants and to help make furrows when planting seeds. There are two basic types and, after a time, you will have both in your arsenal. The most common is often called a grubbing hoe; it has a wide steel blade at the end of a long handle. It is used to dig deep into the soil, removing weeds by their roots. A newer and somewhat easier version is called an oscillating, pass-through, or scuffle hoe; there are several versions of it. Most have a steel loop, flat on one side, at the end of a long handle, and they can be pushed or pulled. Rather than *digging* the entire root, a scuffle hoe passes ½ to 1 inch below the soil line, *cutting* the roots off. Other designs of scuffle hoes have heart-shaped steel blades that are also pulled just below the surface cutting the roots off. Other types of hoes include the collinear, swan neck, Reisch hoe, and onion hoes.

The advantage to a grubbing hoe (sometimes called an "eye" hoe) is that, in addition to pulling out the roots, you are cultivating soil at the same time allowing good nutrient and water penetration into the soil. A scuffle hoe does cultivate but because many plants don't like their surface roots to be disturbed, a grubbing hoe is a good choice. You will have to decide which hoe is best for you in your particular situation.

Pitchforks

A pitchfork can be an invaluable tool in the garden. You can use it backwards (tines down and drawing the pitchfork towards you) to "rake" up weeds and to scoop up the debris into the compost pile. A pitchfork can also be used to break up soil clumps in the garden prior to sowing seeds, and the handle can be used to create a shallow seed furrow.

Lifting or Turning Forks

Perhaps one of the most misunderstood, and most underutilized, tools in the gardener's collection is the lifting fork. Unlike the pitchfork, which has five to seven round tines, a lifting or turning fork has four to five flat, pointed bars with a "T" handle. The turning fork, as its name implies, is used to dig and turn soil over, instead of using a shovel. After the soil is lifted and turned, this fork is used to break up any clods of soil. The turning fork can also be used to harvest root crops (such as potatoes, turnips, and peanuts) without cutting the roots. The lifting fork is inserted into the soil, and, in several swift, lifting motions, it lifts the roots out of the soil. There is very little bruising to the roots while the soil sifts through the fork. To divide overgrown perennials, two forks are placed back-to-back into a large clump of daylilies, liriope, or so forth; the clump can be gently pulled apart causing little, if any, injury to the plant roots.

Pruners, Loppers, and Saws

To complete any gardener's tool chest, you need something to cut branches and harvest fruit. Hand pruners come in a variety of styles, and it seems that someone is always trying to improve on the time-tested standards. Pruners are available in just two basic styles: the anvil or pinching style and the scissors style. The anvil type has a single blade and a flat surface that cuts a branch off. If someone gives you these pruners as a gift, immediately give them to someone else. The blade on this style become dull very quickly and is virtually impossible to sharpen. After time, the blade becomes so dull that rather than cutting the branch off, the anvil pruner simply pinches the branch off, causing damage to the remaining part of the branch. The scissors type, as its name implies, has two bypassing blades that create a nice, sharp cut. The blade can easily be sharpened after a day's work and good models even have replaceable blades. Hand pruners should only be used when the branches to be pruned are less than ½ inch in diameter. For branches ½ to ¾ inches in diameter, use loppers. These long-handled pruners have scissor type blades also, and because the long handles can provide the needed leverage to cut larger pieces of wood, they are a useful tool. Anything more than ¾ inch in diameter requires a saw. The most common type of saw is a folding handsaw. The blades are very sharp and folding the blade into the handle when the job is finished will protect the blade, as well as the gardener.

Miscellaneous Tools

There are few other things you need as time goes on. A good garden hose is worth its weight in gold. Do *not* try to save money on this garden tool. Inexpensive versions will kink (why spend all your time in the garden trying to unravel the hose?); the brass connectors at either end will bend or, worse, separate from the hose altogether; and a cheap hose will spring leaks. Start with at least a ⅝-inch hose made of good rubber that has some heft to it. Later, you may buy a ¾-inch hose with heavy brass connectors, but at first, buy what you can afford. Please, when you buy your hose also buy a water breaker designed to water plants, and a hose-end water valve. Water straight out of the hose will wash small seeds and seedlings away. Most breakers come attached to a long, aluminum watering wand that will help to reach those hard-to-get spots. Keep the water nozzle used to wash cars in the garage where it belongs; its spray is too powerful and will wash seeds and seedlings away.

Watering cans, like shovels, are something you have for a long time so make sure you get one that works just like you want it to. You can pay a good sum for one, but the plastic versions can work just as well. (Put the expensive galvanized or copper versions on your birthday wish list.) The ideal watering can will have a good detachable "rose" (the device where the water comes out), the front half of the top opening should be covered (to prevent water from gushing out over the top when you tip the can), and it should have measurements marked on the side to aid in measuring fertilizer.

At first, I thought gardening boots were a luxury, but after wearing out several pairs of tennis shoes, I learned otherwise. Good garden boots have a stiff, steel arch that helps immeasurably when you use your foot against the shovel to dig holes. Believe me, your arches will thank you at day's end. Good boots will also have reinforcement rubber along the outside of the arch and at the protruding ankle bone location on the inside of your foot. Finally, if you spray chemicals of any kind, rubber boots protect your feet and legs from chemical contact and can be cleaned with soap and water. (Chemicals are absorbed and their toxicity is intensified when you use leather shoes or boots.)

VEGETABLES & FRUITS

Growing food in Florida may be one of the most gratifying and satisfying voyages in your gardening saga. Eating fresh food that you have grown, often from seed, and nurtured to maturity is a remarkable voyage. The best news is that you did it. You know what has (or has not) been sprayed on the fruit and vegetables you are about to eat. You know the work involved in bringing food to the table (if you didn't eat all the peas out in the garden first). You saved your family's hard-earned money by growing food at home. And when you go inside after a long day in the garden and look in the mirror at your smudged face and dirty fingernails, you can be proud. Fellow gardeners, I salute you!

BEAN

If you have a vegetable garden in Florida you have to have beans. Bush beans, pole beans, green beans, wax beans, French beans, lima beans—all perform well in Florida gardens. Beans are a great way to introduce children to gardening because they may be the easiest of vegetables to grow. In my family, we often grow pole beans on bamboo poles, creating a little teepee "hideaway" for the younger folks. It's not unusual to find children tucked inside reading a book. Snap beans used to be called "string" beans because of the tough fibrous string on the back of the pod that had to be removed before cooking. Newer varieties don't have the "string."

When to Plant

In North Florida beans are best grown from March through November. In Central and South Florida plant beans beginning in February through May and again from August through October, thus escaping frosts and the hottest months. Plant a new row of seeds every ten to fourteen days to have a fresh supply of beans every week.

Where to Plant

Plant beans in a location that receives at least eight hours of full sun a day. Beans will provide a virtually limitless bounty if you take the time to prepare a good, compost-rich seedbed. And, if they are grown in good soil and receive ample water, beans can be pest free. Beans are a good candidate for growing in containers provided they get adequate light and plenty of water.

How to Plant

As with any legume with a deep taproot, beans do not like to be transplanted. Direct sow them in the soil where you plan to grow them. If you insist on growing them in pots first, use biodegradable pots that can be planted directly in the soil without disturbing the beans' roots. Plant in rows 18 inches apart, and 6 inches apart in the row. Beans do not perform well in wide row plantings. When the new growth emerges from the soil (three to five days after they're planted), the bean seedlings are often the favorite food of birds, especially brown thrashers. They will break off the tender seed that emerges with the new leaves, which will kill the new sprout. My daughter's 30-inch-long lifelike plastic lizard will scare them off most years but aluminum pie pans attached to strings and allowed to twirl in the air will work, too. If neither appeals to you, simply plant a few more seeds after the remaining seedlings get a little taller. Go easy on the fertilizer—more beans are killed by too much fertilizer than too little. Too much fertilizer also produces more leaves and fewer beans.

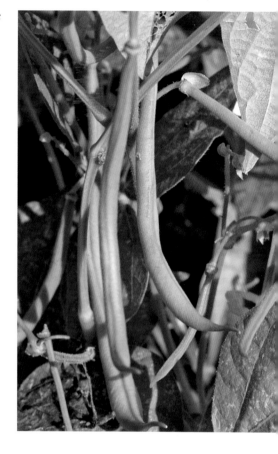

Care and Maintenance

If you are looking for a carefree plant, beans are it. If beans are prone to any disease, it is rust; tiny orange pustules will appear on the undersides of the leaves and will cause the leaves to drop off prematurely. The best way to prevent rust is to make it a habit to avoid walking through or handling bean plants while they are wet. Handling them will transfer the disease from one plant to another via water droplets. Wait until a plant's leaves and stems are totally dry before handling them. Fertilize every four weeks with a general-purpose fertilizer or one specific to your particular soil as determined by a soil analysis. Bean beetles, which can be identified by their copper color with black spots, sometime infest bean plantings. Immature larvae are yellow or orange with spines on their backs. Both adults and larvae eat the green "leafy" part of the leaf between the veins. Remove them manually or spray with insecticidal soap or rotenone.

Additional Information

Bush beans are harvested while the bean pods are still tender and the beans have not fully formed inside. For bush beans, filet (French) beans, and bush lima beans, pull the entire plant, harvest the pods, and throw the foliage and stems into the compost pile. It may seem different than what you're accustomed to, but if you plant beans every ten to fourteen days you will have plenty of bush beans for the table. Bush beans (those that grow to about 18 inches tall) come in a wide variety of colors and forms. Green beans and wax beans (yellow beans) are the easiest to grow and should be picked when the pods are no more than 6 to 7 inches long while they are still tender. The best varieties for Florida include 'Bush Blue Lake 274', 'Commodore Improved', 'Contender', 'Greencrop', 'Roma' (Romano form), 'Tendergreen Improved', and 'White Half Runner'. The best wax beans are 'Improved Golden Wax' and 'Cherokee Wax'. 'Royal Burgundy Purple Pod' is the best purple variety (burgundy colored beans are the same and will change to green when cooked). Raw, young green, wax, and purple beans look colorful when added to salads or served individually as crudités with a dip. Soybeans are difficult to shell; a good 5-minute soaking in boiling water will allow the beans to "pop" out the end.

Pole beans, unlike bush beans, produce many crops in one season (provided you pick every pod) and they are easier to harvest. Pole beans can grow to 8 feet tall and need some sort of support to grow on. Most often, two poles are placed at either end of a row and wire is placed at heights of 5 to 6 feet between the posts. Strings are then *gently* and *loosely* attached to bean seedlings below the leaves and then to the wire. The beans will naturally climb up the string. Good varieties of pole beans include 'Kentucky Wonder', 'Blue Lake', 'Kentucky Blue', 'Asparagus Yard Long', 'White Half Runner', 'Romano' (Italian), 'Purple Podded', and 'Big Mama' (lima).

Shell beans are harvested when the beans are fully formed in the pod but are still tender. Shell beans can be allowed to dry in the pod before harvesting for dry bean storage.

Don't forget lima beans! They can be eaten fresh, canned, dried, or frozen. Use 'Dixie Butterpea Speckled', 'Jackson Wonder', 'Fordhook 242', 'Burpee Improved', 'Eastland', 'Giant Calico', 'Henderson', and 'Big Mama'.

Italian beans are flat and are often used in soups and stews. Unlike other beans, they can be picked and used in soups even after they get a little tough.

French (or filet) beans are tiny, tender beans picked when they're 3 to 4 inches long and can be cooked or eaten raw. 'Maxibel', 'Petite Filet', 'Delinel', or 'Rolande' are good choices.

'Painted Lady' is a climbing bean (with an edible pod) that will produce a bean pod but is generally grown as a decorative variety for covering gazebos or arbors. The flowers are red-and-white bicolored, and a plant can grow to 18 feet long.

> Once bush beans are planted they don't need any additional fertilizer. Pole beans and lima beans enjoy a little more "juice" after the blossoms begin to appear.

BEET

Before you say it, I *know* not everyone likes beets. Their deep, earthy flavor may be an acquired taste but they are a very versatile vegetable when cooked in soups, served warm with a little raspberry vinaigrette, or used fresh in a cold salad. If you have only eaten beets from a jar or can then perhaps growing your own beets might change your mind. Their colors run the gamut from deep "church pew" red to yellow, white, and even striped red and white. Don't forget the beet leaves can be eaten in salads or cooked like spinach. Beets are high in a wide array of vitamins and minerals.

When to Plant

Beets are a cool-season crop and should be planted from September through March in North Florida and from October through March in Central and South Florida. They are tolerant of a little frost (short of hard freezes) and can also withstand a few warm days, making them a very long-season crop.

Where to Plant

Plant beets in full sun, in a well-tilled, well-drained soil free of rocks and stones. Beets can sometimes look stunted, which is often caused by soil pH outside the beet's comfort range of 6.2 to 6.7.

How to Plant

Each little beet seed actually contains the beginnings for three to four seedlings. So don't be surprised if three little plants sprout from the ground where you only planted one seed. To prevent crowding, it is essential that you thin the seedlings to one plant every 3 inches. Otherwise, the roots will be small and difficult to use. Soak the seeds overnight in warm water (I use an insulated thermos bottle) and sow the next day. Plant individual seeds ¼ inch deep and expect to see sprouts in seven to ten days. To prevent root maggots, sprinkle the row with a small amount of wood ash (1 cup for every 10 feet of row) from your fireplace. Space the rows anywhere from 12 to 18 inches apart.

Care and Maintenance

Beets are particularly sensitive to a lack of water. If you want big healthy roots, make sure they get plenty of water, especially during dry spells. Follow the directions based upon a soil analysis, but a general rule of thumb is fertilize the seedbed before the seeds are planted and again after the beets reach a height of 3 to 4 inches. Flea beetles are a problem from time to time but a light sprinkle of rotenone dust will make quick work of them.

Additional Information

Beet greens are best harvested when they are 5 to 6 inches tall. The roots can be harvested anytime during the growing season but they are best when they are less than 2 inches in diameter. If they are any larger than that they can get woody and are difficult to eat.

Hands down, 'Detroit Dark Red' is the best deep red variety. 'Burpee's Golden' is just that—a beautiful, deep-golden color. For a little novelty try the heirloom variety 'Chioggia'; when it's cut across the root, it has alternating red and white stripes (great for salads) and turns solid red when cooked. Other good varieties include 'Cylindrica', 'Early Wonder', 'Green Top Bunching', 'Piatta D'Egitto', and 'Yellow Detroit'.

BROCCOLI

Despite being disparaged by a certain past president, broccoli, when prepared properly, is a delicious vegetable. Unfortunately, some people cook the pure life out of it by covering it with water and cooking it until it leaves the saucepan limp and lifeless. It is the unopened flower head that we eat, and a well-grown broccoli "head" can easily reach 6 to 7 inches in diameter. When the primary head is removed, smaller florets appear in the lower leaf nodes and can continue to produce for another 30 to 45 days.

When to Plant

Make no mistake—broccoli is a cool-weather crop. If an early-maturing variety is planted at the onset of cooler weather, a second crop can be planted and will grow until warm weather returns. (Be sure to rotate to another location within the garden if you plant a second crop.) But if it gets too much heat the plants will begin to flower and set seed (called "bolting") and it will be unusable.

Where to Plant

Plant broccoli in full sun, in well-drained, moist soil with added organic matter (compost, leaves, peat moss, and so forth). A soil acidity in the range of 6 to 7 is best to prevent root diseases.

How to Plant

Broccoli is very easy to grow from seed. Place one or two seeds in a small flowerpot or seedling tray with good potting soil ¼ inch deep and cover with fine soil. To prevent seeds from washing away while watering, place the container inside a larger one containing shallow water and water from the bottom up, removing the pot when the soil becomes saturated. Seedlings will appear in four to seven days. If more than one seed sprouts, thin to one seedling per container. Keep the seedlings in full sun and prevent the soil from drying out. Once the seedling has developed three new leaves that look like the mature leaves, plant the seedling directly into prepared garden soil. Broccoli needs plenty of room to grow properly, so don't try to squeeze many plants into a small space. Space plants 24 inches apart in the row and place each row 24 inches apart. Anything spaced less than this means you are wasting your efforts.

Care and Maintenance

Once planted, broccoli is easy to grow. Give it plenty of water, and feed it every two to three weeks with a general-purpose fertilizer of 5-5-5 or 8-8-8. It is a shallow, rooted plant, so be very careful about deep cultivation. Once the heads have matured, but before the individual flowers begin to expand, cut the center head about 6 inches below the flower head. If you continue to feed and water as before, small flower shoots (florets) will begin to sprout and can supply

more broccoli, albeit smaller, for four to five more weeks. Watch for aphids on the undersides of the leaves that often migrate to the central head. To remove the small insects before cooking simply soak the flower head in salted water for several minutes. The dead aphids can be washed off with a kitchen sink sprayer. Watch for armyworms when seedlings are first set out into the garden. A simple 3-inch collar of heavy paper secured with a paper clip and pushed partially into the ground around each transplant will keep the worms away from the stems.

Additional Information

Several varieties of broccoli are available but some of the best include 'Packman' (an early season selection), 'High Dividend', 'Green Comet', and 'Green Goliath'.

BRUSSELS SPROUTS

When I first saw Brussels sprouts when I was eight years old, I thought they were tiny cabbages growing on a stalk. As it turns out, I wasn't far off. As a member of the same family, the taste is similar to that of cabbage and some even say, of broccoli. A planting of ten to twelve individual seedlings is usually enough for a family of four. Getting them to a size large enough to produce harvestable quantities may take a little longer than some gardeners have patience for, however.

When to Plant

This is a cold-season crop and should planted from October through February. Seeds should be started indoors or under cover forty five days prior to transplanting into the garden soil; by then, the seedlings should have three to four pairs of true leaves.

Where to Plant

Plant Brussels sprouts where they will get plenty of sunshine (a minimum of eight hours), in enriched, well-drained soil. Give them room to grow, although the stalk where the little buds grow is only 1½ inches in diameter. It's the leaves at the top that are the plant's power supply, and they need plenty of space. Too little sun will cause the plants to stretch and the sprouts will be small, if any are produced at all.

How to Plant

Plant as seedlings 24 inches apart, in rows 24 inches apart. Don't worry if the seedlings fall over once they are planted. Brussels sprouts are famous for laying down before they decide to grow upright. Staking is not necessary even though each plant can reach a height of 36 inches.

Care and Maintenance

Brussels sprouts are carefree plants. The new growth at the top and the sprouts may attract aphids, but a simple spray of water from the garden hose usually takes care of that situation. If they persist, a light dusting with rotenone will solve the problem. Growing plants in full sun with adequate moisture and regular feedings will allow the plant to defend itself. Keep the pH in the neighborhood of 6.0 to 6.8. Brussels sprouts are heavy nitrogen feeders so add additional nitrogen to your standard fertilizer application every two to three weeks to keep them going strong. If your fertilizer contains a few minor elements, especially boron, so much the better. You will get stronger buds and the stem won't get hollow. Brussels sprouts are shallow rooted so be careful when cultivating.

Additional Information

Before you plant, make certain you are committed to growing Brussels sprouts for the long term. Of all the vegetables, they can take the longest to produce a harvest and they need plenty of room to grow properly. The

little sprouts mature from the bottom of the stalk up. To harvest, simply twist the individual sprouts off the stalk when they are about ¾ inch in diameter and firm. Small sprouts can be eaten but it takes more of them to make a meal. When they grow too large, they get fibrous and woody and their flavor is much stronger. Remove the lower leaves and buds to encourage more sprouts and leaves. Many gardeners will pinch out the growing shoot when the lower sprouts begin to mature. This encourages many sprouts to ripen along the stem. Try 'Jade Cross' and 'Long Island Improved' for best production in Florida.

CABBAGE

Of all the members of the Brassica family, which includes Brussels sprouts, cauliflower, and broccoli, cabbage may be the least finicky of the cool-season crops to grow in the home garden. It's a great plant to include in a beginners garden because it is so easy to grow, and there are numerous unique cabbage varieties to keep the more advanced gardener intrigued. Other than needing a frequent application of fertilizer, cabbages can be grown just about anywhere and can be harvested at any stage.

When to Plant

Cabbage hates warm weather and will "bolt" (begin flowering) when temperatures get too warm. (They can also bolt when it gets too cold, but that's rarely a problem in Florida.) Plant one crop in late fall and plant another crop 30 to 45 days later to stagger the harvest. Trust me, one family *does not* need ten cabbages at the same time! Stop planting in March.

Where to Plant

Plant in full sun, in average, well-drained soil.

How to Plant

There are two schools of thought on how to plant cabbages. I once read that to grow cabbages properly you mustn't till the soil prior to planting. The advice was to simply remove the weeds and transplant seedlings into hard, unimproved garden soil. Another time, I read that you must till the soil deeply, add organic matter to a depth of 6 to 8 inches, and plant the seedlings in the prepared soil. After planting cabbages utilizing both methods, I didn't notice any difference. Lucky for us, cabbages don't know how to read. However, you must anticipate the eventual size of the plant (read the seed package or label when buying transplants) because different types of cabbages need different spacing. Cabbage can be direct sown into the ground but must be thinned to proper spacing to achieve proper growth. Spacing seeds or transplants too close together will yield small, weak plants. Give them room to grow.

Care and Maintenance

Well-drained soil, lots of water, and regular applications every three weeks of fertilizers high in nitrogen is the prescription for healthy cabbage. Keep the weeds away because they compete for the water and nutrients. Occasionally after planting, armyworms will cut the tender stems of the new sprouts or newly planted transplants during the night, making them look as though a tiny lumberjack sawed his way through the garden. A 3- x 5-inch index card cut in half lengthwise, attached end to end with a paper clip or staple, and then pushed halfway into the ground will create enough of a barrier to prevent damage from the worms. Once the seedlings get a little older (and a little tougher), the collars can be removed.

Additional Information

Many different types of cabbages are available and some of the best information about which cabbage does best in your area may come from your fellow neighborhood gardeners. Ask around for their ideas; you'll be surprised how helpful that neighbor you never talked to before can be. Other than asking a neighbor, try 'New Jersey Wakefield' (whose head grows to a point), 'Copenhagen Market', and 'Bonnie's Hybrid' to start. For a red cabbage variety, try 'Mammoth Red Rock'; and for a densely curled cabbage, plant 'Savoy Chieftain'.

Chinese cabbages are the "pretty boys" of the cabbage world and many can even be used in ornamental plantings instead of bedding plants. 'Michihili' is without a doubt the best, followed closely by 'Jade Pagoda', 'Mei Oing Choi', and 'Rubicon'.

CANTALOUPE

Is there anything in the world more refreshing on a hot, Florida summer day than eating an ice-cold cantaloupe? Only a big scoop of vanilla ice cream dropped in the center could make it better. I am often asked why I got into gardening and it may very well be that eating a cantaloupe freshly picked off the vine is what showed me how great the difference between home, grown versus store-bought is. If you haven't attempted to grow cantaloupe because you don't have the space, believe me, it's worth the effort. However, given their nomadic nature, this plant really should not be considered for small gardens.

When to Plant

Plant seedlings or seeds in mid- to late February or after the danger of frost has passed. The earlier you can get them in the ground (but avoiding any chance of frost), the better your chances of growing ample-sized fruit before the bugs invade with warmer weather. Start seeds indoors three weeks before the last anticipated frost in spring.

Where to Plant

Plant in full sun, in well-drained, organically enriched soil. Depending on the variety selected, cantaloupes take up lots of room. For gardeners with small spaces try some of the bush forms (see page 33). Good air circulation is a must to fend off pesky disease organisms.

How to Plant

Given that weeds often grow faster and better than the vegetable you're trying plant, applying a weed barrier of some sort is helpful when growing melons. Seeds or seedlings can be planted either in rows 48 inches apart, with individual plants set 24 inches apart, or in hills 48 to 60 inches apart, with four to five seeds per hill. Place black plastic or landscape fabric over the entire area in which you want the vines to grow, or place a single layer of newspaper covered with coastal hay immediately next to the plants and wherever the vines are expected to grow. The vines will grow over the weed barrier without weed competition. If you use plastic or landscape fabric, cut a slit in the plastic and plant the seedlings or seeds as described. Give the seedlings at least 1 inch of water per week.

Care and Maintenance

Sometimes, cantaloupes will be visited by slugs and bugs that bore into the fruit. Much of their damage can be reduced, if not eliminated, by placing any half-grown fruit on a board or atop a recycled tin can. In addition, cantaloupe can be grown on a vertical support system similar to that of pole beans and the fruit supported by recycled nylon stockings or panty hose. Using this method, slugs are almost never a problem and the fruit stays clean and easy to monitor for picking at the right time. One last thing, as the fruit begins to ripen, hold off on watering a little. The fruit tastes better if cantaloupes don't get too much water late in the game. Cantaloupes are ready to harvest when the fruit separates easily from its stem and/or the netting on the outside of the fruit turns from green to tan.

Cantaloupes are heavy feeders and need plenty of soil moisture to perform well. Give each plant ½ cup of a 5-0-5 fertilizer ratio or fish emulsion three weeks after planting and again after the flowers appear.

Additional Information

The hybridizers have been busy with cantaloupes, but despite their best efforts I still think 'Ambrosia' is the best; the flavor is intense and the vines are resistant to diseases. Once you have conquered the standard varieties consider other members of the melon family including banana melons, Crenshaw, French hybrids, casaba, Jenny Lind muskmelons, yellow canary melons, and Ogen melons. For small areas, try 'Minnesota Midget' cantaloupes—they have 3-foot-long vines.

CARROT

If you have ever pulled a carrot out of the ground, washed it off with water from a garden hose, and munched on it, you know how sweet and crisp homegrown carrots are compared to the store-bought ones. After tasting their first garden carrot my children later would routinely run out into the garden after school to graze on the myriad fresh vegetables. Come to think of it, I used to do the same after my father introduced me to freshly picked peas. With our four children, carrots were the breakthrough veggie, followed by beans, peas, lettuce, and broccoli.

When to Plant

Carrots can be planted anytime between September to mid-March. Two to three sowings during that period will provide roots that are tender and sweet.

Where to Plant

Plant carrots where they will receive at least eight hours of full sun, in a well-drained soil that is free from any rocks, stones, and roots.

How to Plant

A carrot is one of those vegetables that require just a little bit of extra care for good production. First, carrot roots tend to fork rather than have that straight, store-bought look when they reach any sort of obstacle such as roots of neighboring trees or shrubs, rocks, pebbles, and even irrigation pipes. It's important that you enrich the soil the best you can, fluff up the soil with a spading fork or rototiller to a depth of at least 12 inches, and remove any of these obstacles. Next, lay the handle of a rake or hoe in the prepared space and gently press the handle into the fresh soil to create a shallow furrow ¼ inch deep. Carrots often take two to three weeks to germinate, and it's difficult to remember where you planted them. To get around that, simply plant radish seeds 12 inches apart and ½ inch deep in the furrow. The radish seeds will germinate in two days and act as living "markers" for the carrot seeds. Plus, the radishes can be harvested in thirty days without harming the newly sprouted carrot seed. After planting the radish seeds carefully sprinkle a small amount of carrot seed into the furrow every 2 to 3 inches apart. Do *not* cover the seed. Repeat that sentence. Then, gently water the seed with a watering can, which will cover the seed just enough to make them happy without burying them too deep.

Care and Maintenance

Regardless of how careful you were, you probably sowed too many seeds. To grow properly, the carrot seedlings must be thinned to one plant every 3 inches. Trust me, this is probably the hardest thing to do in vegetable gardening but is absolutely critical if you want fully and properly formed roots. You can gently pull the seedlings sideways or simply snip the extra seedlings off at ground level with a pair of scissors; both methods reduce root damage to the remaining seedlings. Carrots that grow too long past their prime will become woody and are inedible even in soups. Plant three crops during the cooler months, four weeks apart. At the end of their growing season, carrots require less water, and too much water can cause the roots to crack.

Additional Information

It's essential to rotate the location of your carrot crop to different spots in the garden every year. Carrots planted every season in the same location will encourage an infestation of wire worms, a tough-skinned maggot that bores into the root, ruining it. Just to be on the safe side, when you till the soil in preparation for sowing seed, sprinkle a fair amount (1 cup to every 10 feet of row length) of wood ashes from your fireplace onto the soil and incorporate into the mix. The ashes will repel root worms.

'Nantes Half Long' carrots perform well in Florida, as do 'Chantenay Royal', 'Imperator 58', and 'Tendersweet'. If you like the unusual, try 'Cosmic Purple' and 'Snow White'.

CAULIFLOWER

Gardening is often about the little miracles that happen when you work in the dirt. One day you plant a tiny, vulnerable seedling a mere 2 inches tall, and after only six to eight weeks you can harvest a snowy white head of cauliflower that's more than 8 inches in diameter, weighing in at more than 3 pounds. Eat cauliflower raw with salad dressings, steam it with a little butter, use it in casseroles—you decide! It's one of the most versatile vegetables you can grow and also one of the easiest.

When to Plant

Direct sow cauliflower seeds or transplant seedlings any time between September through January. Cauliflower, unlike many of its cabbage relatives, can take moderate frost but not hard freezes, so protect it from extreme temperatures.

Where to Plant

Plant cauliflower seeds or seedlings in well prepared and composted soil with high water-holding capacity and a pH of 6.0 to 6.5. Site in locations where they will get at least 8 hours of full sun. Adding a little magnesium sulfate, either by itself or as part of the general fertilizer, will produce bigger yields. Follow the fertilizer container's instructions for the correct amounts.

How to Plant

Direct sow seeds ½ inch deep or plant seedlings. Space in rows 18 inches apart and individual plants 18 inches apart for proper air circulation and to prevent overcrowding. To grow cauliflower to its best ultimate size, the leaves must have plenty of room to manufacture energy, so the more room you give them, the better. Plants grown too closely together will be small and will produce small heads called "buttons."

Care and Maintenance

Cauliflower is grown much like one grows cabbage: lots of water, plenty of sun, and high-nitrogen fertilizer every three weeks. Weeds compete for nutrients and water so keep the rows as weed free as possible. For many years it was said that you must gather the leaves when the curd is about the size of a softball, cover the head with the leaves, and secure with a rubber band. The reason was to keep sunlight off the curd to help keep the curds white (a process called "blanching"). With newer varieties like 'Snowball', the growers have developed leaves that naturally cover the head and blanching is not necessary. Unlike its broccoli relative, once the main head has been harvested, a cauliflower plant will not produce side shoots so the entire plant can be pulled up and added to the compost pile. Cauliflower rarely has any pest problems. A few holes chewed in the leaves by worms usually aren't of sufficient quantity to impact production. Regular additions of fertilizer are important to maintain

good plant quality. Adequate soil moisture *must* be maintained to produce good flower heads. Inconsistent watering regimens will reduce overall curd quality and size.

Additional Information

Because of its self-blanching attribute, 'Snowball' is at the top of my list. The heads are uniform and tightly grown. On the less traditional side, 'Brocoverde' is a broccoli/cauliflower cross and its light-green flower head is spiky with individual florets. 'Cheddar', as the name implies, is a yellow form of cauliflower, and 'Violet Queen' displays a rich, deep-purple color. All make wonderful additions to salads or dips. Purple heads turn green when they're cooked (as do purple beans).

CELERY

Unfortunately, most home gardens don't include celery. It's a shame because the flavor of homegrown celery has an intense, fabulous flavor. Plus, the sheer joy of growing your own and later adding it to soups, stews, and salads is very gratifying! If you are looking for the big, fat, crunchy celery with perfectly grown long stalks, the homegrown type may not be for you. But, if you are ready to step up and try a vegetable that is a little more difficult to grow, celery is a good choice. An ice-cold gazpacho during the summer just wouldn't be the same without celery.

When to Plant
Plant celery beginning in July with a last planting in December. Celery takes 120 to 140 days to mature.

Where to Plant
Plant celery in well-prepared, composted soil with a pH of 5.8 to 6.8 in a spot that receives at least 8 hours of full sun. Wherever you plant celery, make certain that plenty of water will be available throughout the growing season. Celery needs highly fertile, well-enriched soil ideally amended with lots of peat moss and well-rotted manure.

How to Plant
Celery seeds are so tiny that planting them outside is almost futile. Instead, plant two to three seeds in a container and barely cover them with soil. Mixing seeds with sand and sprinkling the seed/sand mixture on top of potting soil works well, too. Watering from the bottom usually works best so you don't wash the seeds away. When the seedlings are about 2 inches tall or have three pairs of true leaves, thin each pot to only one plant. Continue to grow the seedlings indoors until they are ready to plant in the garden. Generally, this is when they are about 6 inches tall. Transplant the individual seedlings into the garden in double rows 2 feet apart, with 6 to 8 inches between the double rows and individual plants set at 8 to 12 inches apart in the rows.

Care and Maintenance

Water, water, water, and then water some more, especially during the hot summer months. Celery plants that are allowed to go dry develop dry, stringy, and tough stalks suitable only for stews and soups—*not* for eating raw. With the amount of water necessary to grow celery, that inevitable wet-weather pest, slugs, can become a real problem. They won't kill a plant but they will devour the leaves and make the plant look unsightly. Because I prefer to avoid using chemicals around vegetables, I use beer traps instead (which gives me an excuse to drink whatever is left). Celery stalks can be harvested at any time, and if you want white, tender stalks, tie them up with twine and harvest as needed. Blanched stalks will be less bitter. Celery doesn't like the cold so protect it when the weather

gets cold. Even if cold weather damages a few of the outside stalks, the interior stalks will be fine.

Additional Information

Of all celery, a form called "cutting celery" is very easy to grow and the leaves are used in salsa, soups, stews, and with mixed vegetables. Try some in tomato juice! 'Giant Pascal', 'Stokes Golden Plume', and 'Golden Self Branching' varieties will produce the traditional celery plants like those found in grocery stores.

COLLARDS

Mention Florida gardening and my mind flashes to swept front yards, rickety white picket fences, and collards in the vegetable garden. The ever-present collard plants standing tall in the Florida sun is a symbol of self-sufficiency, strength, and southern pride. Once, an older friend of ours invited us to her house for some "sun tea" (although it turned out there was very little tea and quite a bit of Wild Turkey whiskey in the sun tea). When we were ready to leave, she kindly gave us a bunch of collards that she had grown in her garden, tied up with the biggest rubber band I have ever seen. She was so proud of the greens she had grown and I was proud to accept her heartfelt gift of something she had grown herself.

When to Plant

Collards can withstand both heat and all but the most severe cold weather, so feel free to plant them whenever you have the notion.

Where to Plant

Like their cabbage relatives, plant collard seedlings in full sun, in well-drained soil with a pH of 6.0 to 6.8. Give them *plenty* of room; plant individual seedlings 36 inches apart, in rows 36 inches apart.

How to Plant

Collards can be direct sown in the garden ½ inch deep utilizing the proper spacing or by planting transplants. If you're planting in the middle of summer, make certain the seedlings or transplants don't get a chance to wilt from a lack of water.

Care and Maintenance

Collards don't require much care. Occasionally, aphids will try to eat the new growth, but a strong stream of water will wash them away. Cabbage butterfly larvae will often eat holes in the leaves. They can be removed manually or a light dusting of Dipel® (*Bacillus thuringiensis*) or rotenone will do the job.

Additional Information

The best varieties for Florida include 'Yates Strain', a very large but low-growing variety with broad, thick, heavy leaves; and 'Georgia Southern', a variety that grows to 36 inches tall and can withstand a variety of soil conditions. A high-yielding variety of excellent quality when cooked, 'Georgia Southern' is the old standard for Florida. Collard leaves, known as collard greens, grow along a tall, inedible stem. The leaves are picked from the bottom up and should be selected before the leaves get large and tough. The leaves should then be chopped up into tiny pieces (every part of the leaf is used) and cooked for an hour or more with a ham hock, or any other smoked, inexpensive meat, for the best flavor. If collards are grown without a straw weed barrier, make certain you wash the leaves

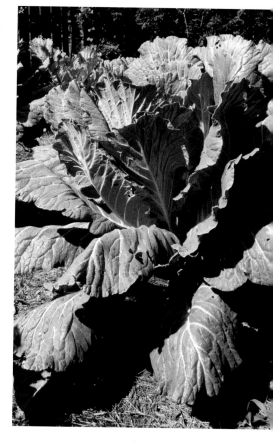

thoroughly three or four times to remove the grit and dirt. Collards are best eaten fresh but they can also be frozen after blanching for a short time (three to four minutes per pound).

CORN

When you think of summer, you think of growing corn—that is, everywhere but in Florida. Given the summer heat in Florida, sweet corn should be planted from October until April (depending where on the peninsula your garden is located) when the nighttime temperatures are cooler and the daytime temperatures aren't oppressive. To be quite honest, given the sheer number and kinds of bugs that attack corn foliage, tassels, and fruit (if they get that far), most gardeners decide after one growing season that it's easier to just buy a few ears at the local market. The bottom line is, growing corn is *not* easy in most areas of Florida. Another problem when planting corn is deciding which variety to grow. There are many, many varieties of sweet corn that can be grown in Florida, and they come in three basic types: super sweet (which has the longest storage time); normal sugary (which has the shortest storage time); and sugary enhancer (medium storage time). Corn can also be divided by color in each of these three types.

When to Plant

In North Florida plant sweet corn from February to April, in Central Florida plant corn from January to April, and in South Florida plant corn from October to March.

Where to Plant

Plant sweet corn in full sun in well-drained soil with a pH of 6.0 to 6.5. In the absence of a soil test, apply 3 to 4 pounds of 12-0-12 or similar analysis fertilizer per 100 square feet to establish a basic fertility level. Sidedressing with a high nitrogen fertilizer late in the growing season is also advisable. Soil temperature for normal sugary can be in the 60°F range (plus or minus), while the sugary enhanced and the super sweet will not germinate until the soil is much warmer. When growing super sweet corn it is important that there be no other corn plants close by (300 feet away is the minimum). Super sweet corn cross-pollinates readily through the air and if the super sweet corn is contaminated by pollen from normal sugary or sugary enhancer varieties, the super sweet won't taste as good. Start with fresh seed every year; even under the best storage conditions, corn seeds will only last two years. With the super sweet corn seeds, reports indicate that the extended storage can actually alter the corn's ultimate quality.

How to Plant

Did you ever shuck an ear of corn only to find that the kernels weren't fully formed or they were formed sporadically on the cob? Corn is pollinated by the wind so it's important that corn be planted in "blocks" rather than in long rows to increase the opportunities for pollination. Blocks of corn help ensure that pollen will fall directly below to the silks of the ears. With long row planting, any pollen hitting the ear silk is a hit-or-miss proposition, and proper pollenization might not take place.

Plant sweet corn 1 inch deep, 6 to 8 inches apart, and in rows that are 30 inches apart. When the new growth emerges from the soil (three to five days after planting) the corn seedlings often are the favorite food of birds (especially brown thrashers). They will break off the tender seed that emerges with the new leaves, killing the new sprout. My daughter's 30-inch-long, lifelike plastic monitor lizard will scare them off in most years, but aluminum pie pans attached to strings and allowed to twirl in the air will work, too. If neither appeals to you, simply plant a few more seeds to fill in the blank spots after the remaining seedlings get a little taller.

Care and Maintenance

Let me make it known: corn requires babysitting. Large quantities both of water (1½ inches per week) and fertilizer are required to produce full, healthy ears. Make sure weeds are removed as soon as possible so they don't compete for water or nutrition. The tassel is the part that emerges from the top center of a corn plant and contains the pollen. The tiny "hairs" that emerge from the top of each ear of corn are called silks and each strand of silk is connected to a single kernel of corn. It is the silk that accepts the pollen grains from the tassel above to fertilize the corn kernels. To enhance the chances of the pollen reaching the silks, try shaking the entire corn plant several times a day when the pollen first appears. That will increase the chances.

Not only do weeds compete for water and nutrients, they harbor a wide selection of pests. Fall armyworms are a corn plant's worst enemy. They get into the whorl of the plant, often eating the leaves before the plant has a chance to produce a tassel. They also burrow into the ears and eat the kernels. Another important pest is the corn earworm. An adult female lays an egg on the newly emerged corn silk and the worm burrows into the ear, eating the kernels. Rotenone or Dipel® lightly sprinkled inside the plant whorl or on the ear silk once per week will lessen the problem. And, both products are organic. Spinosad is a new highly effective organic insecticide against caterpillars that does not harm beneficial insects.

Once a worm burrows into an ear of corn, the home gardener can do very little, although some have had luck squirting mineral oil down into the silks after the worms have been discovered. Genetically altered corn has been developed that is resistant to both armyworms and corn earworms but it has not been approved for organic gardens. Raccoons somehow know that you plan to pick the corn the next day and will take a bite of nearly every ear the night before. Of all the methods to repel them, raccoons are immune to almost every one except an electric fence.

There are two ways to check for ripeness. When the silks of an ear of corn turn from a "blonde" color to brown all the way to the husk, the ear is ready to pick. Just to be sure, though, pull the husk back a bit to make sure that the kernels are fully formed at the top of the ear. Also, a kernel should squirt "milk" when you press it with your thumbnail. Sweet corn remains in the milk stage for a relatively short period; check the ears frequently. Corn that is too immature will ooze a watery material, while ears that are too old will have a tough, doughy kernel. To lengthen corn's shelf life, immerse the ears in ice-cold water to slow the breakdown of the sugar to starch. The old-timers will tell you that water should be boiling on the stove when you pick corn and that you should *run* back to the stove to cook it. Seriously, more than half of the sugar is converted to starch in the first twelve hours after picking.

Additional Information

Recommended yellow corn varieties include 'Golden Cross Bantam', 'Early Sunglow', 'Sweet Riser', and 'Kandy King'. The best white varieties for Florida are 'Silver Queen', 'How Sweet It Is', and 'Sweet Ice'. Of the bicolor varieties, 'Peaches and Cream' and 'Seneca Dancer' perform the best.

CUCUMBER

Growing cucumbers in Florida is all about timing. Cucumbers like it warm, but not *too* hot and humid—the foliage will die from mildew. They don't like it *too* cold—they'll stop producing when it gets too cold. Don't get me wrong, cucumbers of *all* kinds are worth the effort, but sometimes it's difficult to remember how you grew that one perfect crop. That's where the garden journal comes into play. Reviewing the pages where you wrote down all the details about your garden may save a lot of time and disappointment later.

When to Plant

Cucumbers like warm soil to germinate. In North Florida plant seeds directly into the garden from August to September for a fall garden, and plant from February to April for a spring garden. In Central Florida plant seeds in September for a fall garden and from January through March for a spring garden. South Florida has an extended growing season; plant seeds for a fall garden from September to October, for a winter garden from November to December, and in January for a spring garden. It's generally too hot and humid in South Florida for a summer crop of cucumbers.

Where to Plant

Plant cucumbers in full sun in well-drained, enriched soil with an ideal pH of 5.8 to 6.5. Keep in mind that cucumbers will grow in soils with a pH outside of their preferred range, but they just won't be as productive.

How to Plant

The old standby is to direct sow the seeds ½ inch deep into prepared soil in rows 36 to 48 inches apart and the seeds 8 to 10 inches apart. An alternate method, and my favorite, is to grow the vines up strings, like pole beans. Using this method the "cukes" stay clean, they can be seen more easily, and thus can be harvested at the proper time. By growing them upright they have better air circulation, are easier to fertilize, weeds aren't a problem, the plants require less space, and you don't step on the vines to harvest. Utilize the same spacing between the plants and rows.

Care and Maintenance

The most serious problem by far is powdery mildew. Powdery mildew can be lessened using organic methods by increasing air circulation, reducing overhead watering, and timing daily watering to occur in the early morning so the plants have a chance to dry off. It's also important to never walk among the plants while they are wet—diseases can be transferred via wet clothes and skin. During warm, humid nights a light, powderlike dusting will appear on the upper surfaces of the leaves, causing the leaves to drop off prematurely, ultimately killing the plant. Oils such as Neem and Sunfine Ultraspray work well to prevent powdery mildew but they cannot be used together or when temperatures reach 90°F. Serenade® is an organic fungicide that can be used on cucumbers; it must be applied every seven days once the disease has been identified. Serenade®

can be applied up to, and including, the day of harvest. Immunox® (Myclobutnil) is a systemic fungicide registered for cucumbers that both protects and cures powdery mildew; it must be applied every seven to ten days once the disease has been identified. Ordinary sulfur and copper applied every seven days works well, too.

When the plants reach 4 inches tall, add a high-nitrogen fertilizer (bloodmeal, cottonseed meal, and so forth) or water the plants with fish emulsion. Check the garden daily for harvestable fruits. If mature cucumbers are left on the vine, all production for that particular plant will stop.

Additional Information

For standard slicing cucumbers 'Straight Eight', 'Dasher II', and 'Cherokee' work fine. For pickling cukes try 'Ohio MR 17' and 'Pixie'. 'Burpee's Bushmaster' works great in smaller gardens. Hobby greenhouse owners can grow cucumbers indoors that don't require pollinators. Good greenhouse varieties include 'Toska', 'Fabulous', and 'Sweet Success'.

EGGPLANT

My experience is that you either love eggplant or you hate it. There never seems to be any ambivalence. So, if you can't stand them, turn the page. If, however, you have a passion for eggplant and the numerous dishes that can be made with it, read on. I have won over more than a few eggplant loathers to fanciers just by showing them pictures of the wide range of different types that can be grown in Florida, with colors ranging from deep purple-black to polar white, and from egg-sized to 3-pounders. For an average family, 6 plants are enough. (Really, how much eggplant can you eat?)

When to Plant

Eggplant is a heat-loving plant. It loves heat so much that when eggplant is grown in cool temperatures it simply languishes in the cool, damp air until the heat is turned up. Don't plant eggplant too early or it will just sit there and stare back at you. Eggplants are best planted as seedlings from June to September.

Where to Plant

Plant eggplant in full sun in average, well-drained soil. Keep eggplant out of moist, mucky soils.

How to Plant

Eggplants are best planted as seedlings, *not* directly sown from seed into the garden. However, the uncommon varieties are usually only available as seed. Most garden centers won't carry the oddball variety seed and you will have to search them out. Do it; it's worth the effort. Sow the seeds ¼ inch deep, six weeks prior to your anticipated outdoor planting date. Set individual transplants 30 inches apart in 30- to 36-inch-wide rows. The smaller fruiting types can be spaced closer together.

Care and Maintenance

Eggplants are virtually pest free. Occasionally, aphids, cottony cushion scale, flea beetles, and spider mites will stop by, but only when the plant is stressed by too much or too little water. A simple soap or Neem oil spray will eliminate the bugs but it's just as easy to prevent them by keeping the plants stress free. In the absence of a soil analysis, a 12-0-12 fertilizer applied 3 to 4 pounds per 100 feet of row is sufficient. Apply the same amount halfway through the growing season and again immediately after the first fruit is picked. Giving eggplant too much fertilizer will delay its fruit set. To prevent the heavy fruits from lying on the ground, pound a sturdy ¾-inch x 48-inch-tall bamboo pole into the ground beside each plant and *gently* tie the individual branches to the pole using heavy garden twine or 1-inch-wide strips of old sheets or other fabric. The tall pole will seem like overkill at first, but as the plant grows you'll be glad you started out with the taller pole. Although eggplants can withstand drought, fruit production is severely curtailed if the plants are permitted to go without sufficient water. Keep the soil moist and add a

layer of mulch to conserve available moisture. Small yellow fruits that never mature is a sure sign of too little water; simply double up on the watering and the bush will begin to produce full-sized fruit again. Larger yellow fruits mean that the eggplants are overripe and should be discarded. No more than four to six flowers should be allowed to set fruit per plant. If too many flowers appear, clip some off.

Additional Information

Harvest the fruits when they are still glossy using pruning shears or a sharp knife. Leave the calyx (the green star at the top) on the fruit to prolong its shelf life. Varieties suitable for Florida include 'Black Beauty' (stocky and black); 'Cloud Nine' (stocky and white); 'Calliope' (stocky and purple-and-white striped); 'Casper' (long and white); 'Florida High Bush' (long and black); 'Green Goddess' (long and green); 'Machiaw' (slender and light purple); 'Rosa Biancha' (round and white with blush of purple); and 'Apple Green' (egg shaped and light green).

ENDIVE

Endive is one of those vegetables that, unless you have eaten them, you really wouldn't miss. For many years I would pass it over in the market thinking it was simply another variety of lettuce. And, as everyone knows, lettuce is just . . . lettuce. This is so not true. Just as lettuce has different flavors and textures, endive can really perk up an otherwise drab salad. Forget the boiled eggs, croutons, tiny pieces of ham, or *anything* else that you put in a salad to make it a little more interesting. Once you add endive, especially endive grown in your garden, it will quickly become a staple in your cool-weather garden.

There are two types of endive: the broad-leaved form (also called escarole) that's used in salads and the narrow-leaved form (called Belgian endive) that has swept the gastronomic scene by storm. The latter can be used as a tender, succulent, exotic leaf to scoop gourmet dips or used as a base for a wide variety of fresh epicurean delights. Place a freshly made crab dip or caviar on a single leaf of Belgian endive and drift off into foodie Shangri-La. The broad-leaf form adds interest to the average salad because of its noticeable "bite" as you eat it. Many people enjoy this added layer of interest in a salad but some don't. Try endive one time to determine which group you belong to. Belgian endive's outer leaves are bitter and have more bite than those on the inside, which are extremely tender and mild with a very fresh flavor.

However, growing Belgian endive is a very precise and difficult process. It requires a gardener to dig the roots of the plant 120 days after the seed has been sowed. The roots are then replanted in pure sand and grown without light for another month. It can all get very complicated, and for that reason, only the escarole growing techniques will be discussed here.

When to Plant

Endive is a cool-weather crop and needs days below 75°F and cool evenings in which to grow. If there are any warmer temperatures then the plant will "bolt" (go to seed) and become very bitter and unpalatable. In North Florida, endive can be grown from September through April (with protection in freezing temperatures);

in Central Florida, from December through March; and in South Florida, from December through February. Endive can be transplanted into the garden by sowing three to four weeks earlier than the garden planting date.

Where to Plant

Endive benefits greatly from a richly prepared soil high in organic matter with a soil pH of 5.8 to 7.0. Although it requires cool temperatures, it also requires full sun of *at least* 8 hours to grow properly. Any amount less than that and the escarole leaves will be thin and not as robust as you would like.

How to Plant

Plant escarole in single rows or in wide row planting (broad-leaf endive performs better in wide row planting than the Belgian form does). Plant fresh seed in rows ¼ inch deep or thinly sow seed over a carefully prepared wide row bed 18 to 24 inches wide, and gently cover with fine soil. Tamp the seeds carefully with a hard tined garden rake or hoe to gain good seed-soil contact, and gently water with a watering can or a hose with a water breaker on the end of it. The seedlings will emerge in five to seven days. Thin to 6 inches apart.

Care and Maintenance

Keep endive well watered as it grows, and fertilize regularly (every three weeks) with a fertilizer high in nitrogen.

Additional Information

Broad-leaf endive should be blanched in the garden; as they begin to grow, gently place a lightweight board or dark fabric over the plant for several hours during the day. This will allow the leaves to remain bright white and makes the leaves taste a little less bitter. Recommended varieties include 'Tres Five Maraichere', 'Rull Heart', and 'Salad King'.

ENGLISH PEA

English peas are easy to grow in all areas of Florida *provided* they are grown in the proper season. Make no mistake about it—peas are a cool-season crop and like daytime temperatures that are cool and nighttime temperatures that are even cooler (although short of frost). The variety of peas that can be grown in the home garden is limited only by the amount of space. English snap peas, snow peas, and sugar snap peas can all be grown in Florida. Fresh-off-the-vine peas taste like candy compared to those bought from a grocery store. Trust me, once you have tasted fresh peas from the garden you will look forward to the English pea planting season.

When to Plant

In North Florida plant peas from January through March. In Central and South Florida plant English peas from September through February.

Where to Plant

Plant peas where the plants will receive a minimum of 8 hours of full sun. The plants perform best in well-enriched soil that has been deeply tilled.

How to Plant

English peas including snap, snow, and edible podded can be grown on a tall support device similar to climbing beans or as a bush. Many varieties of the bush form benefit from some support to keep the fruits off the ground. Mesh fencing placed between a double row planting 6 inches apart works very well. After soaking the seeds overnight in warm water, plant them 2 inches apart in rows 30 inches apart. When the new growth emerges from the soil (three to five days after they're planted), the pea seedlings are often the favorite food of birds. They will break off the tender seed that emerges with the new leaves, killing the new sprout. Aluminum pie pans attached to strings and allowed to twirl in the air will work well to scare them off.

Climbing peas produce multiple crops (provided you pick every pod) and are easier to harvest. Climbing peas can grow to 6 feet tall and need some sort of support. Most often, two poles are placed at either end of a row and wire is placed at heights of 5 to 6 feet tall between the posts. Strings are then *gently* and *loosely* attached to the pea seedlings below their leaves and then to the wire. Pea vines will naturally climb up the string. For shorter varieties of peas 18 to 24 inches tall, pound a 36-inch stake into the ground at either end and stretch a 24-inch-tall piece of one-inch chicken wire from pole to pole. At 2- to 3-inch intervals lace a pole through the wire mesh and pound into the ground. Mulch heavily to maintain soil moisture. Both forms benefit from a slight mounding of the soil against the stems for added support.

Care and Maintenance

Peas like moisture but not wet feet. Soaking the seeds before planting will require less water initially, but as the flowers bloom and pods develop, the plants will require more water. As you water more, keep a sharp eye out for slugs. Peas are one of their favorite foods, so the addition of slug traps filled with beer works well to trap them. Aphids can also be a problem on the tender new growth, but they can be washed off with a stiff stream of water. Adding too much fertilizer will produce nice, new growth but at the expense of fruit.

Peas are ready when the pods begin to bulge slightly. Pick the pods just moments before cooking; the sugars will change to starch very quickly.

Additional Information

'Little Marvel Improved' is by far the most popular English pea grown in Florida. The vigorous plant grows to 18 inches tall and produces loads of pods. 'Sugar Snap' is another popular variety and the entire pod and peas within can be eaten raw or cooked. Other good varieties include 'Wando', 'Oregon Sugarpod II', and 'Green Arrow'.

GARLIC

Given that you can cultivate garlic simply by breaking off a clove and sticking it in the ground, one would think growing garlic in the Sunshine State would be easy. Even though our temperatures are perfect for gardeners, garlic is more accustomed to growing in colder climates and our warm winters may throw a wrench into things.

Garlic comes in two basic types: hardneck and softneck. You can forget growing hardneck types in Florida. They like very cold winters, cool springs, and mild summers. The hardnecks include the categories of porcelain and purple stripe garlic. If you live in Florida and you see these names in a catalog description, just move on to the softneck group.

When to Plant

Plant garlic cloves anytime cold weather is on its way. They enjoy the cold weather and after growing all winter, they can be harvested by early summer. It's important that they grow in cool soil as long as possible. When our weather begins to heat up, the garlic matures and the growing portion of the garlic's life is over. If a bulb matures before it's finished growing you will harvest small garlic bulbs.

Garlic tolerates different weather conditions. Just remember, every year you grow garlic will be different from the year before. Depending on the weather, rainfall, temperatures, planting date, and so forth, your garlic may be stronger or weaker in taste, hot varieties may become mild, and mild varieties may become hot.

Where to Plant

Plant garlic in good, deep, rich, loamy soil in full sun. Garlic is very self-sufficient and can get what it needs out of the soil. Stay away from dry, tight soils and grow in soils with a pH of 6.5 to 7. Garlic enjoys moist soil but will not tolerate standing water for even the shortest period of time. If it's given too much nitrogen the bulb will produce good foliage but only small bulbs.

How to Plant

If you have sandy soil, add organic material to it so it will hold water a little longer and provide a good friable (easily crumbled) soil. Garlic is very susceptible to a wide variety of pathogens but a little work upfront will help later as the bulb grows. Here's a little tip: Combine seaweed and baking soda (1 tablespoon each) in a gallon of water. Place individual cloves to be planted in the solution; leave overnight. Then, soak the cloves in rubbing alcohol for five minutes. Remove the cloves from the rubbing alcohol and plant directly into the ground; place a 2-inch layer of mulch on top. (The cloves will later grow through the mulch.)

Care and Maintenance

Garlic is very easy to grow after the soil preparation and inoculation is complete. Just keep the weeds down and fertilize every two weeks with a seaweed/molasses combination (1 tablespoon per gallon of water) every two weeks until harvest. Harvest when the bottom one-third of the leaves turns brown and only the top four or five leaves are still green. It's important to harvest the bulbs when the soil is dry, so stop watering one to two weeks before harvest. If it looks like rain, throw a tarp over the bed. Dry the bulbs in a cool, dark place with lots of ventilation. Garlic bulbs are very susceptible to bruising at this stage so be careful how you handle them—don't throw them or handle them roughly. Clean the bulbs down to the last paper skin that wraps around the individual cloves, and cut the dried leaves off. Garlic can be stored up to nine months, depending on the variety, at room temperature. Garlic stored in a refrigerator will sprout prematurely and will not last long.

Additional Information

Good varieties for Florida include 'Early Italian Purple', 'Inchelium Red', 'Kettle River Giant', 'Siskiyou Purple', and 'Transylvanian'.

KALE

Admittedly, I never considered kale to be an important vegetable. In fact, for years the only kale I grew was the beautiful ornamental flowering kale used as a bedding plant. It wasn't until I started cooking in earnest that I realized how adaptable kale is in a variety of recipes ranging from soups to side dishes. Kale has quickly risen to the top of my "must have" vegetable list, and, if you give it try, I think it will rise on your list, too.

When to Plant

A cool-season crop, kale should be planted in the cooler months, primarily from September through March. A light frost is not a bad thing; it will only sweeten kale's flavor.

Where to Plant

Kale is not very fussy about soil, and wherever it's planted it seems to thrive and be perfectly happy. If possible, however, direct sow seeds ¼ inch deep or plant transplants in full sun with rich, water-retentive soil with a pH of 5.5 to 6.5. For transplants, start seeds indoors five to six weeks prior to the expected outdoor planting date.

How to Plant

Kale can be planted using the wide row method with rows 48 inches wide and the individual plants 14 to 18 inches apart in the rows. Otherwise, kale is planted in rows 24 inches apart, and 18 inches apart in the row. There are many different selections of kale and spacing depends solely upon the variety you plant.

Care and Maintenance

Give kale full sun, plenty of water, and periodic applications of fish emulsion fertilizer and it will provide tasty leaves throughout its growing season. Leaves that are grown on well-tended plants will be sweet and tender; those allowed to dry out will often be bitter and tough. The leaves can be picked based on color—dark and heavy means the kale is tough and bitter, while rich green leaves are sweet and ready for cooking. The leaves are picked from the bottom, encouraging new leaves to grow at the top. The newer, tender leaves can be eaten raw in salads. Like many other cooking greens, kale is susceptible to many of the same pests, such as aphids and slugs, but generally these are not serious problems and most can be removed with a strong stream of water. A 2- to 3-inch layer of organic mulch will moderate soil temperatures, keep weeds under control, and conserve water.

Additional Information

Good varieties of kale for Florida include 'Dwarf Blue Curled Scotch', 'Red Russian Kale', and 'Yates Blue Curled'. 'Nero de Toscana' is a unique looking kale that can also be used as an ornamental in mixed containers or in the vegetable garden.

Kale is very high in betacarotenes; vitamins A, C, and K; potassium, iron, and calcium, and it's an excellent source of fiber. Patients taking many of the anticoagulation drugs should avoid kale because of its high vitamin K content (which promotes blood clotting, thus reducing the effectiveness of the anticoagulation drugs). Kale was popular during World War II in Great Britain because of its high vitamin content, which supplemented a poor diet resulting from wartime food rationing.

KOHLRABI

Mention the vegetable "kohlrabi" in a conversation and chances are good that very few people will know what you're talking about. That's a shame, too; kohlrabi may be one of the most underutilized and fun plants to grow in the garden. Unlike beets or turnips, which hide their "bulb" beneath the soil, kohlrabi has a light-green, 3-inch-diameter, spaceship-looking bulbous growth with dark-green leaf sprouts coming out of its top that appears just above the ground. (In German, the word *kohl* means "cabbage" and *rabi* means "turnip.") Being unusual, however, it not it's only claim to fame. The bulb is harvested by cutting it off just above the ground. It's peeled like a potato and either eaten raw as crudité or gently steamed to be served with cream sauces. Some say it has a very mild broccoli or cabbage taste while others say it tastes like celery with a nutty flavor. The leaves can be harvested and added raw to salads; they have a slightly spicy taste. Kohlrabi are very easy to grow and will surely elicit a question or two as your friends stroll through your garden.

When to Plant

Grown only in cool seasons, direct sow kohlrabi seeds in September and continue through March on three- to four-week intervals. It matures in 45 to 55 days depending on the variety selected. It can withstand significantly cold weather and even a little frost.

Where to Plant

Kohlrabi enjoys full sun when planted in well-prepared, water-retentive soil with a pH of 5.8 to 6.5.

How to Plant

Direct sow kohlrabi seeds ¼ inch deep in rows that are 18 inches apart. Thin kohlrabi seedlings to 6 inches apart in the row or plant using the wide row method three wide with the same individual plant spacing of 6 inches. If the seedlings are not thinned the resulting aboveground bulb will be small and unusable.

Care and Maintenance

Kohlrabi is one of the easiest plants to grow and has no serious pests or diseases. Occasionally, aphids will stop by but a strong stream of water will wash them away. Sometimes the bulbous aboveground growth will get a black moldy spot, which is indicative of using too much water. Remove the infected plant and reduce the amount of water to stop the problem. It's important to make successive plantings every three to four weeks during the growing season. If kohlrabi is left to grow too long, it will get woody like overly mature carrots and will be unusable.

Additional Information

Good varieties of kohlrabi for Florida include 'Early White Vienna', 'Kolibri' (perhaps the prettiest of kohlrabi with its intense, deep-purple color), 'Grand Duke', and 'Early Purple Vienna'. For the more unusual varieties try 'Kossak' (which grows to 10 inches in diameter) and 'Superschmelz' (which can withstand less water than others without getting pithy). Kohlrabi is high in potassium, Vitamin C, and fiber.

LEEK

Once you taste a leek, you'll wonder how you ever survived without them. Sweeter and milder than any onion, leeks are a favorite among chefs the world over for their amazing diversity in a wide variety of recipes. Braised, steamed, sautéed, and grilled, leeks can be eaten raw in salads (after a very brief blanching) and featured in soups. Leeks are so easy to grow and harvest that once you try a few leeks in the garden, you will be hooked on them forever. You will never look at the ordinary onion in quite the same way again.

When to Plant

In October, direct sow seeds ½ inch deep in compost-rich soil in full sun. Leek seeds will germinate in ten to fifteen days.

Where to Plant

Although leeks enjoy getting plenty of water during the growing season, they cannot tolerate water-saturated soil or standing water for even the shortest period of time. Plant leek seeds in October, and you'll be able to harvest five months later. However, leeks, like onions, can be harvested at any stage in their growing cycle and used raw or cooked.

How to Plant

Once the seeds have sprouted and the plants have grown to 12 inches tall, carefully dig them up and plant them into the bottom of a 10-inch-deep trench (just like you do when growing potatoes), 4 to 5 inches apart. The real taste treat of leeks is found in their tender, bright-white growth at the bottom of each stalk. To achieve this delicacy, you must blanch the stalk (prevent the sunlight from reaching the bottom of the plant). As the plant grows, mound soil to just below the point where the leaves begin to separate and form leaves. Another, and easier, method is to direct sow the leek seed as you do any other vegetable crop, thin to 5 inches apart, and pull surrounding soil around the stalk just up to where the leaves begin to separate. A final method is to transplant pencil-sized transplants into 6-inch-deep x 2-inch-wide holes. Trim the roots to 1 inch long and gently drop the leeks into each hole. Watering the transplants will wash enough soil into the hole for the leek to grow, and an occasional hoeing will eventually fill the hole so the plant is blanched.

If dirt gets into the leaf fan, the grit will be very difficult to remove prior to eating the leek. If you find grit (or expect it's there because dirt got into the leaf fan), simply remove several outer layers of the white skin with its attached green leaves. Beginning 2 inches from the bottom of the stalk, cut entirely through the stalk. Turn a quarter of a turn and cut through the stalk. Rinse with copious amounts of water to remove the grit.

Care and Maintenance

Given plenty of water and regular feedings three weeks apart of a 15-0-15 fertilizer during the growing season, leeks typically will form bright-white blanched stalks nearly 2 inches in diameter. The "secret" is to maintain regular feedings and to keep them well watered. If the plant becomes dry at any time, it will stop growing for a time and will begin growing again only after the feeding and watering resumes.

As a leek plant grows it can get a little unkempt; the leaf tips can be trimmed by up to one-half to maintain a tidy plant.

Additional Information

Good varieties of leeks for Florida include 'Poncho', 'Sherwood', 'King Richard', 'Tivi', and 'Verina'.

LETTUCE

If you have a vegetable garden of any size, any kind, anywhere, you *must* have some sort of lettuce. It is a staple of healthy eating and is one of the easiest plants to grow. There are so many different kinds and shapes of lettuce that it's mind-boggling. Tall, short, wide, upright, green, striped—the list goes on and on. It's probably the first vegetable that young gardeners grow because it sprouts so quickly and sustains their curiosity over a long period of time. Planting lettuce, growing lettuce, and eating lettuce are all about instant gratification. It is also about color and texture. Some of my favorite lettuce varieties are those that "perk up" an otherwise boring green salad with their intense reds and shades of green. When I was growing up we had iceberg lettuce. That's all. Now, that's not bad and I remember eating entire heads of iceberg lettuce right out of the refrigerator. Once I moved away from home, however, I realized that there was another world out there, a world of 'Black Seeded Simpson', and 'Deer Tongue', and 'Cardinal' and . . . well, you get the picture.

When to Plant

Lettuce is a cool-weather plant, and it will be bitter when it's grown in warm weather. In North Florida lettuce is planted from September through October and again from February through March. In Central Florida plant lettuce from September through March. In South Florida plant lettuce from September through January. If cold weather is imminent, cover lettuce with row cloths or old blankets to retain ground heat. Plant short rows of lettuce every two weeks to ensure you have enough to last throughout the growing season.

Where to Plant

Plant seeds and seedlings in well-composted, deeply tilled, well-drained but still water-retentive soil that receives at least 8 hours of full sun.

How to Plant

Lettuce of all kinds can be planted either by sowing seeds

directly into prepared soil or by setting out transplants. Plant seeds indoors four to five weeks prior to planting outdoors. Use fresh seed every year and place partially used seed packets in the refrigerator for sowing later in the season. Lay the handle of a rake or hoe in a well-prepared bed and gently press the handle into the fresh soil to create a shallow furrow ¼ inch deep. Carefully sprinkle a small amount of lettuce seed into the furrow every 2 to 3 inches. Barely cover the seed with fine soil. *Gently* water the seed with a watering can just enough to wet the seed and make them happy without burying them too deep. Lettuce seeds will sprout in five to seven days.

Regardless of how careful you are, you'll more than likely sow too many seeds. Once the lettuce plants grow their third or fourth pair of "true" leaves, the plants must be thinned to a distance described on the seed packet (it's different for different kinds of lettuce). Thinning can be done by gently pulling the extra seedlings sideways out of the soil or by clipping the seedlings off at ground level; both methods reduce root damage to the remaining seedlings. Trust me, thinning is probably the hardest thing to do in vegetable gardening, but it is absolutely critical that you do so if you want fully and properly formed lettuce plants. Lettuce performs best in soils that have been highly enriched with rotted manure and fertilized well before planting with high nitrogen fertilizers such as bloodmeal and cottonseed meal.

Care and Maintenance

Lettuce is an average feeder. Water with a little starter fertilizer when planting seedlings and fertilize every two weeks during the growing season with a general-purpose product. Lettuce matures in fifty days so fertilizing after the initial application at planting often isn't necessary. This, of course, depends upon whether adequate nutrients were added to the soil prior to planting the seeds or transplants. If lettuce plants are kept too wet, slugs can be a problem, but slug traps baited with beer usually does the trick. Also, placing boards next to lettuce plants will encourage the slugs to hide beneath the boards after the sun comes up. The slugs can be removed manually from underneath the boards and destroyed.

Additional Information

Lettuce can be subdivided into four main groups: crisp head, Cos or romaine, Bibb (sometimes called butterhead), and leaf.

Crisp head is the most difficult lettuce to grow because of its long growing season requirements and it has a tendency to bolt or flower when the temperatures increase. Slow-bolting varieties are available, and adding a layer of mulch beneath the plants will help reduce fluctuations in soil temperatures. Mulching also helps keep dirt and grit off the leaves. Standard crisp head varieties for Florida include 'Iceberg', 'Ithaca', 'Great Lakes', and an heirloom variety called 'Hanson

Improved'. More uncommon and smaller but equally good crisp head lettuce varieties include 'Bronze Mignonette' (slow to bolt); 'Prizehead' (its inner leaves are green and outer leaves or reddish brown); and a French heirloom variety called 'Rouge d' Hiver'.

Cos or Romaine varieties for Florida are some of the most plentiful and colorful varieties. My all-time personal favorite lettuce variety, 'Freckles', has regular green leaves speckled with bright red spots. It can really perk up a salad and when I serve it at dinner parties everyone wants to know about it. Another unusual variety is 'Cimmaron Red', which has green leaves inside the head and deep red to magenta leaves on the edges. Other more common but equally good varieties include 'Parris Island' and 'Dark Green'.

Bibb lettuce may be the most tender of all the lettuce varieties and produces well-formed, flat heads of exceptional quality. Bibb lettuce varieties are formed the best and perfectly shaped when the seedlings are spaced properly in the initial planting. Good performers include: 'Bibb', 'Big Boston', 'Buttercrunch', 'May Queen', and 'White Boston'. A French heirloom variety named 'Merveille des Quatre Saisons' is a red-tinted butterhead variety. 'Baby Star' produces 5-inch-tall heads of shiny green leaves, with a Romaine flavor.

Leaf lettuce is far and away the largest group and is the easiest to grow. 'Black Seeded Simpson' is the old standby and it's still very popular. Others include 'Red Sails', 'Oak Leaf', 'Ruby Red', 'Salad Bowl' (red and green varieties), and 'Tango'. 'Deer Tongue' is an American heirloom variety that dates to 1740; it has wonderful taste and texture.

MUSTARD

If any plant describes vegetable gardening in the Deep South it's mustard greens. Mention the words, and cheese grits, fried fish, hushpuppies, and "pot licker" come to mind. (We'll talk more about pot licker later.) If there is an easier vegetable to grow in a Florida garden I don't know what it is. Mustard greens will thrive, and even flourish, in the worst of soils provided adequate water and sun are available. It seems as if every seed will germinate when given a chance, and when someone says that a particular seed is easy to sprout, you will often hear them say, "Those seeds will come up like mustard."

When to Plant

In North Florida plant mustard seed from September through May. In Central and South Florida plant mustard from September through March. If it's grown in the long, hot season, mustard with "bolt," or go to flower, which means the leaves will be inedible (because they are bitter).

Where to Plant

Although mustard greens will perform well in any ordinary soil, it grows best in organically enriched soil with a pH of 6.0 to 6.8, in a location in full sun.

How to Plant

Plant short rows of mustard every two weeks in order to harvest a succession of tender greens. Direct sow the seed ¼ inch deep, 8 inches apart, in rows that are 24 inches apart.

Care and Maintenance

For a constant supply of tender greens it is important to encourage mustard to grow quickly. Make sure it has plenty of water and plentiful amounts of high-nitrogen fertilizer, manures, or compost to promote the fast growth of tender, green leaves. Water plants during dry periods; otherwise, the greens will be bitter. Keep mustard plants well weeded; weeds compete for water and fertilizer and harbor hiding spots for pests. Occasionally, aphids and cabbage worms can be a problem, in which case a light dusting of rotenone with solve the problem.

Additional Information

Although literature says that mustard greens can be eaten raw, my experience has been cooking mustard greens is the only way to eat them. Pick individual leaves from the bottom (like collards) or harvest the entire plant. During the summer months, a teaspoon of sugar in the cooking water will take away the bitterness. Nearly everyone I know places a smoked ham hock or neck bones in with the leaves for better flavor. Mustard is very high in vitamins A and C, iron, and calcium and also contains antioxidants and beta-carotene. For that reason, every bit of the cooking liquid is good for you, including the dark green liquid left in the pot after cooking.

The liquid is called "pot licker or "pot liquor," and it is often sopped up with a biscuit or added to peas and poured over white rice. Mmmmmm.

Talk to the ol' timers and they will tell you that 'Florida Broadleaf' and 'Southern Giant Curled' are the best mustard greens to grow; both mature in about 45 days. 'Big Red' is just like 'Florida Broadleaf' except that it is a deep maroon color. 'Misuna' is a decorative mustard with finely divided leaves; it has a spicy flavor and can be used raw or cooked. 'Tatsoi' is an Asian mustard with dense whorls of compact leaves; it matures in fifty five days.

OKRA

If you live in Florida you need to grow okra for several reasons. First, it's one of the few vegetables that will grow in Florida's summer heat and humidity. Give okra plenty of water and ordinary soil and it will repay you with hundreds of tiny okra pods. Second, okra is one of those vegetables that deserves a chance. Even if you don't like okra, it grows so well and is so pretty as a plant (it's a member of the hibiscus family) that you could grow it as an ornamental. Finally, it's important to try at least one new vegetable every year and this may just be the year for okra in *your* garden. Pick the little 2-inch pods, slice them up with some green pepper and fresh tomato, and you have a meal. Plus, fried okra is a southern tradition, and where would gumbo be without okra?

When to Plant

In North and Central Florida plant okra seed directly into the ground from March through July or August. In South Florida plant okra from August through September.

Where to Plant

Plant in the full, hot, blazing sun—just make certain there is plenty of water nearby. Okra will exceed even your wildest expectations when grown in well-drained, composted (and thereby water retentive) and deeply tilled soil. Avoid wet, poorly drained soils.

How to Plant

Direct sow okra seed 1 inch deep after the danger of frost has passed and the soil has warmed up a bit. Okra planted in cool soil will sit there; the seed *will not* germinate until everything starts to warm up a bit. If you want to get a jump on the season, plant individual seeds in peat cups indoors, give them plenty of bright light, and transplant outdoors when the soil temperatures are warm to the touch. Give okra plenty of room—plant seed 24 inches apart in rows 36 inches apart.

Care and Maintenance

It took me a little while to get used to okra but once I did, I became a real fan. I recommend both growing the plant and using the little pods in cooking, with *little* being the operative word. Show no mercy: you must be unrelenting when it comes to picking okra. Once the pods get beyond 3 inches long they are virtually inedible, so it's important that you pick okra every day, or no less often than every two days. If you are only growing a few plants, it may be necessary to store the pods in the vegetable drawer in a zip-lock-type plastic bag until you have enough to cook. Refrigerated okra will last at least five to six days. Once the unpicked pods are allowed to get more than 3 inches long, the plant will think it's done its job and will stop forming seedpods (which is what you are eating). In

well-drained soil, you can't water okra too much. Harvest okra with handheld clippers; do not twist the pods off! Also, most varieties have pods that have very fine little "spines" that can irritate your skin so wear gloves.

Additional Information

The old standby 'Clemson Spineless' is just that—spineless. If ever you grow any other variety you will appreciate the spineless part. Other varieties include 'Alabama Red', 'Baby Bubba' (which is perfect for small gardens and containers), 'Cow Horn', 'Evertender', 'Little Lucy' (which is another dwarf, but this one has burgundy foliage, stems, and pods), 'Red Burgundy', and 'White Velvet'. Don't you love that name?

ONION

Onions, shallots, bunching onions, and chives are easy to grow in Florida. Bulb onions come in a variety of colors, including white, yellow, and red; red is the sweetest of the group. Shallots have a more refined, less harsh flavor compared to onions, and bunching onions have green tops and small, slender white onions at the bottom. Chives are very easy to grow and can be grown either in pots on the windowsill or in the ground. Onions and its many relatives can be harvested and eaten at any stage in their development.

When to Plant

Onions prefer cool weather. In North, Central, and South Florida plant all types of onions from September through March.

Where to Plant

Onions enjoy full sun in a well-prepared, deeply tilled sandy loam or muck soil. Any amount of organic matter will enrich the flavor and increase the size.

How to Plant

Bulb onions that have been grown from seed the previous year are purchased in bulk by the pound and are called "onion sets." The bulbs should be the size of a large marble. Individual onions are placed halfway into the prepared soil, pointed side up, 2 inches apart in a row. After about eight weeks, thin the row by pulling every other onion out; they can be eaten as fresh scallions or boiled. The extra space between the remaining onions will give them plenty of room to grow. Onions can be double planted in a row; that is, set in two smaller rows 3 to 4 inches apart next to each other and 18 to 24 inches between these two rows. "Transplants" are just that, onions that you have grown from seed earlier in the summer and then transplanted out into the garden. Make certain that when you buy seeds from mail-order sources you order "short day" onions, not the "long day" onions that would be grown in northern states. Another method is to direct sow seeds into the prepared seedbed. This method is usually reserved for bunching onions, which are also known as scallions. Plant them ½ inch deep, and thin when they get about 4 inches tall. Eat any thinned onions.

Onions can also be planted using the newspaper-and-straw method. Lay a single layer of newspaper over a prepared seedbed, cover lightly with straw, and water the seedbed. While the newspaper is still wet, gently push the onions through the newspaper halfway into the soil, and grow as you would otherwise. The thin layer of newspaper and straw will virtually eliminate weeds.

Care and Maintenance

The biggest problem with onions is keeping the weeds away. Not only are they unsightly and a nuisance, weeds compete for water and fertilizer. Cultivating is difficult around the small, thin onion plants so extreme care is needed when weeding. I've learned the hard way about proper fertilization of onions. For years, my onions were always sub-par. Then, someone told me that onions were heavy nitrogen feeders. Ever since, I have added a 12-0-12 fertilizer about every three weeks or a water-soluble 20-0-20 every week, and my onions have never looked better.

Additional Information

For standard bulbing onions try 'Crystal Wax Bermuda' (flat and white); 'Excel' (flat and yellow); 'Red Creole' (red-skinned with a strong flavor); 'Granex White' and 'Granex Yellow' (very large bulbs with mild flavor); and 'White Lisbon' bunching onion (a popular salad onion with long white stems and no bulb). For a real twist try 'Crimson Forest' bunching onion; it's a standard salad onion but it has a beautiful burgundy color. 'Barletta' onions are used primarily for pickling and with shish-ka-bobs. Shallots are sometimes difficult to find, but if you look hard enough you can find 'Matador' shallots from France; they are a very fine addition to any garden.

PARSLEY

Parsley is the poster child for using fresh garden herbs to create high-flavor, low-calorie meals. And if there is an easier plant to grow in the garden than parsley, I haven't grown it yet. Seeds are simply direct sowed into an organically rich soil mix or planted into individual pots and later transplanted to the garden (or a container). The flavor of freshly cut parsley is indescribable. The great thing about parsley is that *everyone* can grow it wherever they live. My sister keeps a small pot of it growing on her windowsill even in the middle of winter in Ohio. In Florida, parsley grows outside, in full sun, twelve months a year including our summer months of intense heat and humidity. I hope I have convinced you—you *need* to grow some parsley.

For those of you who also enjoy butterflies, parsley is a primary food source for the black swallowtail butterfly. Parsley grows and flowers over a two-year cycle, and it's the flowers that bloom in the second year that attract the butterflies to encourage them to lay eggs on the foliage. By adding new plants to your garden every year, you can have several one-year plants (for you) and several two-year plants (for the butterflies). It's a win-win situation, and you can enjoy the butterflies as you work in the garden.

When to Plant

Parsley can be grown year-round and can be sown into the garden at any time. In North Florida, parsley will have to be protected from freezing temperatures.

Where to Plant

You can plant parsley just about anywhere you want, provided you give it a spot with plenty of sunlight (at least 8 hours), lots of water, and regular feedings of fertilizer. It is very tolerant of dry soil and its drooping leaves and stalks act as a good barometer for the rest of the garden that everything needs a deep drink. Unlike many other vegetables that are slow to start growing again after it becomes a little dry, parsley starts right where it left off and grows its little heart out. In Florida, parsley will grow well at least two full years and blooms in the fall of its second year. So, place parsley in a spot in the garden where you won't be stumbling over it as you plant, harvest, and remove other vegetables during the growing season.

How to Plant

Parsley seed benefits from a good soaking before being planted into the soil. After soaking overnight, plant the seeds ¼ inch deep directly into the garden furrow, 2 to 3 inches apart, in rows 14 inches apart. Another way to plant parsley is to generously sow seeds in potting soil placed in 4-inch pots; transplant the entire group into the garden four to six weeks later. Depending on how much parsley you use in cooking, an 8-foot row is generally plenty for a family of four. Parsley is a larval plant for many butterflies and for that reason I don't mind that the striped caterpillars eat a few of the leaves and stalks. In fact, if I know that they are in the neighborhood, I'll plant a few more plants to have enough for the family and the caterpillars, too.

Care and Maintenance

Parsley is very easy to grow, and if watered and fertilized regularly with a general-purpose fertilizer they will grow without any care.

Additional Information

Parsley comes in two models: the Italian flat and the curled leaf. Both are grown the same way, and both will grow for about two years before flowering. Selection of either type is simply your personal choice.

PEANUT

Sometimes, it's just plain fun to grow something unusual in the vegetable garden, just to say that you have done it. That's the way I felt about peanuts the first time I grew them. I didn't have a clue how peanuts grew or when they grew, and I certainly didn't know how to harvest them. But try, I did. Since that first time some twenty years ago, a summer garden in my yard wouldn't be complete without them. It's another way to introduce children to the joys of gardening, as well. Let's face it; what kid can avoid smiling when they see peanuts turned over with a spading fork for the first time?

When to Plant

Plant certified seed peanuts (available from most feed stores and mail-order sources) in early summer after the spring garden has been harvested.

Where to Plant

Plant peanuts in well-prepared, deeply tilled sandy loam soil. For garden areas that are new locations for peanuts, place ¾ cup of an 8-8-8 fertilizer per every 10 feet of row.

How to Plant

Individual peanuts are shelled and the seeds (also called "kernels") are planted 1½ inches deep, 8 inches apart, in rows 24 inches apart. The seeds germinate in seven to ten days. After reaching a height of 14 to 16 inches tall, a peanut plant will begin to produce bright-yellow, pea-like flowers near the bottom of the plant.

Care and Maintenance

It is important to keep the area directly beneath and around peanut plants free from weeds. While the plants are blooming, gently cultivate the soil beneath the plants to keep the soil soft and workable for the next stage in the peanut plant's lifecycle. Make certain that the soil is well watered at this stage, to a depth of 6 to 8 inches deep, and do not allow it to dry out. After a flower is pollinated the ovary produces an elongated stalk or "peg" that grows to, and into, the ground. The pegs continue to grow into the soft soil, and it's there, about 2 to 3 inches underground, that peanuts are produced. Peanuts continue to grow until maturity, when the entire plant turns yellow and is ready for harvest.

Additional Information

Once a plant has turned yellow, use a spading fork and gently dig around each plant, lifting the entire plant as you work. Gently knock off any soil you can without knocking off the individual peanuts. Hang the entire plant in a dry, warm shed or garage. After the peanuts have dried for two weeks, remove the individual peanuts from the fibrous roots and continue to dry for another two weeks. Once they have completely dried, store them in a mesh bag in a cool, well-ventilated space until you roast them. From planting to harvesting, the entire process takes about four to five months, depending on the type and variety of peanut you grow. The variety 'Valencia' is the one usually grown in Florida backyard gardens. Peanuts are usually roasted in the shell, but they also are excellent boiled. To make boiled peanuts, simply boil them immediately after harvest. Otherwise, peanuts must be roasted before they are eaten.

PEPPER

Peppers are great plants for the summer vegetable garden because they are very easy to grow, and they can be grown in the ground or in containers. And—big plus—they enjoy the heat and humidity of Florida summers. There are many different types of peppers and you can cook with them so many different ways. Bell peppers by far are the most commonly grown; however, if you are looking for hot and spicy peppers, the list is virtually limitless. The hardest part about growing peppers may be deciding which pepper to grow!

When to Plant

Peppers enjoy warm temperatures. Plant seed into peat pots three weeks before the last anticipated frost. In North and Central Florida plant pepper plant transplants outdoors from February through March and again from July through September. In South Florida plant peppers outdoors from August through September.

Where to Plant

Plant peppers in locations where they receive at least 8 hours of full sun and where there is an ample water source close by. Although peppers are not particular about soils, they perform best in compost amended, well-drained soil. The soil pH should be about 6.5.

How to Plant

Peppers are very easy to grow by seed and seeds are much less expensive than transplants. Sow seeds indoors three to four weeks before the last anticipated frost of the season. Recycled seed trays or biodegradable pots work best. Fill the containers with a good, sterilized soil mix and press the seeds $1/8$ inch into the soil mix. Cover the seeds with fine, sifted soil mix. Label every pot or tray with a plastic marker and a china marker. Because the fine seed can be washed away by a strong stream of water from a watering hose, it's best to water the seeds from the bottom. (This is the reason why it is very difficult to grow peppers from seed sown directly in the garden.) Place the entire tray or peat pot into another, larger tray filled with shallow water and allow the soil mix to absorb as much water as it can; usually fifteen minutes is enough time. Afterwards, place the container in full sun or indoors in bright light. Water using this method every day until the seeds pop out of the ground, usually in five to seven days. Place newly germinated seeds in a little more bright light every day over a period of two weeks until they are growing in full sun every day. Once you see roots growing out of the pot or you can see roots twirling around in the bottom of a seed tray, they are ready to be planted into the garden, generally when they are about 6 to 8 inches tall.

Plant the individual plants using the recommended spacing on the seed packages. For sweet bell peppers, for instance, plant individual plants 18 inches apart in rows 24 inches apart. For many of the larger varieties, however, more space will be required. Some peppers can reach a maximum height of 4 feet and can get 4 feet wide. Peppers also like a little sulfur when they are planted, so place a few (five or six) matches in the bottom of the planting hole, and place the transplant directly on top. Complete the planting as you would any other transplant. I am not kidding; this really works.

Care and Maintenance

Peppers are major feeders at all stages of their growth, and if I have learned *anything* over the years it's that peppers like a little bit of fertilizer frequently. An 8-0-8 fertilizer applied every three weeks is ideal. Peppers like moist, but not wet, soil, and dry soil can limit fruit production. A good layer of mulch will help moderate soil temperatures and retain moisture. Cultivate lightly to keep weeds out of the pepper patch. As the peppers begin to set fruit reduce the nitrogen fertilizer and increase the level of potassium. Too much nitrogen will produce loads of green leaves at the expense of little or no fruit production. Peppers can produce many fruit on a single plant at the same time. If allowed to stay on the plant, green peppers will turn red and their taste will be sweeter. The sheer weight of the fruit can cause a pepper plant to fall over. Before they have a chance to do that (and possibly break off at the ground), place a $^3/_8$-inch x 24-inch bamboo stake or similar tall stick into the ground and gently and carefully attach the main stem to the stick. Strips of hook-and-loop tape work very well and can be adjusted, if necessary. I caution you about using plastic coated wires—they can scrape the stem allowing disease organisms an opportunity to get a foothold. Strips of fabric work well, too.

Occasionally, aphids can be a problem, especially on emerging growth. A firm stream of water is usually sufficient to wash them away.

Additional Information

If you plan to store seed from your peppers for the following year, make sure you separate the hot and mild varieties in the garden. Peppers are self-pollinated but sometimes bees will stop by after they have visited another plant. The mix in flavors won't affect this year's fruit but may in the cross-pollinated seeds.

There are too many different pepper varieties to mention all of them. However, some of the best in each category include:

Standard sweet varieties: 'Yolo Wonder', 'Cubanelle', 'Sweet Banana', 'Early Calwonder', 'Keystone Resistant Giant', 'Purple Beauty', 'Pimento'

Hybrid sweet varieties: 'Big Bertha', 'Gypsy'

Standard hot varieties: 'Caribbean Red', 'Chili Jalapeno', 'Habenero', 'Hungarian Yellow Wax', 'Long Thin Cayenne', 'Serrano Tampiquero', 'Scotch Bonnet'

Hybrid hot variety: 'Super Chili'

> ### Why do the flowers on my pepper plants fall off?

Peppers are very sensitive to temperatures and fruit set is best achieved when daytime temperatures are between 70 to 80°F plus/minus and when nighttime temperatures are in the 60 to 75°F range. Poor pollenization can also be a cause. With fewer and fewer pollinators around to help out, bud drop of peppers is becoming a real problem To help with pepper pollenization, interplant pepper plants with flowers that attract bees such as marigolds, wishbone flowers, African daisies, and so forth. The more pollinators there are, the less bud drop will occur. Although there is no significant data to back it up, many gardeners think that poor air circulation might also be a cause of bud drop. By placing peppers on the outside rows of a garden rather than deep inside among taller plants, the plant will get better air circulation and less bud drop. It's important to maintain consistent irrigation levels and keep the pepper plants moist but not overly wet. Be careful not to apply too much nitrogen fertilizer on peppers; the extra nitrogen will produce lots of new growth but at the expense of flower buds. Finally, place one teaspoon of Epsom salts in a quart of water and spray the open flowers to encourage fruit set.

POTATO

Potatoes are fun, easy to grow, and they are good for you.
The bottom line is that they are just plain entertaining. Dig
a trench, throw an "eye" (the sprouting part of the potato) in
the ground, and watch them grow. Every time I grow a crop,
whether they are the big Idaho potato baking type or the cute
little Irish red type, the entire process fascinates me. Years ago,
while I was living in Tallahassee, I gave a tour of a vegetable
garden to a few Girl Scout Brownies. When I asked them about
what they knew about growing plants it was clear that they
had never set foot in a food garden before. When asked, not
one of the ten girls had a clue where potatoes came from other
than the ever-popular "grocery store" response. We encouraged
them to drop to their knees and dig in the soil, apparently
for the first time. Lo and behold, what did they find? Tiny
potatoes. You should have seen their eyes light up! Since then,
whenever I have asked someone to dig potatoes for the first
time, I get the same response. Soon thereafter they want to
know about how to grow lettuce, and tomatoes, and beans, and
. . . you get the picture. And so it begins.

When to Plant

In North and Central Florida plant potatoes from January
through March. In South Florida plant them from September
through January.

Where to Plant

Plant potatoes in full sun with compost- or manure-enriched,
well-drained soil. Potatoes can grow well in muck but not in
soil that is constantly wet.

How to Plant

Growing potatoes for the first time is a fascinating process.
First and most important, use potatoes that have not been
treated with hormones to prevent them from sprouting (such
as those found in a grocery store). "Seed potatoes" are available
from local feed stores or through online web sources. Locate a
potato "eye" (a small, dark-colored depression on the potato's

skin). With a sharp knife, remove a ¼ inch "scab" (including an eye) from the potato. The scab should be about 1 inch in diameter, including the eye and some of the white of the potato. Dust the scabs with sulfur dust or allow the scab to dry for several days. Dig a 6-inch trench 4 to 6 inches wide and 6 inches deep; place a scab in the trench every 8 to 10 inches apart with the eye facing up, and cover with 4 inches of soil. Rows should be 36 inches apart. In ten to fourteen days the scabs will sprout and new growth will emerge from the soil.

Care and Maintenance

Once the sprout reaches 8 to 10 inches in height, pull the soil up around the sprout leaving just the top leaves above the mound. (Add a few handfuls of an 8-0-8 fertilizer in the soil to be mounded as you work.) As a potato continues to grow, keep pulling the soil up to the sprout until there is a mound about 12 to 14 inches high. It is in the mound where the stem, now surrounded by soil, will sprout to produce potatoes. Tubers in the mounded soil can be harvested when the foliage begins to turn yellow. For smaller potatoes, harvest anytime during the growing season. Potatoes have no real problems except an occasional potato beetle, and they can be scared away with rotenone dust.

Early varieties of potatoes are ready to harvest when their flowers bloom.

Additional Information

For Florida the best varieties include 'Kennebec', 'Yukon Gold', 'Gold Rush', and 'Red Pontiac'. Other varieties that are fun to grow include 'French Fingerling', 'Adirondack Red', 'Adirondack Blue', and 'Russian Banana'.

PUMPKIN

At one time or another I think every gardener who grows vegetables dreams about growing pumpkins. When new gardeners ask me about growing them, I try to remain positive, but the reality is they take *lots* of room to grow. If you have plenty of space, then have at it! For those with smaller spaces, the smaller pumpkin varieties are just fine. Just be aware that pumpkins need *lots* of water, too. If supplying water is a problem then you'd better look for something else to grow. If your supply of water is plentiful, then having a pumpkin maturing into a nice fruit ready for Halloween carving is just around the corner.

In my case, I usually remember that I want to grow pumpkin about two weeks before Halloween, and I get mad at myself for not starting early enough. I promise myself that *next* year will be different. One year, I actually went as far as purchasing a package of pumpkin seeds only to realize when I got home that I was already two months late. Next year will be *the* year—you can count on it.

When to Plant

To have pumpkins ready to harvest by Halloween, you have to plant the seeds July 1. Planting any vegetable, let alone pumpkins, at that time is fraught with risk—bugs and diseases are at their high point. If you are growing pumpkins for pie making, it's better that you plant immediately after the danger of frost has passed in your area and try to beat the pest invasion. It can be done but the timing is critical. You can get a head start by planting pumpkin seeds in peat cups three to four weeks before the last frost, and then planting them outdoors as quickly as you can after that.

Where to Plant

Pumpkins need lots of room (100 square feet per plant), full sun (at least 8 hours), well-drained and well-composted soil, and lots and lots of water. Pumpkin plants *do not* tolerate wet, poorly drained soil or standing water even for the shortest period of time; it will put the plants into a tailspin.

How to Plant

Given the space needed to grow pumpkins and the number of weeds that would enjoy living in the same space, pumpkins are best grown on black plastic to eliminate weed competition. Place a 10-foot x 10-foot piece of black plastic over the garden space and pin into place. Make a 6-inch "X" in the center of the plastic and plant three seeds into the exposed soil. The seeds should germinate in five to seven days. After the seedlings reach 4 to 5 inches tall, remove all but the strongest seedling.

Care and Maintenance

One plant will produce one pumpkin in a 10-foot x 10-foot garden space. Pumpkin vines will produce a pumpkin 110 days after the seeds have been sown into the soil. That's why seeds should be

planted about July 1 to have a pumpkin ready for Halloween. Diseases and insects are a real problem so be prepared to spray a variety of chemicals weekly (pages 250 and 259) to keep the plant alive and well.

Water and sunlight are the key ingredients. An application of 10-10-10 fertilizer (½ cup) every four weeks is needed to keep the fruits and vines growing well. One cup of 10-10-10 fertilizer added to the initial planting area has very positive results.

Additional Information

Good varieties of pumpkins for Florida include 'Connecticut Field', 'Spirit', 'Half Moon', 'Big Moon', 'Howden', and 'Jackpot'. For pumpkin pies, grow 'Small Sugar'. For small pumpkins try 'Apprentice', 'Bumpkin', and 'Munchkin'.

RADISH

Sometimes, salads can be so drab and unappealing. Many people simply throw a few lettuce leaves in a bowl, sprinkle them with dressing, and call it a salad. But salads can be much more than that given the different varieties of fresh vegetables you can grow and add to them. For example, radishes are a main component of any salad in our house. But, if you only know the little, red, round radish from the local markets, well then, you're in for a real surprise.

When you open any seed catalog or visit an online site selling vegetable seeds, you will be *amazed* at the number of different radishes that are available now. Recently, I counted seveteen different varieties in just one catalog. Radishes are now available with different heat intensities, in different colors, and in different sizes. Second only to growing parsley, radishes have to be one of the easiest vegetables to cultivate. Because they are so easy to grow, and the seeds are relatively inexpensive considering the number you receive in a seed package, it's a great vegetable to help children get started in gardening. Many radishes can be harvested only forty-five days after sowing the seed. When they're planted at weekly or biweekly intervals, radishes can keep a child's attention over many months.

When to Plant

In North Florida radishes can be planted from April through November. Radishes don't like intense heat (which translates into hotter bulb flavors), so in Central and South Florida plan to sow them from October though April.

Where to Plant

Radishes are very forgiving of a variety of soils. They can grow in any natural soil in Florida (including South Florida's rockland soils) and can be planted in a wide variety of containers filled with a good quality potting soil. Because they are so small, radishes are a perfect candidate for planting in mixed containers with flowering annuals and perennials; just harvest before the flowering plants "fill in." Radishes still need full sun like other vegetables and they need ample water to prevent a harsh flavor (which sometimes can be caused by too little water).

How to Plant

Radish seeds are easy to handle and should be planted 3 inches apart in a furrow or broadcast evenly in a wide planting bed and covered with ¼ inch of fine soil. Thin the wide row of seedlings to 3 inches apart when the seedlings produce their second pair of true leaves. Radishes can be used as "marker" vegetables. Carrots are notoriously slow to germinate and sometimes get "lost" in the garden. Plant a radish seed every 10 to 12 inches in the carrot row to mark the location of the carrots. Once the radishes have matured forty-five days later, they can be harvested; in the meantime, the carrots will have grown tall enough to be seen.

Care and Maintenance

Just make sure radishes get adequate water so the soil remains moist but not soaking wet. Radishes that are allowed to go dry will have a much more intense, harsh, and bitter flavor; and keep an eye on the number days since you planted the seed. Although it may be fun to watch a radish plant grow to 18 inches tall with a fist-sized bulb, ones that large aren't very tasty. Harvest radishes within ten to fourteen days of the harvest schedule printed on the seed packet.

Additional Information

For traditionally sized and flavored radishes, try 'Sparkler' and 'Cherry Bell'. For more exotic shapes and colors, try 'White Icicle', 'Fire and Ice', 'Watermelon', and 'Zlata'.

RUTABAGA

Looking like a turnip on steroids, rutabaga is a root crop that can be grown throughout Florida in the cooler months of the year. It resembles a turnip root except that is it much larger, and the flesh inside is a beautiful golden yellow instead of white. Rutabagas can be baked, diced, mashed, creamed, glazed, fried, added to casseroles, stews, or soups, or served raw in salads. The leaves can also be eaten, but frankly, they aren't that good and need lots of seasoning to make them palatable. It's one of my favorite vegetables with a delicate sweetness and flavor that hints of the light freshness of cabbage and turnip. It has a distinct "bite" to the root but only mildly so compared to that of a turnip. There are only 40 calories in 3½ ounces of rutabaga, making it a great vegetable for snacks. It is low in sodium, very low in saturated fat and cholesterol, and is a good source of dietary fiber. Once harvested, rutabagas can last in a refrigerator for up to one month.

They are easy to grow in the garden but do take some time to grow—up to ninety days before initial harvest. As with most root crops, it's best to keep your eye on the harvest dates to be certain that the root isn't allowed to grow much after its "due date." Otherwise, the root gets pithy and woody and cannot be eaten. If you have never eaten a rutabaga, you might want to try a few from the market before you set aside valuable garden space for a vegetable you might not like.

When to Plant
Throughout Florida, plant rutabagas in October or November.

Where to Plant
Unlike their cousin the turnip, rutabagas really enjoy a well-prepared, compost-enriched soil. They can be grown in single rows, wide rows, and even in containers. Given that a rutabaga root is 85 percent water, they enjoy a regular drink of water and lots of sunlight. Once well established, rutabaga can withstand wet soils for a short time but cannot tolerate standing water.

How to Plant

Plant the seeds in well-prepared soil, ¼ inch deep. In wide row plantings, cover with ¼ inch of soil, and later thin to 5 inches apart after the seedlings grow the second pair of true leaves. Tamp the soil firmly after planting the seed to achieve good seed-soil contact and gently apply water. The seedlings should emerge within five to seven days.

Care and Maintenance

It's important that you rotate any root crop's location in the garden every year and rutabaga is no exception. Just like turnips and carrots, wire worms can be a problem if root crops are planted in the same location every year, so rotate the planting locations in your garden to prevent an infestation. As an added measure, liberally sprinkle wood ashes from a fireplace (no charcoal briquettes, please) in the furrow or over the wide row before planting to further reduce the chances of an infestation.

The leaves will often be eaten by a number of small insects, but they rarely eat enough to decrease the quality of the harvestable roots. If the leaf holes really bother you, an application of rotenone powder or Neem oil will take care of the problem.

Additional Information

Good varieties of rutabagas suited for Florida include 'American Purple Top', 'Macomber', 'Purple Top Yellow', 'Long Island Improved', 'Sweet Russian', 'Laurential', and 'Zwaan's Neckless Purple Top'.

SPINACH

Versatility is the key word when talking about spinach. It can be eaten raw, steamed, added to pasta dishes, and used in dips. Once you get few of the details down it's easy to grow, and a few rows a can feed a family of four without much work. In addition to using it in the vegetable garden, its wrinkled, emerald-black leaves work well as a border plant in the landscape or as a filler plant in a mixed container of bedding plants and perennials.

When to Plant

Spinach is a cool-weather plant and "bolts," or goes to flower, when the weather turns warm. Most spinach is planted in the fall and it will continue to grow until warm weather returns. In North and Central Florida plant spinach from October through November and in South Florida plant spinach from October through January. If you plant successive crops of spinach every three weeks you'll be able to harvest a continuous crop.

Where to Plant

If you ever need to improve your garden soil with compost or manures, spinach would be the crop to do it. Rich, deep loamy soil that drains well will produce crisp green leaves for harvesting. Full sun is a must and so is moist, but not wet, soil. Spinach prefers locations with good air circulation. If that's not possible in your garden, try growing spinach in aboveground containers or in raised beds.

How to Plant

Spinach can be direct sown into the garden or started from seed indoors four weeks before planting in the garden. For transplants, plant the seed ½ inch deep in biodegradable containers and keep the soil moist for good germination. Transplants can be planted out when the seedlings are 3 to 4 inches tall. When planting seed outdoors directly into the garden, soak seeds overnight in water and plant 3 to 4 inches apart. Later, thin to 6 inches apart in rows that are 24 inches wide. Spinach lends itself to wide row plantings.

Care and Maintenance

Spinach likes to be fed a little bit at frequent intervals. Fertilize with a general 12-0-12 fertilizer every two to three weeks and keep the soil moist. An occasional liquid feed of 20-20-20 wouldn't hurt, either. Remove weeds often to reduce the competition for food and water. Harvest the single, outside leaves of spinach or cut the entire plant for cooking. Mulching with hay around the plants will reduce weeds, conserve water, and reduce the amount of dirt and grit that splashes up on the plants during rainstorms. As the weather begins to warm up watch for flower stalks and harvest immediately, otherwise the foliage becomes very bitter quite quickly. After it's been washed, fresh spinach can be refrigerated in an airtight container for up to one week.

Additional Information

Spinach is rich in calcium, iron, and vitamin A. There are several different kinds of spinach. Of the crinkled leaf varieties 'Bloomsdale Longstanding' performs well in Florida. Good medium savoyed varieties include 'Melody' and 'Vienna'. 'Tyee' is a good, slightly savoyed spinach with very upright leaves that help it stay cleaner than most others. Good, plain-leaf varieties for Florida include 'Giant Nobel', 'Space', and 'Olympia'.

SQUASH

Of all the vegetables, I must admit squash is my favorite. There are so many different kinds that one never grows tired of it. It can be prepared in a nearly infinite number of ways and that makes it a preferred vegetable of chefs around the world. Stir-fried, baked, sautéed, grilled—the list of preparation methods is endless. It's also very, *very* easy to grow. Just stick a few seeds in the ground and forty five days later you'll have edible fruit. That's why it is so popular in children's gardens, too; it grows fast and the fruit are easy to find during harvesting. I encourage you to try some new squash varieties in your garden this year. It's a great way to learn more about growing plants, and a new vegetable on the dinner table might be a nice change!

When to Plant

The traditional terms of summer and winter squash really don't mean a thing in Florida. Let's talk about summer squash first. In North Florida summer squash should be planted from March through April and again from August through September. In Central Florida summer squash is planted from February through March and again from August through September. In South Florida summer squash should be planted from January through March and again from September through October. Now let's talk about winter squash (which is usually the vining type). In North Florida plant winter squash in March and again in August. In Central Florida plant winter squash from February through March and in South Florida plant winter squash from January through February and again in September. Whew! That's a lot of squash.

Where to Plant

Plant squash in full sun in a compost-enriched, well-drained soil that has been deeply tilled and which has a pH of 5.8 to 6.8.

How to Plant

Although our northern friends plant squash in hills, in Florida they are planted in rows just like other vegetable crops. The use of hills in northern gardens allows the seed to dry out and stay above any wet soil, a problem we don't generally have here. Plant two or three seeds every 36 inches apart, in rows that are 36 to 48 inches apart. Five to six fruit-producing plants are enough for an average family.

Care and Maintenance

Although they are very easy to grow and care for, squash plants do have a few problems that may arise. The number one problem is stem borers. Very large, cream-colored worms burrow into the thick but hollow squash stems and ultimately kill the vine beyond the spot where the pest has eaten. A light dusting of rotenone every two weeks will deter stem borers. Once inside the stem they can be detected by their light-green "frass" (a somewhat nicer word for poop) found on the outside of the stems. If stem borers are caught early enough, the home gardener can carefully cut an infected stem open lengthwise with a sharp knife and kill the worm. Piling 2 to 3 inches of dirt in mounds on the cut vine will cause the vine to root at those locations and will help overcome any borer damage. Once a worm is inside a vine, insecticides will not work. Worms will sometimes bore into the fruit, as well. A light dusting of rotenone on a regular basis will deter these pests, too.

The other serious problem for squash is powdery mildew. As a result of our warm, humid nights, a light, powderlike dusting will appear on the upper surfaces of the leaves causing the leaves to drop off prematurely, ultimately killing the plant. One method of control is prevention. Plant mildew-resistant varieties if they are available (unfortunately, only a few are available at this time), and avoid those varieties that are regularly susceptible. Planting in full sun, watering in the mornings, and selecting sites with good air circulation will help. Applying horticultural oils (such as Neem and Sunfine Ultraspray) copper and sulfur work well to protect plants and eradicate powdery mildew *but* they cannot be used together nor should they be used when temperatures reach 90 degrees F. Serenade® is a new organic fungicide that can be used on squash and must applied every seven days once the disease has been identified. Serenade can be applied up to and including the day of harvest. Immunox® (Myclobutnil) is a systemic fungicide registered for squash that both protects and cures powdery mildew on squash; it must be applied every seven to ten days once the disease has been identified.

Additional Information

Do not try to pull the fruits off a squash vine; instead, cut the fruit so there are 1 to 2 inches of stem remaining. (Squash store better (longer) if their stems are left on.) Remember, both summer and winter squash can grow in fall and spring, but for the sake of simplicity I will use "summer squash" (those with a tender skin) and "winter squash" (those with a tough, hard skin) for descriptive groupings only. Good varieties of summer squash for Florida include early 'Prolific Straightneck', 'Summer Crookneck', 'Peter Pan', and 'Early White Scallop'. Good winter varieties include 'Spaghetti', 'Table King', 'Table Queen', 'Table Ace' (acorn), 'Waltham', and 'Early Butternut'. Good Florida zucchini varieties include 'Cocozelle', 'Spineless Beauty', 'Black Beauty', 'Gold Rush', 'Eightball', and 'Caserta'.

> Winter squash is ready to harvest when the skin is hard enough so that a scratch from a thumbnail will not leave a mark.

For different types of squash try 'Ambercup', 'Bonbon', 'Bush Delicata', 'Calabaza', and 'Golden Hubbard'. But, like I said, there are hundreds of varieties so keep planting to find your favorites.

➤ *Can I save the seeds of squash for planting next year?*
Yes, provided they are not hybrids. Remove the hard seeds from mature squash and allow them to dry in the sun, turning them daily so they dry evenly. Remove any pulp and store the seeds in a resealable plastic bag in the bottom of the refrigerator. Inspect the seeds periodically, and remove any seeds that have mold on them. Seeds stored in this way can be used for several years.

➤ *Can I eat squash flowers?*
The flowers of squash are delicious and are sometimes sautéed over high heat with the small squash fruits still attached. The flowers can also be filled with a slivered almond-ricotta-parmesan cheese mixture and broiled briefly in the oven.

STRAWBERRY

If ever there were a sweeter berry than a strawberry, I don't know what it would be. One of my favorite memories growing up was the delicious aroma of strawberries in the air riding along the sandy roads through Plant City (near Tampa) in the springtime.

The air was heavy with the deep, rich scent and afterwards I was determined to learn how to grow them myself. I have since learned how to do it, and I still enjoy the springtime ritual of riding through Plant City in the spring.

Just a word of caution, however. If you enjoy fresh strawberries, think how much the bugs, slugs, birds, spider mites, mice, raccoons, and a possums like them, too. As with sweet corn, I encourage you to grow strawberries once or twice, but chances are you will find that going to the store or to a strawberry festival may be much easier and less costly!

Where to Plant

Plant in full sun in rich, very well-composted, well-drained garden soil with a soil acidity of 5.5 to 6.5.

How to Plant

Bareroot, single-crown strawberry plants planted in the fall will produce up to three cycles of berry production, with the most abundant in the spring months. The cycles can be interrupted by frost and water availability. Strawberry plants are grown in raised linear beds about 8 inches high. Drip irrigation or soaker hoses are placed 2 to 3 inches below the top of the soil. If you cover each row with an opaque, polyethylene plastic it will control weeds, keep the fruit clean, and conserve water. Small slits are made in the plastic in an alternating pattern 12 inches apart along the row and 12 to 18 inches wide, and the plants are planted into the soil beneath. It is very difficult to grow strawberries any other way given their long growing season and the abundance of weeds in Florida gardens. The only alternative would be to use newspaper and coastal hay (with or without mounding the soil and with or without soaker hoses).

Care and Maintenance

A fertilizer formula containing nitrogen (N), phosphorus (P), and potassium (K) is essential for successful strawberry growth and fruiting. Two pounds of a 10-5-10 or similar garden fertilizer with micronutrients (such as zinc, copper, iron, manganese, and boron) per 10 feet of row should be incorporated into the bed before planting. At least half of the nitrogen should be slow release. Protect fruit and flowers from temperatures below 32°F by covering them with old blankets or commercially available polypropylene row covers.

Strawberries are the favorite among many pests. Birds, field mice, raccoons, and so forth can be repelled by placing fine mesh bird netting over the plants. The netting won't bother the strawberries but it infuriates the animals. For slugs, a very common pest, beer traps work best. For spider mites and insects, apply Neem oil as necessary. For spider mites, at least three applications will be necessary five days apart to keep them under control once they are discovered.

Additional Information

Recommended varieties for Florida include 'Camarosa', 'Sweet Charlie', and 'Festival'. All three varieties produce attractive, flavorful berries suitable for eating fresh or for freezing. 'Camarosa' has been the most productive variety in North Florida, while 'Festival' has been the most productive variety in Central Florida. These varieties are capable of producing one to two pints of fruit per plant over the season.

SUMMER PEA

It's confusing, I know, but in Florida you can plant two types of peas. The first is the English pea; that's the kind that is green, sweet, and grown in the cooler seasons of the year. The second is the summer pea, which are similar to beans and can be eaten fresh or dried to be used later. Black-eyed peas and purple hulls are examples of summer peas. Summer peas are usually long and narrow, with tiny beans or "peas," and they enjoy the hot, humid summer months. Summer peas and a few other vegetables, such as okra, sweet potatoes, peppers, and peanuts, are about the only things that can take the full sun and summer heat of Florida. People from our northern neighboring states may think it seems odd not to plant anything in the summer, but that's Florida—it's just too hot and too humid for most vegetables.

When to Plant

Plant the seeds when it's hot—the hotter, the better. Once soil temperatures reach 70°F, it's pea planting time. In North and Central Florida plant summer peas from March through August. In South Florida plant summer peas from August through April.

Where to Plant

Plant summer pea seeds in full, hot, steaming sun in a location that receives at least 8 hours, more if you can get it. Summer peas will grow in just about any kind of soil from rich organically improved soils all the way to the other end of the spectrum—muck. They are not fussy plants and will grow just about anywhere, provided they have sun and water.

How to Plant

Summer peas are easier to grow than radishes. Plant the seeds 1 to 2 inches deep, 3 to 4 inches apart, in rows that are 30 inches apart. The seeds will germinate in five to seven days. The peas will be ready to harvest in eighty to ninety days. Summer peas must be planted directly into garden soil—do *not* transplant.

Care and Maintenance

Fertilize the plants once a month with a general-purpose 8-0-8 fertilizer, or fertilize according to the results of your soil analysis. When new growth emerges from the soil the bean seedlings are often the favorite food of birds, especially brown thrashers. They will break off the tender seed that emerges with the new leaves, which will kill the new sprout. My daughter's 30-inch-long, lifelike plastic monitor lizard will scare them off most years but aluminum pie pans attached to strings and allowed to twirl in the air will work, too. Another prevention is to have a good, barking dog or a vigilant cat. Many of the pea pods can be eaten like snap beans if they're picked early enough. Otherwise, the pods should be allowed to grow until the peas inside the pods are fully formed. Shell them like English peas.

Additional Information

Summer peas are easy to grow and even easier to cook. Just place dried beans in a pot and cover with water; let it stand overnight. The next day, pour the water off, add new water to cover, add a ham hock or neck bones, and season to taste. Make some corn bread, too, to sop up the leftover liquid. Wow!

Varieties of summer peas that perform well in Florida include 'Brown Crowder', 'California Blackeye', 'Knucklehull Purplehull', 'Mississippi Silverskin', 'White Acre', and 'Zipper Cream'.

SWEET POTATO

If you are looking for a problem-free summer vegetable that requires very little care then sweet potato is for you. These tender, sweet, orange tubers and their vining, heart-shaped leaves thrive in Florida's summer heat. All you have to do is prepare the soil properly before planting and walk away. Sweet potatoes are grown from tip cuttings of growing tubers and not that long ago a gardener would simply take cuttings of the vine tips, called "slips," and plant them directly into long, mounded hills. Then the growers came out with rooted slips in bundles of twenty five, which made life much easier; with the old way you had to watch the new cuttings to make sure they didn't dry out. Now, however, slips are considered old fashioned. Growers now put cuttings in plastic, nine-count cell packs. When you buy them they are fully rooted and ready for planting out into the mounds. Isn't technology grand?

When to Plant

Plant sweet potatoes from March through June throughout Florida.

Where to Plant

Plant in full sun, in mounds of compost-enriched soil. Be sure there is an ample water supply nearby.

How to Plant

Create 10-inch tall, 12-inch-wide linear mounds with surrounding garden soil. A little 10-10-10 fertilizer (2 to 3 pounds) sprinkled on the soil used to make the mounds should be enough for the entire growing season. Place the rooted slips into the top of the mound 12 to 14 inches apart in rows that are 48 to 60 inches apart.

Care and Maintenance

Once the slips are planted, make certain that the plant receives enough water to produce large tubers. In the final two weeks reduce the amount of irrigation the plants receive. The tubers can be harvested at any time during the summer, but they are finished growing when the vines begin to turn yellow. Cut the vines away from the mounds and gently lift them, shaking carefully to remove the soil. The tubers that have grown in the mounds can be eaten after two or three days of "curing" in the sun. The only real problems with sweet potatoes are deer; deer will walk a hundred miles to eat sweet potato vines. Let them eat all they want; deer eating the vines every so often won't have an adverse effect on the size or quality of the tubers. Store the tubers in a cool, dry location.

Additional Information

For Florida the best sweet potato varieties include 'Beauregard', 'Hernandez', and 'Picodito' (boniato). Sweet potatoes perform best where the soil has been turned over two to three months prior to planting. This reduces the number of nematodes and helps any plant debris that was turned under to decompose. Soils with high levels of nematodes (more than 2 percent) are not well suited for sweet potato production and planting in that location will result in cracked tubers. Avoid garden areas that have been allowed to go fallow or where sweet potatoes have been grown in the last three years. Sweet potatoes will continue to grow as long as there are green tops. For that reason, sweet potatoes can be harvested anytime their size fits your particular need.

SWISS CHARD

There is something satisfying about growing greens in the home garden. I guess it's like having money in the bank; as you walk through your garden you know at the very least you won't starve no matter how tough things get. Swiss chard is a staple in any fall garden and on the dinner plate it complements just about everything. Many people eat it raw in salads like spinach and just about everyone eats it cooked with a piece of smoked meat for additional flavor.

When to Plant

Swiss chard can be planted as early as mid-September; but, given Florida's heat, the quality can sometimes be less than desired. Seeds can be started in biodegradable pots in late September and planted out into the garden in mid-October. Plant three to four successive plantings in 15-foot-long rows of chard, three weeks apart, to provide an adequate supply for an average family.

Where to Plant

Plant in full sun in compost-enriched, deeply tilled soil with a pH of 6.0 to 6.8. Swiss chard prefers to have moist, but not wet, soil, so be certain an adequate supply of water is nearby.

How to Plant

Plant Swiss chard seeds directly into the garden every 4 to 5 inches apart in rows that are 24 inches apart. Soak seed overnight in warm water and plant the seed ½ inch deep. One seed will produce several seedlings when it begins to sprout so it is necessary that the small seedlings be thinned to 12 inches apart. Seedlings grown in biodegradable pots should be planted 12 inches apart when the seedlings reach a height of 6 inches.

Care and Maintenance

Swiss chard is grown like spinach or mustard. If the seedlings don't sprout uniformly, interplant with more seed to make a complete row. A standard 12-0-12 fertilizer applied every three weeks will provide adequate nutrition. Apply a layer of hay or leaves to maintain adequate soil moisture, to keep the foliage free of dirt and grit, and to minimize weeds. Not only do weeds compete for nutrients and water, many of the critters that can eat the leaves on Swiss chard begin their life cycle in weeds. Swiss chard should be harvested like collards—the leaves at the bottom of the plant are picked first. Picking from the bottom encourages new growth on top.

Speaking of bugs, Swiss chard doesn't have many pests. If the soil is kept too wet, slugs can be a problem, but they are easily eliminated with beer traps. Wide boards placed near the base of the plants will attract slugs, too. Simply flip the board over in the morning and eliminate the slugs that have accumulated beneath the board during the evening.

Additional Information

In addition to its other good qualities, Swiss chard is a handsome vegetable that can also be used as an attractive border plant in the landscape. Most notably, 'Bright Lights' has large, broad stems with orange, red, yellow, and light-green stems. Other good chards include 'Erbette', 'Monstruoso', 'Fordhook Giant', 'Italian White Ribbed', and 'Ruby Red'.

TOMATO

If you mention the words "vegetable garden," often the first thing many people think about are tomatoes. Juicy, firm, vine-ripened tomatoes. Of all the vegetables, tomatoes are king in the garden. More people grow tomatoes than any other kind of vegetable. (Technically tomatoes are fruits, but let's not get into that.) They can be grown indoors and outdoors, in the ground and in containers—even in hanging baskets! Tomatoes can grow several feet tall or fewer than 12 inches tall and still produce loads of fruit. There are *hundreds* of different varieties to choose from, and because tomatoes are so easy to place in your garden, the most difficult is trying to decide which variety to grow.

Let's talk for just a minute about how tomato plants grow. They can be divided into two main groups: indeterminate and determinate. Knowing these terms will save you time in the garden later. If ever you have grown tomato plants, you know that most grow and grow and then grow some more. More often than not they grow taller than the stake you tie them to, or they grow taller than the cage you placed them in. The majority of tomato seeds sold today are the vining type of tomatoes, which is the "indeterminate" type. That means, given adequate water and fertilizer, they will grow to an indeterminate height. Then there are the "determinate"-type tomatoes, and, if you haven't guessed by now, they grow to a (genetically) determined height (usually 4 to 5 feet tall) and stop. Determinate tomato varieties are great because you know at what height the tomato will stop growing and thus, the length of stake or the size cage you will need.

One more thing; have you ever noticed the letters "VFN" after the variety name on the plant label? The "V" stands for Verticillium wilt (which is a deadly tomato disease); the "F" is an abbreviation of Fusarium wilt; and "N" stands for nematodes. When these letters, and occasionally a few others, appear on a label it means that hybridizers have created a built-in resistance to these problems and the plants have a better chance of survival in the garden.

When to Plant

It seems the "when to" part of growing tomatoes is a little tricky in Florida. In most areas of the country, tomatoes are planted in the spring and allowed to grow all summer. If you haven't already guessed it, that's not true in Florida. In North Florida plant tomatoes from February (after the last frost) through March (so they will produce loads of fruit before the heat sets in). Plant again in August (so the plants will produce fruit before first frost). In Central Florida plant tomatoes from January through March and again in September. In South Florida plant tomatoes from August through March.

Where to Plant

Plant tomatoes in a location where they will receive at least 8 hours of full sun. More is better and less will cause the plant to "stretch," and it will produce low-quality and fewer fruit. Tomatoes can tolerate a variety of soils; just make certain the soil is compost rich and well drained. Tomatoes prefer constantly moist soil; inconsistent moisture will produce poorly formed fruit just like cucumbers. Tomatoes will not tolerate soggy or wet roots. If you are planting in containers on a patio or terrace, be sure to plant them where the roots have plenty of room to grow. A deep, 24-inch-diameter container or larger works best.

How to Plant

Tomatoes are very easy to grow from seed and can be sown indoors six to eight weeks before the danger of frost is past. Sow individual seeds in a high-quality, sterile potting soil and grow in full sun until planted outdoors. More often than not when customers buy ready-to-plant transplants in the store they overlook the tall and spindly plants and buy the short, stocky plants instead. Actually, the taller plants are better. Tomato plants should be planted deep into garden soil; they are the only vegetables that can be. A deep, narrow hole is best and only 4 inches of a tomato plant should poke its head out of the hole. Backfill the planting hole with native soil and good compost to a height 2 inches *less* than the original soil line to create a water reservoir. Because it is planted so deep, in addition to the roots at the bottom of the plant, roots will also form along the entire length of the stem. This allows more water and nutrient absorption.

Care and Maintenance

The less you fuss with tomatoes, the better. Tomatoes are highly susceptible to a variety of diseases and any activity that reduces contact with dirty, germ-ridden human hands is a good idea. Do not pick tomatoes or groom plants when the leaves are wet; that's when they are particularly vulnerable to transmission of diseases. Blossom drop is the result of cool temperatures (below 55°F), hot temperatures (above 90°F), not enough water, and too much nitrogen fertilizer.

Tomatoes are commonly attached to wooden stakes with stout twine or thin straps of remnant cloth tied into a figure-eight shape. Hook-and-loop strips designed for outdoor use work very well, too. I prefer cages made from concrete sidewalk reinforcing wire (often available for free at construction sites), formed into a tall column, and placed around a newly planted tomato plant. As the stems grow they are pushed into the column and the stems/leaves are supported by the wire mesh. This method requires minimal gardener-to-foliage contact. A gardener friend of mine once made a cage of one-inch chicken wire to grow his tomatoes. The tomatoes grew very well, but he couldn't get the fruit through the chicken wire!

A common method of growing tomatoes in the South is the wire-and-string method, which is similar to the system one would use to grow pole beans. Place a stout, 6-foot-tall pole at either end of a planned tomato row and place a heavy wire across the top of the poles, stretching the wire from pole to pole. After planting the tomato plant, gently tie heavy string to the lower stem of a tomato plant, and attach the other end to the wire. As the tomato grows, simply tie the tomato stems to the upright string. Another method of staking tomatoes is called the "Florida weave." It starts out with two very stout poles located at either end of the row as described, but in addition, smaller-diameter poles are pounded into the ground along the row every 2 feet apart. Heavy garden twine is then woven back and forth from one end of each row at 6-inch intervals to create a basketlike effect. The tomatoes are planted along the row and as they grow, the stems are "woven" in and out of the supporting twine.

> Use a thin piece of cloth to wind a figure-eight shape between the stem of a tomato plant and its stake. The cloth will support the plant but will also allow it to move with the wind when needed.

Additional Information

Deciding which tomato to grow is based on a variety of criteria such as how much space you have, the size of tomato plant you ultimately want to have, whether you want to grow modern versus heirloom varieties, and so forth. Several varieties that perform well in Florida are:

Indeterminate (large fruit) - 'Better Boy' (VFN), 'Bonnie Best' (North and Central Florida only), 'Bragger', 'San Marzano' (plum shaped)

Indeterminate (small fruit) - 'Red Cherry', 'Sweet 100', 'Sweet Chelsea', and 'Husky Cherry'

Determinate (large fruit) - 'Walter' (F), 'Sun Coast' (VF), 'Floramerica' (F), 'Flora-dade' (VF), 'Duke' (VF), 'Sunny' (VF), and 'Celebrity'

Determinate (small fruit) - 'Floragold', 'Florida Petite', 'Patio', and 'Micro Tom'

TURNIP

Can you have a garden in the South and not grow turnips? I have to confess I am a real fan of turnips, but I also have to come clean. For half my life, I used to throw the tops away and eat only the roots. It wasn't until I was in my mid-30s that I tried eating the tops, when an old-timer walking by my house while I was sitting on my porch pointed out that I was throwing out the wrong part. Since then, turnip greens, with a few diced roots and a ham hock, are one of my favorite meals. Add some cracklin' cornbread to sop up the pot licker on the bottom of the pan and you're livin' the high life! For the Irish in us, turnips are perfect in lamb stew and cooked with corned beef. Mashed turnips make a great side dish, too.

When to Plant

In North Florida plant turnips from January through April and again from August through October. In Central Florida plant them from January through March and again from September through November. In South Florida plant turnips from October through February.

Where to Plant

Turnips are the least fussy of all southern garden plants. Give the plants full sun (8 hours minimum) and plenty of water in well-composted or manure-enriched, well-drained, and deeply tilled soil and you're home free. To prevent the occasional root maggot, sprinkle the soil with a little wood ash from a fireplace (one cup to every ten feet of row) over the soil before planting the seed. Leaf-eating worms are also sometimes a problem. A light dusting of rotenone or Dipel® will make them disappear. When too much water is added to turnips, slugs can be a pest, but beer bait traps can make quick work of them.

How to Plant

Direct sow turnip seed ½ inch deep, 2 to 3 inches apart, in rows 24 inches apart. After they are about 3 inches tall, thin them to 3 inches apart. Because turnips are a root crop, they don't perform well when they are transplanted. If you want to grow primarily tops and not roots, turnips can be planted closer together.

Care and Maintenance

Keep the plants weed free and cultivate regularly but lightly. A layer of coastal hay between the rows will also reduce weeds and prevent soil and grit from splashing up on the greens. Every three weeks or so feed the turnips with a water-soluble fertilize, containing some minor elements, including boron. Harvest turnips when they are about 3 inches in diameter; any larger and they are likely to be woody and tough to eat.

Additional Information

'Purple Top White Globe Turnips' are by far the most popular turnip for both greens and roots. If you are interested primarily in growing turnips for their tops only, then try 'Seven Top', 'Southern Green', 'Shogoin', and 'Topper'. For varieties for which you want to grow the roots, try 'Golden Ball', 'Just Right', 'Lunga Bianca A Colletto Viola', 'Tokyo Cross', and 'White Lady'.

> *What are the two kinds of turnips?*
The rutabaga is considered by some to be the yellow turnip or the Swede, and the white turnip is the "true" turnip. The true turnip includes the 'Purple Top' and 'White Lady' cultivars. Both belong to the Brassica family, which also includes cabbage, broccoli, Brussels sprouts, mustard, and cauliflower. All members of the Brassica family contain very high levels of vitamin C and, according the researchers at UC Berkley, they provide potent antiviral, antibacterial, and anticancer properties.

WATERMELON

Florida provides the perfect growing conditions for producing watermelon: well-drained soil, a long growing season, plentiful sunlight, and abundant rainfall. The multitudes of semi-trailer trucks running down the roads loaded to the brim with bright-green watermelons is a testament to that. Watermelon fields in Florida are like peanut fields in Georgia or cotton fields in Alabama—it's a sign of who we are. We are proud to be able to grow them in such quantities. In fact, Florida is the nation's leading producer of watermelons in the United States and, from December through April, Florida is the *only* producer of watermelons in the entire country.

When to Plant

Watermelons grow best when daytime temperatures are between 70° to 85°F; they can tolerate temperatures up to 90°F. In North Florida that means planting seeds from March through April and again from July to August. In Central Florida plant seeds from January through March and again in August. In South Florida watermelons can be planted from January through March and again from August through September.

Where to Plant

Watermelons can grow in a wide variety of soils but they have a tough time growing in muck soils. The soil pH should be in the 6.0 to 6.5 range, but they can tolerate a pH as low as 5.0. Plant watermelon seeds in full sun with an ample water supply nearby. They are thirsty plants.

How to Plant

Seeds planted 1½ inches deep, 36 inches apart, in rows that are 7 to 8 feet apart will provide the best possible yields. Watermelons reach maturity within 80 to 100 days after planting seed, depending on the variety. Given the amount of water necessary to grow ample-sized fruit and the fact that competing weeds also like the same water, many gardeners will stretch black plastic over the garden and plant the seeds *through* the plastic as described. The plastic eliminates the weed problem, conserves moisture, and keeps the fruit clean. A thin layer of newspaper covered with coastal hay will work too, and it can be tilled under when the season is over.

Care and Maintenance

Aphids are the primary insect pests affecting watermelons grown in Florida. Normally, these are not a huge problem on most vegetables, but aphids are vectors for a variety of viruses that can directly affect watermelon production. Cucumber beetles also carry viruses. For that reason it's important that aphids and cucumber beetles are controlled. Dusting rotenone in the late afternoon or at dusk, when the pollinators are least active, is most effective. Any worms that feed on the fruit are called rind worms. Beet armyworms and cabbage loopers are the worst rind worms, and they can be controlled with Dipel® (*Bacillus thuringiensis*).

Additional Information

There is no sure way to determine when a watermelon is ripe. Generally, when the fruit is ripe, the bottom of the melon will turn a bright golden yellow. Additionally, look for the tendril closest to the fruit—when the tendril turns from green to brown, more often than not the melon is ripe.

For large watermelons in Florida try 'Jubilee' (also known as 'Florida Giant'), 'Crimson Sweet', and 'Charleston Grey 133'. For smaller varieties or "icebox melons" try 'Sugar Baby' and 'Mickeylee'.

AVOCADO

Personally, I don't think it's a coincidence that many avocado varieties ripen at the same time that college football season starts. Guacamole is a staple at our house during the fall gridiron season and you can't get any fresher than by going out to the backyard a week before the big game to pick a few avocados. Sushi couldn't exist without the California roll and its avocado contents, and a summer salad with ripe, buttery avocado is just the thing to cool down a hot afternoon. In addition to fruit production, avocado trees make good landscape specimens, ranging in height from 30 to 60 feet tall depending on the variety.

Where to Plant

Traditionally, avocados were only planted in the warmest areas of the state, primarily the southeastern and southwestern corners. With the advent of hybridization and the introduction of cold-hardy selections, avocados can now be grown in cooler areas of the state, as well. Regardless of where you live, follow the guidelines found in the chart that follows and talk to gardeners in your area to determine whether or not planting avocados is a viable option. Plant avocados in full sun and be sure to give them plenty of room. For the first four to five years make certain to water during prolonged dry spells.

How to Plant

In areas where the soil depth is shallow, planting an avocado tree will take some work. Hand picks, augers, or backhoes will do the job. Any underlying hard rock will have to be removed to twice the depth of a containerized rootball and three times its width. Plant the rootball 1 to 2 inches above the soil line to compensate for settling. In areas where flooding can be a problem, plant an avocado tree on mounds of native soil (2 to 3 feet deep by 10 to 12 feet wide) and install as described. In sandy soils plant as you would any containerized rootball but do not add any amendments (such as peat moss, top soil, and so forth) to the backfill.

Care and Maintenance

Nutrition for avocados can be a little confusing because there are different amounts and types of fertilizers added to the underlying soil at different stages of an avocado tree's life. During its first three years, fertilize an avocado tree with 1 cup of a 10-10-10-4 (NPKMg) fertilizer every two months. A generic palm fertilizer will also work. After its first three years, four fertilizer applications per year are recommended (in increasing amounts proportional to the size of the tree)—but never exceed 20 pounds per year. One more thing: four times in the spring and summer during a tree's first four years, apply a foliar spray from a hose-end sprayer containing, copper, zinc, manganese, and boron. After its fourth year, a spray of zinc, manganese, molybdenum,

and boron during spring and summer will do the trick. Finally, watch for iron deficiencies that will appear as a general yellowing of the leaves. A granular application of chelated iron will soon correct any problems (but foliar sprays of iron won't help).

Additional Information

Oddly enough, avocado fruits do not ripen on the tree. Generally, the fruit is picked when it's at its maximum size (as noted on the following chart), but this can change from year to year depending on weather conditions. I use this simple test at home: when you think the fruit is ready, pick the largest fruit and leave it on a table without refrigeration. If the fruit softens within four to eight days the remaining fruits on the tree are ready, too. On the other hand, if the fruit gets wrinkly or becomes rotten, it's not ready and you can test again in a week or two. That's the great thing about avocados—they don't all have to be picked at the same time. But remember, once they are harvested, expect them to ripen within four to eight days. One more thing: when you select an avocado variety for your garden, why not select several that have different ripening seasons, if you have room? When you refer to the chart you can see that avocados have a wide range of dates to maturity. Ideally, it would be great to have early, mid-, and late maturing varieties in your garden.

I haven't said anything about critters because avocados have only a few diseases and bugs that can affect the appearance of the fruit but they seldom reduce the number of fruit produced. Loopers, aphids, thrips, and scale are sometimes a problem, but if the trees are well fed and watered they hardly ever have serious problems.

> *Why do my avocados have brown strings?*
Often, younger trees will produce fruit with "strings," which will become less prevalent as the tree matures. Also, many avocados have strings based on the amount of oil content in the fruit. The more oil, the fewer strings the fruit will have.

> *How do I grow avocados from seed?*
About half-way down an avocado seed insert toothpicks at equal distances from each other; place the broad end of the seed in a glass of water. Once the seed has sprouted to 6 inches tall, cut the stem to 3 inches. Allow it to grow to 12 inches and cut to 6 inches. Plant the 6-inch-tall plant in a small flowerpot with good soil and place in bright sunlight. When the plant reaches 18 inches tall the tree can be planted into the ground. Remember, however, that most avocados are hybrids and will not resemble the parent plant or fruit.

Variety	Season of Maturity	Fruit Weight (ounces)	Cold Tolerance	Production
'Simmonds'	mid-June to mid-Sep	16-34	Low	Moderate
'Russell'	July to mid-Aug	16-24	Very tender	Moderate
'Brogdon'	mid-July to mid-Sept	8-12	High	Moderate
'Choquette'	Dec to mid-Jan	18-40	High	High
'Monroe'	Dec to mid-Feb	24-40	Moderate	High
'Day'	mid-Jul to mid-Sep	8-16	High	High
'Winter'	mid-Oct	8-12	High	High
'Lula'	mid-Nov to early Mar	14-24	Moderate	High
'Mexicola'	mid-May to mid-Jun	6-8	High	High
'Hall'	mid-Nov to early Feb	20-30	Moderate	Moderate
'Marcus Pumpkin'	early Oct to mid-Nov	30-48	Moderate	Moderate
'Pollack'	mid-Jul to mid-Sep	18-40	Low	High
'Bernicker'	mid-Jul to late Aug	18-32	Low	Moderate

BANANA & PLANTAIN

It may be cruel, but when I hear the national weather service
report that snowstorms have swept through the Midwest,
I often call my sister to tell her that I picked a fresh banana
for my corn flakes and had fresh-squeezed orange juice for
breakfast. Then I ask, "So, how is the weather in Cleveland?"
Edible bananas can range from 4 to 18 feet tall and are very
easy to grow where heavy freezes are not a problem. In the
more northern areas of the state, many smaller but equally fine
banana varieties can be grown in pots and brought indoors
when cold weather passes through. Consider this, though,
when you think about Florida's winter weather: wherever you
are in Florida, it's still warmer than it is in Cleveland.

Where to Plant

Plant bananas and plantains where the temperatures are
hot, generally in the 75° to 85°F. range; fruiting is best at
temperatures of 80° to 85°F. Full sun to part shade is required
for growth, and full sun is best for fruit production. Bananas
can withstand wide ranges in soil acidity, from 5.5 to 7.0, but
they require well-drained, deep soils enriched with plenty of
compost. Do not locate banana plants where flooding occurs;
occasional flowing water won't hurt the plant long-term but
standing water is life threatening.

How to Plant

In South Florida plant bananas from March to May. Elsewhere,
wait until the spring drought is over and plant when the daily
rain showers begin again. In the rockland soils of southeast
Florida, where the soil profile is shallow, planting a banana will
take some work. Hand picks, augers, or backhoes will do the
job. Any hard rock will have to be removed to twice the depth
of the containerized rootball and three times its width. Plant
the rootball 1 to 2 inches above the soil line to compensate
for settling. In sandy soils dig a hole in well-prepared soil and
place the top of the rootball 2 inches above the native soil
to compensate for settling. In both soil types, mulch well to
maintain adequate soil moisture and to reduce weeds.

Care and Maintenance

Bananas are virtually trouble free provided they receive adequate sunlight, are planted in well-drained, highly enriched soil, and receive plenty of water. There are a few diseases that affect bananas but these are more common on large commercial farms than on single backyard plants. A regular fertilizer regimen should begin when a banana tree grows two new leaves after planting. Later, as the plant grows, it should be fertilized monthly with a 6-2-12-2 (NPKMg) at a rate of 1 to 2 pounds for every three to four stemmed plants. Once a banana plant grows five stems it should be divided and the process started again. An annual nutritional spray containing manganese and zinc will help. For proper fruit production, bananas need at least 1½ inches of water per week.

Additional Information

Good fruit-producing bananas include: 'Manzano' or 'Apple' (14 feet, zones 9-10); 'Dwarf Cavendish' (6-7 feet, zones 8-9); 'Dwarf Orinoco' (6-8 feet, zones 7b-10); 'Dwarf Red' (6-7 feet, zones 8-9); 'Goldfinger' (14 feet, zones 8-9); 'Blue Java' (12 feet, zones 8-10); 'Lady Finger' (14-16 feet, zone 9); 'Mysore' (10-14 feet, zones 8-10); 'Rajapuri' (8-10 feet, zones 8-9); and 'Williams Hybrid' (8-10 feet, zones 8-10).

Don't throw away the banana peels. Cut them into three inch pieces and bury them near eggplants, peppers, and tomatoes. The tomatoes will enjoy the potassium.

BLACKBERRY

Blackberries have always performed well in the northern and central areas of the Sunshine State, and several new varieties have made growing them even easier. There are two main types of plants: erect and trailing. Trailing types, also known as dewberry or boysenberry, have long stems and need a support of some sort on which to grow. The erect types have stiff stems and grow to 4 to 6 feet in height. They are the easiest to grow given their low-maintenance requirements. Regardless of the type you plan to grow, give them ample room and enjoy some blackberry jam!

Where to Plant

Blackberries like mildly acidic, well-drained soil. Add a good layer of organic mulch to moderate soil temperatures, conserve water, and to keep the weeds down. Although the plants themselves can withstand very cold temperatures (to the mid-teens), the flowers are very susceptible to cold temperatures and will not fruit if they get even a touch of frost.

How to Plant

Blackberries are often are sold bareroot, that is, without soil or a container. If this is the case, plant in the cooler months of the year (December to February), and plant immediately after you purchase them. Clip the roots to 6 inches long and set in a hole 7 to 8 inches deep. The crown of the plant (just above where the roots begin) should be set slightly higher than the level of the native soil. Alternate adding soil from the planting hole and watering until the hole is filled to remove any air pockets that might injure the roots. For containerized plants (which can be planted anytime), dig a hole a little larger than the plant, set the rootball slightly above the native soil level, and fill the hole with unimproved native soil.

Care and Maintenance

All blackberries produce fruit in summer. Trailing types ripen earlier, the berries are smaller, and the clusters of fruit are more open than the erect types. After the first year, prune the primary canes to 36 inches to initiate new cane development from below. Blackberries produce fruit on one-year-old canes, so the more you prune, the more berries you will have. However, don't prune more than one-third of the canes down to the ground in a single season.

Additional Information

A thornless variety named 'Apache' has made the lives of gardeners everywhere a little less painful. Its fruits are glossy black and blocky, and the canes are more erect than most so a trellis won't be needed. 'Arapaho' and 'Navaho' are very similar to 'Apache' and the fruit quality is quite good, maybe even better. 'Chester' is another good thornless variety; it's very cold hardy and a semi-erect type. 'Chickasaw' produces the sweetest and greatest number of blackberries of any variety available but, unfortunately, this variety has a good number of thorns. The canes are erect.

> *What's the difference between blackberries and raspberries?*
  There isn't much difference. One sure way to tell is to look at the fruit after it is picked. Raspberries will leave a "plug" on the plant and the berries will have a hole at the top. Blackberries will not leave the plug and therefore the fruit is complete (with no hole).

> *My blackberry plant produces many leaves; can I do anything with them?*
  Blackberry leaves contain powerful antioxidants, and tea made from dried leaves can be used to treat inflammation of the mouth and throat and is reported to be helpful in reducing blood sugar levels. Try one heaping tablespoon to one cup of water, steep for ten minutes, and sweeten to taste.

BLUEBERRY

Blueberries are a surefire sign that summer has finally arrived and that the accompanying heat will be with us until fall. Blueberries are harvested from late spring to early summer. Our warm winters throughout Florida make it important to purchase varieties of blueberries that have been specifically grown for Florida gardens. Either rabbiteye or southern highbush blueberries can be grown in Florida, depending on your location. Give them a try; a blueberry smoothie on a hot summer day always hits the spot.

Where to Plant

Plant blueberries in highly acidic soil, pH from 4.0-5.5, that is high in organic matter and well drained to a depth of at least 24 inches. Although blueberries need 45 inches of rain each year, they will die if their roots are flooded or stand in water for even the shortest period of time. Blueberries must have full sun and cannot be planted near hardwood trees (because the blueberries will produce less fruit), and they should be located at least 20 feet from a house or other structure. Wherever you plant them give them plenty of room. Rabbiteyes can reach 12 inches tall and 8 feet wide. Southern highbush are a tad smaller. A space 10 x 10 feet for rabbiteye or a 6 x 6-foot area for southern highbush will work just fine.

How to Plant

The best time to plant blueberries is during winter. Unlike most landscape plants installed in Florida gardens, adding plenty of sphagnum peat moss to the planting hole will help the shrub get a good start; a good 2-gallon bucketful added to the native soil and backfilled into the hole will do the trick. Be sure to plant the top of the rootball 1 to 2 inches above the native soil level to compensate for settling.

Pine bark may be the best friend of blueberries. Composted types work best but any form will do. Place a 2-foot-wide band around every plant after it's planted and continue even after the plant has been established. As the bark breaks down, it releases acid and improves the soil even more.

Care and Maintenance

Once the plant has become established, blueberries enjoy a little fertilizer often. Use 2 pounds per plant of 12-4-8-2 (NPKMg), four times per year beginning in April. Apply the fertilizer in a 2-foot circle around the plant and maintain a good layer of mulch. After the first year, increase the amount by 1 ounce each year for four years and spread the fertilizer in a 4-foot circle in the final year. After that maintain the 4 ounces per application in a 4-foot circle around the shrub.

Additional Information

Generally, the blueberries grown in Florida are not fruitful and require cross-pollination with other varieties of blueberries. If you live in Central or South Florida you should grow southern highbush blueberries (their early flowering makes them susceptible to early frost in northern areas of the state). Good southern highbush blueberry varieties include: 'Emerald', 'Gulf Coast', 'Millennia', 'Sharpblue', 'Jewel', 'Star', and 'Windsor'. Good rabbiteye early varieties are: 'Beckyblue', 'Bonita', and 'Climax'. Mid- to late maturing varieties are more productive than the early types and good varieties include: 'Brightwell', 'Powderblue', 'Tifblue', and 'Woodruff'.

> *My blueberry bush produced so many berries I couldn't eat them all. Can I freeze some for eating later?*
> Yes, you can freeze blueberries. After picking the berries, place the *unwashed* berries on a cookie sheet and freeze until they're frozen solid. Once they're completely frozen, place the berries in an airtight container or plastic bag and store in the freezer until you need them. Thoroughly wash the berries before using them.

CARAMBOLA

Even if carambola, also known as star fruit, didn't produce its delicious, golden-yellow, ribbed fruit, I would plant it as a small landscape tree. It never gets very large (less than 20 feet tall), and it has an upright, round habit that makes it a good candidate for a small yard. Or, even better, it is a good street tree that can be planted between the sidewalk and the pavement. The tree gets its name because its fruit, when cut, is in the shape of a star. The fruit is slightly waxy and it's been said the juice tastes like a combination of papaya, pineapple, and orange flavors. Mmmmm.

Where to Plant

Plant a carambola tree in full sun and in well-drained soil. Although the carambola can withstand some cool weather, it prefers the hot and humid climate of Central and South Florida. While too much water will hinder fruit production, a carambola will not tolerate drought. Make certain you have ample water nearby—give it at least 1 inch of water per week. If the leaves begin to wilt or fold up during the day, the tree is not getting enough water. Depending on the variety, many star fruit trees will produce several crops of fruit a year.

How to Plant

Carambola trees are nursery grown in plastic containers throughout Central and South Florida and therefore can be planted anytime. Remember—plant in full sun with a source of water nearby. Dig a hole twice as deep and as wide as the container and place the rootball in the hole so that the top of the rootball is 1 to 2 inches above the native soil level. Water well and add a 2- to 3-inch layer of mulch to conserve water, moderate soil temperatures, and keep the weeds down. If you live where flooding may be a problem, create a mound of native soil 2 to 3 feet high and 8 to 10 feet and plant as described. If you live where there is rockland soil, you'll have to use a hand pick, auger, or even a backhoe to dig the planting hole, depending on the size of tree.

Care and Maintenance

Carambolas are virtually trouble free. Occasionally aphids may invade the new growth but a firm stream of water will wash them off. Fruit flies can be a problem but if you keep the fruit picked they won't stay around where there is nothing to eat. Fertilize young trees with ½ pound per application of a complete 10-10-10-2 (NPKMg) fertilizer six times per year. Trees grown in soils with a high pH should be sprayed with a micronutrient spray containing manganese and zinc.

Additional Information

Good carambola varieties for Florida include: 'Arkin', 'Fuang Tung', 'Kari', 'Sri Kembangan', and 'Thai Knight'.

Star fruits contain high amounts of oxalic acid, so if you have kidney disease it's probably best to leave the carambola fruit alone.

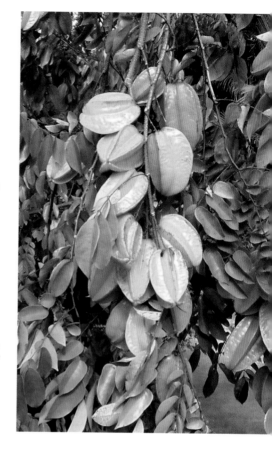

➤ *How do I know when my star fruit is ready?*
The best answer is to pick one and see if it is sweet enough to eat. Otherwise, shake the tree, and any that fall should be ripe. If you try to pick a fruit and it "tugs" back or does not come off easily, then it probably is not ripe.

➤ *How do you eat a star fruit?*
Star fruits do not have to be peeled to be eaten. They can be sliced across the "ribs," which will give you the "star" from which the star fruit gets its name. Or, the fruit can be eaten raw, like an apple, right off the tree. Bon appetit!

CITRUS

When you think of Florida you think of citrus—oranges and grapefruits. For more than 150 years, Florida has been king of the citrus world and it wasn't until the 1980s, when killing freezes swept through the state, that this mainstay of the Florida economy was threatened. Citrus trees were decimated in those freezes as temperatures plunged to 15°F for more than three days. Many commercial trees were not replanted, but being able to grow a backyard citrus tree is one of the real pleasures of living in Florida. With proper planning, citrus can be harvested eight months of the year. From pommelo fruits the size of bowling balls to oranges the size of golf balls, citrus can be fun to grow for the Florida gardener.

Where to Plant

To avoid repeating the devastating freezes of the '80s, dooryard citrus is generally grown south of a line from Daytona Beach to Crystal River. Several citrus selections *can* be grown north of that line, to be sure, but below that line is considered the "safe zone." Citrus of all sorts need sun and lots of it. Citrus can be grown in the three basic soil types found in Florida: sandy soils, flatwood soils, and the calcareous soils of South Florida. Little work is required for trees planted in deep, well-drained soils short of keeping weeds to a minimum or providing an adequate supply of water. The poorly drained flatwoods soils require a little more work such as improving drainage or building 24-inch-tall x 12-foot-wide mounds of good soil for the roots to grow into. In calcareous soils, dig a deep hole three times the depth of the rootball and as wide as is practical and fill it with good soil. Citrus produce the highest yields of fruit if the soil pH is kept in a range of 5.5-6.5.

How to Plant

Purchase citrus trees from a reputable grower that only sells government-certified plants. Traditional spacing of citrus trees has been from 20 to 25 feet apart. Given the small yards where people try to grow them, however, many gardeners place trees closer together and conduct a severe annual pruning. Don't plant them close to a house (25 feet away should be okay) and *never* plant a citrus tree near an existing septic field. Nearly all citrus for sale in garden centers have been grown in plastic containers and can be planted anytime. The key to success when planting a young citrus tree is water. During planting, the soil should be watered in well around the rootball to remove any air pockets. The rootball should be positioned 1 to 2 inches above the native soil level and a basin created from leftover soil should be formed around the tree. Water every day for the first two weeks and taper off as time goes by.

Care and Maintenance

It is very important during their first several years to make certain that citrus trees receive plenty of water. In poorly drained soils, too much water can be a problem, and that's why planting slightly above the native soil helps. Fertilizing citrus has been somewhat of a mystical component in the homeowner's garden although it needn't be. There are two fertilizing regimens; one is for when the tree is young and the other, for when the tree reaches fruit-bearing age. For younger trees, apply a fertilizer with an 8-8-8-2 (NPKMg) ratio. First-year trees should receive five to six applications per year of ½ to 1 pound of fertilizer per application. As a tree gets older (up to its fifth year), the *number* of applications should *diminish* to four per year and the *amount* of fertilizer should *increase* to 4 pounds per application. This schedule produces an abundance of foliage growth at the expense of fruit production. Later, after the tree is established, fruit-producing trees should be fed with an 8-8-8-2 fertilizer three times a year with up to 8 pounds per application for an annual fertilizer application of 24 pounds. A nutritional spray created for citrus is available at most garden centers and should be applied according the manufacturer's instructions.

Additional Information

Weeds compete with citrus trees for nutrients and water and should be removed beneath the entire tree canopy as much as possible. At the very least, keep weeds away from the trunk to reduce the likelihood of stem rot. Although many homeowners use mulch to reduce water evaporation and to modify soil temperatures, mulch should be kept at least 1 foot away from the trunk of a citrus tree for the same reason.

A grapefruit rind placed in the garden will attract slugs and the entire "organic trap" can be disposed of the next morning.

Citrus can be grown in Florida backyard gardens without using any pesticides. Many pests affect the appearance of the fruit but they rarely affect the quality of the fruit. Aphids on new growth, leaf miners on or in the leaves, and mites on the fruit are all aesthetic problems; for the most part, control measures are not required.

CITRUS HARVEST TABLE

Name	Nov	Dec	Jan	Feb	Mar	Apr	May
Fallglo Tangerine	▓						
Robinson Tangerine	▓						
Kumquat	▓	▓					
Red Navels	▓	▓					
Hamlin Orange	▓	▓	▓				
Parson Brown	▓	▓	▓				
Ambersweet Orange	▓	▓	▓				
Navels	▓	▓	▓	▓			
Orlando Tangelo	▓	▓	▓	▓			
Sunburst Tangerine	▓	▓	▓	▓			
Duncan Grapefruit		▓	▓	▓	▓		
Marsh Grapefruit		▓	▓	▓	▓	▓	
Thompson Grapefruit		▓	▓	▓	▓		
Flame Grapefruit	▓	▓	▓	▓	▓	▓	
Star Rubies	▓	▓	▓	▓	▓	▓	
Ruby Reds	▓	▓	▓	▓	▓	▓	▓
White Grapefruit	▓	▓	▓	▓	▓	▓	
Orlando Tangelos		▓					
Sunburst Tangerines		▓					
Dancy Tangerine		▓	▓				
Pineapple Orange		▓	▓	▓			
Murcott Tangelo			▓	▓	▓		
Minneola Tangelo			▓	▓			
Honeybell Tangelos			▓	▓			
Temples				▓	▓		
Honey Tangerines				▓	▓		
Valencias					▓	▓	▓

FIG

It was my fifth grade teacher who introduced me to figs in a world culture class. We were studying Greece and she shared with us food from that area of the world. When I bit into a dried fig I thought it was the sweetest and tastiest thing I had ever eaten—until I ate a fresh fig right off the bush some thirty years later. Naturally sweet and highly versatile, figs can be eaten fresh, in desserts, or as preserves and jams. The list is virtually limitless.

Fig plants from fifty years ago had one big problem: the fruit had a hole in the bottom (opposite the stem) that allowed pollinating insects access to the plants' sexual parts inside. The problem, if you haven't already guessed by now, is that you sometimes ate a bug as well as the fruit. Well, technology is a grand thing and in the last several years plant hybridizers have made it possible for a fig to pollinate itself and got rid of the hole. Figs are now sweet, nutritious fruit without any added protein!

Where to Plant

Plant figs in full to part sun in a location where they have plenty of room to grow—figs can grow to 12 feet tall and 12 feet wide. Well-drained soil with a good layer of mulch is all you need to grow nice, healthy fig bushes. Keep them away from standing water or overly wet soils.

How to Plant

You can still buy figs bare root; that is, the shrub is sold without soil on its roots. Plant bare-root plants in fall. Dig a hole twice as wide and as deep as the root mass and position the top of the rootball 2 inches above the native soil line to compensate for settling. Be extra careful to water thoroughly as soil is added to the hole. Once planting is completed, leave a soil ring around the top of the hole to be used as a water reservoir. Water every day for the first two weeks, reducing the frequency as time goes on. Plants purchased in containers can be planted anytime. For some unknown reason, figs enjoy a dose of calcium every now and then. After a shrub has become established, give a fig plant 1 cup of calcium nitrate under its canopy once a year, increasing the amount as the plant gets larger.

Care and Maintenance

Figs have healthy fibrous root systems so deep cultivation is not recommended. Place a 2- to 3-inch layer of mulch under a shrub's canopy and keep the weeds in check. Fertilize once a month with an 8-8-8 fertilizer during the growing season. Pruning is generally not required. There are no insect pests to speak of but be aware that ripe figs are highly prized by birds.

Additional Information

Head and shoulders above all others, the best fig for Florida gardeners is 'Celeste'. It has small, purplish to bronze fruit (with a closed end), and ripens in July and August. 'Brown Turkey' is also popular but its fruit have a medium-sized eye opening. 'Brown Turkey' ripens from July through fall.

In addition to the old standbys there are many new varieties worth growing. The beautiful 'Green Ischia' fig is a medium-sized green fig with pale-green skin and very attractive strawberry-colored flesh. It has an excellent flavor. This cultivar is a very flavorful, productive variety and, interestingly, birds don't attack because the green fruit blends in with the foliage. One of my personal favorites is the 'Jelly' fig; it's a medium-sized yellow fig with very tasty, very sweet, amber-colored flesh.

GRAPE

You may have heard the terms "scuppernong," "muscadine," or "bunch grape" when talking about grapes in Florida. They are all the same thing, but are described differently depending on where you live. The grapes grown in Florida are unlike the grapes you buy at the store. Instead of thin, sweet skin like those in the supermarket, muscadine grapes have seeds and tough, almost leathery, exteriors. The sweetness of these grapes is in the pulp. Florida-grown grapes can be eaten right off the vine and the juice can make excellent wine.

Where to Plant

Plant grapes in full sun in well-drained soil with a clay base and a pH of 6.0-6.5. Mucky soils or sugar-sandy soil without a clay base are not good locations for growing grapes.

How to Plant

Plant individual plants 8 feet apart in rows that are at least 6 feet apart. Dig a hole twice as wide and as deep as the containerized rootball and backfill with native soil. Make certain that the top of the rootball is 1 to 2 inches above the native soil line to compensate for settling. It is recommended that grape rows be placed on a north-south axis to maximize the sunlight each plant receives.

Care and Maintenance

Pruning grapes can seem a bit mysterious, but once you learn the basics it's very simple. Grapes produce fruit on new wood, so it's important that the plants produce new growth to get good fruit production. However, if there is too much new wood, the grapes will be small both in size and in quantity. First, you must create a trellis system for the grapes to grow upon. Place 8-foot posts every 10 to 12 feet apart, sinking 2 feet of the post in the ground. Run two wires from post to post at heights of 36 inches (3 feet) and 72 inches (6 feet). Site one plant every 8 feet and train one vine to grow straight up to the 72-inch wire. Initially, remove all other shoots. (Sometimes it's helpful to place a long, thin bamboo shoot between the wires and train the fast-growing shoot to it while it is growing.) Once this is done, cut the top off the vine to encourage the development of side shoots. As shoots begin to "break" along the stem, train two sprouts to grow right and left along the wire at the 36-inch and 72-inch levels. It is on these side shoots that the grapes will develop. Continue to remove all other shoots along the vertical stem. Every four years or so it is important to remove the horizontal stems. These can or will be replaced by new vines from spurs that were left near the upright stem. In the first year apply ¼ pound of 8-8-8 fertilizer to each plant. Increase this amount each year until the fourth year when 4 pounds of 8-8-8 will be applied.

Additional Information

Good varieties of purple grapes include 'Conquistador', 'Blue Lake', and 'Black Spanish'. Good green varieties include 'Stover', 'Blanc Du Bois', and 'Suwannee'. 'Daytona' is a good red grape suited for Florida gardens.

> *Where did the word "muscadine" come from?*
> When early settlers arrived in the southeast United States they discovered a wild grape. They were also familiar with a European grape, the Muscat grape, used to make muscatel wine. As time went on they called the local wild grape a muscal grape because of its similar sweet, earthy fragrance. Eventually the word "muscal" became "muscadine."

> *When I was out in the garden I noticed my grapes were ready to pick and planned to do just that the next day. But, when I arrived that morning all the grapes had vanished! Where did they go?*
> Raccoons have an uncanny ability to know when you are ready to pick fruit, and they usually beat you to it. Before the fruit ripens place bird netting, available at garden centers, over the vines to prevent Mr. Raccoon's midnight raid!

GUAVA

One of the many reasons I enjoy Florida is due to all the exotic fruits we can grow in our backyards. Growing and eating guava fresh from the garden is one of those rare pleasures in gardening—its musky, sweet taste is indescribable. While there are a few people who will rise in opposition to its unique flavor, after a little while even they develop a taste for this unique fruit. The shrub is a handsome specimen in the landscape with small (1-inch), fragrant white flowers, and many people place it in the garden regardless of its ability to produce fruit. The fruit's shape ranges from round to somewhat like a pear and in size from 1 to 40 ounces. When a guava is ripe, the peel changes color from green to yellow and the flesh color can be white, yellow, pink, or red. Flavors range from sweet to highly acidic and from strong and sharp to mild and agreeable.

Where to Plant

Make no mistake—guavas like warm temperatures and do not tolerate freezes. Guava plants may be killed when temperatures are lower than 27°F. Plant growth and fruit production stops when temperatures reach 60°F. Plant guava in full sun in well-drained soil with a pH of 4.5-7.0. Guavas planted in soil with a pH above 7.0 will require annual applications of chelated iron. Many varieties of guava can reach 12 feet tall and 14 feet wide so give them plenty of room to grow. Make certain that the planting site does not flood even after hard summer rains—guava trees will not tolerate wet feet for even a short time.

How to Plant

Guavas are often grown in plastic containers and can be planted anytime. In sandy soils dig a hole twice as deep and wide as the rootball. Backfill with native soil so the top of the rootball is 1 to 2 inches higher than the surrounding soil level and continuously add water as you backfill to prevent air pockets. Leave a soil ring around the circumference of the rootball to act as a water reservoir. In muck soils (which are highly organic and wet), create a 24-inch-high and 8-foot-wide mound of good soil and plant the rootball as described. In rock or marl, dig a hole three times the depth and width of the rootball and back-fill with good garden soil. Water a newly installed plant once a day for two weeks and taper off as the plant becomes established. Guavas require 1 to 1 ½ inches of water per week.

Care and Maintenance

Fertilize guavas with 1 pound of an 8-8-8-2 (NPKMg) mixture every two months for the first year, increasing that amount to 5 pounds per application, four times per year after the fifth year. Once the trees have become established, foliar nutritional sprays containing boron, manganese, zinc, and copper should be applied four times per year.

Additional Information

Pink or red guava fruits are picked when the peel begins to turn light green or yellow. The fruits should be allowed to ripen without refrigeration until they're ready to eat. White guavas are picked before they are fully ripe when the skins are light-green before turning yellow. Good pink varieties for Florida include 'Homestead', 'Barbi Pink', 'Hong Kong Pink', and 'Patillo'. Green types include 'Webber', 'Crystal', 'Lotus', and 'Supreme'.

> *I bought an older house in Miami and it came with a 12-foot-tall guava plant in the backyard. It is covered with fruit, but I moved here from Ohio and I don't know how to eat them! Help me, please.*
> Select guavas that are firm but "give" a little when you exert a slight pressure. Wash the fruit thoroughly and eat the fruit just like you did the apples in Ohio!

JABOTICABA

If you are looking for an unusual specimen tree in the landscape that also produces edible fruit, jaboticaba may be the tree for you. Reaching a maximum height of 15 feet, this Brazilian native produces a unique, vase-shaped growth habit with handsome tan and cinnamon-brown flaking bark. It's the fruit, however, that really steals the show. About the size and shape of a large grape, the fruits follow brilliant white flowers that erupt from the main trunk of the tree. The fruits are commonly dark purple or black (with some green-skinned varieties) and have a thick skin with a gelatinous interior and flavor similar to that of muscadine grapes. Because it is so slow growing, many homeowners have begun to use it as a street tree between the sidewalk and the road.

Where to Plant

The freeze tolerance of jaboticaba is highly variable; however, it is generally accepted that they should not be planted where freezing temperatures fall below 28°F. Plant in full to part sun (although part sun will reduce the number of fruit) in well-drained, deep, sandy soil with a pH of 5.5-6.5. It is not tolerant of salt air and does not like soggy soils. Soils that are slightly alkaline should be heavily mulched and drenched semiannually with chelated iron.

How to Plant

Jaboticaba trees are grown in plastic nursery containers and therefore can be planted anytime. Dig a hole twice as wide and as deep as the nursery-grown rootball and place the top of the rootball 1 to 2 inches above the native soil line (to compensate for settling). As the hole is filled with the native soil, add water to remove any air pockets that could kill the plant. For those areas where holes are difficult to dig, create a mound 24 inches deep and 10 to 12 feet wide and plant as described.

Care and Maintenance

Although studies on jaboticaba's nutritional needs are few, an application of a general 8-8-8-2 (NPKMg) fertilizer four times a year is a generally accepted practice. Pests are negligible;

however, deer have been known to eat new foliage and squirrels and raccoons enjoy the fruit. Harvest the fruit when the color is a dark purple or black and is soft to the touch, like a grape. Pruning is rarely needed but they can be trimmed into a hedge without significant reduction in fruit production since the fruit grows directly on interior larger stems and on the trunk of the tree. Roots of the jaboticaba are quite shallow and as a result additional irrigation may be needed to supplement natural rainfall (a good layer of mulch 3 to 4 inches deep will help, too).

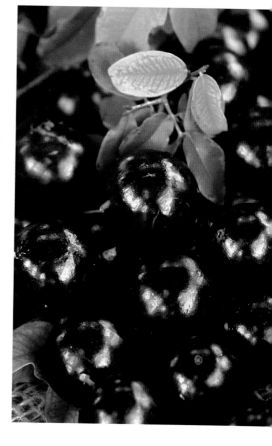

Additional Information

Good varieties for Florida include 'Paulista', a well-developed tree producing very large fruit with a sweet flavor; 'Rajada', an unusual green-skinned fruit with very good sweet flavor; and 'Sabra', a thin-skinned, small fruit variety that is the most popular form in Brazil, which can produce up to four crops a year in South Florida.

> *I enjoy creating bonsai and I was wondering if jaboticaba would make a good specimen.*

Yes, also known as the Brazilian tree grape, jaboticaba is an excellent choice for bonsai work. Jaboticaba has an unusually smooth bark similar to that of the crape myrtle. It is a delicately branched tree with an appealing irregular growth pattern and small, elegant, light-green leaves.

> *I really enjoy the flavor of jaboticaba. Is there anything else I can do with the fruit?*

Jaboticaba fruit can be boiled with water to cover them, and then mashed. The resulting juice can be made into a tart jelly or served as fruit juice. It has been reported to be a very good thirst quencher.

JACKFRUIT

Jackfruit trees, which grow to 18 to 40 feet tall, produce very large fruit—up to 60 pounds!—with a "warty" or bumpy appearance. There are two distinct parts to the cut fruit. The first part is a white pulpy material, often called the "rag," and it is inedible. It is the bright orange, sweet pulp surrounding the seeds that is prized. Though it may take some work to get to, the flavor is well worth it. Jackfruit is a member of the Moracea family along with *Ficus benjamina* and mulberry, so be careful of the latex-like sap that may cause skin irritation.

Where to Plant

Jackfruit is suited for gardeners growing fruit in South Florida where frosts rarely occur because it can be killed at temperatures below 28°F and limb damage can occur even at 32°F. Plant in full sun in areas where flooding is not a problem. Jackfruits are tolerant of a variety of soils ranging from sandy to rocky, including those soils having a high pH. Even though they can reach a height of 40 feet in South Florida, they tolerate moderate to heavy winds. Plant them at least 30 feet from houses and other trees for maximum fruit production.

How to Plant

Jackfruit trees are grown in plastic nursery containers and as a result can be planted anytime. Regardless of your soil type, dig a hole twice as deep and as wide as the rootball. Place the rootball in the hole 1 inch higher than the native soil level and backfill with native soil. Stay away from areas that flood or are constantly wet. For those areas where holes are hard to dig, try creating a 24-inch-tall and 8-foot-wide mound of good soil.

Care and Maintenance

Jackfruit trees can get big—up to 40 feet tall. Pruning is an option and the trees can be kept to a moderate height of 10 to 15 feet without a significant reduction in fruit production. During the first year apply 1 pound of an 8-8-8 plus micronutrients five times. After the first year, gradually increase the amount but, do not exceed 5 pounds per application five times per year. A spray containing boron and manganese should be applied four times per year. Soils with a very high pH should receive an application of chelated iron once annually. Jackfruit trees are virtually pest free, although scale insects can affect the leaves and stems. Control scale by using an insecticidal soap, which is available at most garden centers.

Additional Information

To harvest the fruit, use clippers or loppers to snip the fruit off the tree when the fruit develops a pungent odor. Avoid contact with the sap because it can cause skin irritation and permanently stain clothes. The fruit will ripen four to seven days after harvesting. The orange pulp surrounding the seeds is the tasty part and can be retrieved by first cutting the fruit crosswise with a sharp knife that has been coated with cooking oil. Continue to cut the fruit crossways and extract the seeds. Varieties good for Florida gardens include 'Black Gold', 'Cheena', 'Chompa Gob', 'Honey Gold', and 'Lemon Gold'.

> *Other than its great taste, is jackfruit good for you?*
> Jackfruit is high in vitamin C and potassium. Jackfruit contains lignans, isoflavones, and saponins, which are called phytonutrients; their health benefits are wide-ranging from anticancer to antihypertensive, anti-aging, antioxidant, and anti-ulcer. The jackfruit root is the basis for a remedy for skin diseases and asthma. An extract of the root is taken to cure fever.

> *Do you have a recipe for the tropical "egg roll" I ate as a child?*
> Turon is a Philippine dessert roll made of bananas, jackfruit, and coconut. Cut a banana in half and cover with strips of jackfruit (minus the seeds). Place shredded coconut over all, and sprinkle with a little confectioner's sugar.

LONGAN

An attractive landscape tree, longan also produces large clusters of grape-sized, single-seeded fruit with a sweet and pleasant flavor. The leaves are evergreen and shiny and the bark is dark brown, almost black. In their native China, longans can reach nearly 100 feet tall, although in South Florida heights of 30 to 40 feet are more common and in Central Florida, 15 feet is the norm. New leaf growth on longans is a beautiful wine-red color, and mature leaves are very glossy, making them a welcome addition to any home landscape.

Where to Plant

Longans don't like the cold, and a straight line from Tampa to Merritt Island is as far north as they will grow. Older, well-established trees can survive temperatures to 27°F while younger trees might be killed at the same temperature. Plant longans 40 feet apart in full sun in soil that is well drained, but not wet. Longans do not perform well in organically rich soils.

How to Plant

Longan trees are grown in plastic nursery containers and therefore can be planted anytime. Dig a hole twice as wide and as deep as the nursery-grown rootball and place the top of the rootball 1 to 2 inches above the native soil line to compensate for settling. As the hole is filled with the native soil, add water to remove any air pockets that could kill the plant. For those areas where holes are difficult to dig, create a mound 24 inches deep and 10 to 12 feet wide and plant the rootball as described.

Care and Maintenance

To produce good-quality fruit, three-fourths of the light-yellow to light-brown flower spikes must be removed before or during flowering (from January to March). Similarly, the fruit should be thinned by three-fourths in May to June to increase the size and quality of the remaining fruit. An application of a general 8-8-8-2 (NPKMg) fertilizer four times a year is a generally accepted practice. Make certain that longans receive adequate water during flowering and fruit production. Longans are very wind resistant.

Additional Information

One major handicap of growing longans is their irregular fruiting history. It is not uncommon for longans to produce heavily one year and then skip two to three years before producing again. The fruit ripen in August to September. There are no serious diseases or pests associated with longans, which makes them a great fruit tree for those homeowners wishing to become more "green" in their landscape management. The longan variety 'Kohala' was introduced to Florida from Hawaii and to date is far superior to any cultivar presently grown in the Sunshine State. Other cultivars are under evaluation, but to date none have come close to the fruit quality and fruiting frequency of 'Kohala'. The longan is generally eaten fresh but it can also be canned, just like litchees or rambutans. It can also be used as an ingredient for drinks and liqueurs. Harvest longan fruits by cutting the entire fruit cluster using a sharp knife or handpruners. Pulling individual fruits off the cluster will cause them to perish more quickly.

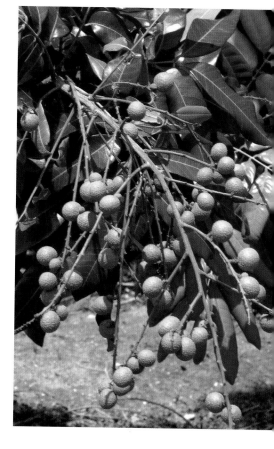

> *Many of my longans mature at the same time. Is there a good way to store the fruit for eating later?*
> Longans should be selected when they are brown. Wrap the longans in a paper towel or thin tissue paper before storing them in a humid environment at a recommended temperature of 34° to 40°F. This will help prevent the longan skin from deteriorating and help maintain its light-brown color.

> *I've heard that longan is good for you. How so?*
> Longan can be made into a wonderful and delicious tonic used by the Chinese as a blood tonic, to nurture the heart, and to add luster and beauty to the skin. It is also thought to have a calming effect on men.

LOQUAT

Even if the loquat didn't produce its marvelous, tart, yellow or orange fruit, gardeners throughout Florida would still use it as a landscape plant. Its bold, highly striated evergreen leaves coupled with a pleasing roundish habit make it a favorite throughout the Sunshine State. Several ornamental selections have appeared on the market in recent years and there are well over 1,000 selections of loquat used for fruit production throughout the world. Generally, loquats flower in the fall and produce fruit in the spring; however, in warmer tropical and subtropical areas of the state, it's not uncommon to harvest two or three crops per year. The fruit is ripe and ready to eat when it's slightly soft when squeezed between the thumb and forefinger.

Where to Plant

Loquat can withstand temperature extremes as low as 15°F without harm, and hot, humid temperatures don't seem to bother the plant (although extremely high temperatures can have an adverse effect on fruit production). Loquats produce fruit best when they're located in full sun. They are not finicky as to soil type; they grow and produce well in soils ranging from deep sand to gravely, rocky soils. They do not like wet or waterlogged soils. Loquats can reach 20 feet tall and 15 feet wide so select a planting location where they will get plenty of room.

How to Plant

Loquats are usually available from garden centers in plastic nursery containers and can be planted anytime. Dig a hole twice as deep and as wide as the rootball, and place the top of the rootball 1 to 2 inches above the native soil line (to compensate for settling). When filling the planting hole, alternate water and native soil as the rootball is covered to diminish the possibility of air pockets in the root zone. For those areas where digging a hole might be too difficult, a mound of garden soil 24 inches tall and 8 to 10 feet wide can be used and the tree planted as described.

Care and Maintenance

Loquats do not require pruning
except to remove an occasional
dead limb after a storm passes
through. One-year-old plants
will need 1 pound of a general
8-8-8-2 (NPKMg) four times per
year spread evenly beneath the
canopy. As the tree gets bigger
the amount can be increased to 5
pounds per application, four times
per year. A micronutrient foliar
spray containing boron, copper,
molybdenum, and zinc can be
applied four times per year. Loquats
grown in alkaline soil will need to
receive chelated iron as a soil drench
twice per year.

Additional Information

Variety	Shape	Peel Color	Fruit Flavor
'Advance'	Pear	Yellow	Sweet-tart
'Champagne'	Pear	Pale yellow-pale orange	Sweet, spicy
'Emanuel'	Pear	Dark yellow-Orange	Sweet, good flavor
'Golitch'	Round	Orange	Sweet
'Juda'	Pear	Pale Orange	Sweet, mildly tart
'Judith'	Pear	Dark Yellow	Sweet
'Oliver'	Pear	Pale Orange	Very sweet
'Thales'	Pear	Dark Yellow-Orange	Sweet
'Thursby'	Pear	Dark Yellow-Orange	Sweet, good flavor
'Wolfe'	Pear	Light Yellow	Sweet, spicy, good flavor

LYCHEE

My first experience with lychee was in New York City's Chinatown. I was getting ready to get on a subway when I stopped to look at the various fruits for sale in one of the district's many outdoor fruit markets. There were several fruits I didn't recognize, and when I asked the vendor which I should try, he suggested the lychee. He told me the bright red, bumpy fruit the size of a large grape had to be peeled, and when I did just that it exposed a clear, gelatinous pulp with a single inedible seed. I popped the entire fruit into my mouth, and my lifelong love of fresh lychee began.

Where to Plant

Lychee trees can grow to 40 feet tall so give them plenty of room. They grow best where temperatures never reach below 28°F and where the winters are dry and cool enough to give the tree a rest. Hard frost will kill young trees but more mature trees can withstand colder temperatures. Grow them in full sun and in soil with a pH of 6.0–7.0. Lychees have a high water requirement to produce superior fruit. The Chinese often grow lychee trees adjacent to ponds or streams to give the trees enough water. The trees enjoy well-composted, well-drained soil with high soil moisture but cannot withstand even short spells of standing water. If high water can be a problem in your area, plant the trees in raised mounds 10 feet wide by 2 feet deep made of good garden soil.

How to Plant

Lychee trees are generally grown in 3- to 5-gallon containers and can be planted anytime. Dig a hole twice the depth and width of the rootball, place the tree into the hole, and backfill with native soil. Make certain that the top of the rootball is 1 to 2 inches above the soil line in anticipation of the soil settling. More lychees have been killed by planting them too deeply than for any other reason. Make a soil ring utilizing the remaining backfill soil and water every day for the first three weeks; taper off watering as the tree becomes established.

Care and Maintenance

Oddly enough, lychee trees respond negatively to high fertilizer regimens—too much nitrogen fertilizer reduces plant growth and inhibits the uptake of other nutrients. An annual fertilizer application of an 8-8-8-2 (NPKMg) is all that is needed. Mature trees can utilize 5 to 6 pounds of fertilizer annually. An annual application of dolomitic lime will also reduce fruit shedding and foliar chlorosis.

Additional Information

Lychees are harvested when they're fully bright red. The entire cluster is harvested and the individual fruits are later clipped from the cluster. If lychees are picked individually, the top of the fruit remains on the tree and the fruit will perish quickly. Lychee trees are not strong enough to support ladder picking (like citrus)

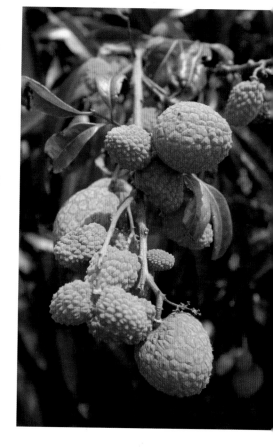

and a long pole with sharp clippers is the tool of choice. Harvest every three to four days to prevent rotting of the picked fruit. Do not harvest immediately after a rain. Both 'Mauritius' and 'Brewster' are good varieties for Florida.

> *As I was eating a fresh lychee the other day I wondered if I could grow a lychee from the large seeds I threw out?*
> Yes, plants can be grown from fresh lychees but not from canned lychees. Within five days of eating the pulp, plant the seed 1 inch deep in a 4-inch pot filled with good potting soil. The seed will germinate in ten to fourteen days. Place in bright light and keep the soil moist. When the tree reaches 18 inches, plant it into the garden.

MANGO

As with other handsome fruit trees, even if a mango tree didn't produce its juicy, delicious fruit, it would be planted as a beautiful landscape specimen. Its long and narrow evergreen leaves (sometimes up to 12 inches long) emerge in the springtime with a brilliant red color. The tree's shape is variable depending on the selection, but most are upright or rounded. A mango tree can live up to 100 years. The single fruits appear at the end of long stems and are best known for their juicy, musky, peachlike flavor. The fruits can be kidney- or oval-shaped and the ripe fruit exhibits colors ranging from green to melon to peach. Average weight is 1 to 1½ pounds, although the fruit of some varieties can grow to 5 pounds each. It is the flesh surrounding the very large, single seed for which the mango is best known. The tough skin contains a milky sap and should not be eaten. Mangoes are very popular in chutneys, fruit salads, and smoothies.

Where to Plant

Mangoes need a frost-free climate. Although mangoes can be seen growing in areas outside frost-free zones, this is due to specific microclimates that allow mangoes to survive. Young trees can be killed when temperatures drop below 30°F, but mature trees can survive fleeting temperatures as low as 25°F. Flowers and small fruits may be damaged or killed if the temperature falls below 40°F for a few hours. In Florida, mangoes can grow to 50 feet tall and require plenty of room. A tree casts deep shade due to its large evergreen leaves and requires full sun and good air circulation. The roots of a mango are quite extensive, though they're not destructive, and need plenty of room to grow. The mango must have warm, dry weather to set fruit. Mango trees tolerate a wide range of soil types, even lightly alkaline ones, but all soils must be well drained and free of standing water.

How to Plant

Mango trees are grown in plastic nursery containers and as a result can be planted anytime. Select an area with deep soil to accommodate the mango's extensive root structure and dig a hole twice as wide and as deep as the rootball. Place the tree in the hole and backfill with native soil, keeping the top of the root ball 1 to 2 inches above the native soil line. Create a soil ring with the remaining soil and water the tree daily for two weeks; taper off watering as the plant becomes established.

Care and Maintenance

Mango trees require a regular application of 8-0-8-2 (NPKMg) during the growing season. Begin the first application after the onset of the fruit but do not fertilize after late summer. Young trees respond best to fish emulsion fertilizer and are otherwise very susceptible to synthetic fertilizers. Synthetic fertilizers can be introduced after the tree has become well established.

Occasionally, thrips, scale, and mealybugs can be noticeable pests but they can be controlled with various horticultural oils and soaps. Although mangoes will ripen on the tree, commercial fruit is considered mature when the shoulder of the fruit fills out and its color begins to change from green to yellow. Some people pick and enjoy the fruit while it's still green, using it in chutneys or even dousing it with hot sauce. Mangos are picked by hand or by using a long picking pole. Mature fruits ripen three to eight days after harvest. Good varieties for Florida include 'Floridan', 'Edward', 'Carrie', 'Van Dyke', 'Carrie Atkins', 'Parvin', 'Dunkin', and 'Keitt'.

PAPAYA

If eating tropical fruit is one of your favorite pastimes but growing them is not, papaya would be a good place to start. They are very easy to grow (there may not be an easier fruit) and provided the tall "trees" get plenty of water and occasional fertilizer, they will produce large, beautiful fruit frequently throughout the year. For North Florida homeowners, you may have to visit those counties farther south for a fresh taste, however. Individual plants can produce fruit for up to twenty years. Papayas are sometimes called the "cantaloupe tree of the tropics" because the taste is very similar and they are often served for breakfast.

Where to Plant

Plant papayas in full sun with average soil in locations where there is no danger of frost. Papayas show signs of cold stress at temperatures as low as 45°F. Papayas can be grown to fruiting size in containers provided the container is large enough, at least 30 inches in diameter, and they get plenty of water and sun.

How to Plant

Papayas can be grown from seed (the sex of the parent will decide the sex of the seed) or planted as nursery-grown container plants. Select seed from known sexed plants, crack the hard seed covering, and dry in full sun. Seeds stored in the refrigerator can remain viable for many years. Plant three to four seeds 1 inch deep in sterile potting soil and wait for germination, generally in two to three weeks. Once the plants reach a height of 4 to 6 inches select the most robust specimen and eliminate the remainder by cutting them off at soil level with scissors or pruners. Place the single seedling into a 1- to 2-gallon container, place the container in full sun, and fertilize with a general liquid fertilizer every two weeks until the roots are well established but not rootbound.

Plant homegrown or nursery-grown plants in average soil ranging from pH 5.5-8.0. Dig a hole twice as deep and as wide as the container-grown plant, and alternate backfilling with the native soil and water until the hole is filled and the top of the rootball is slightly higher than the native soil level. Papaya roots are particularly susceptible to nematodes so refrain from planting them in those garden areas where nematodes have been known to be a problem. Select nursery-grown plants that are 2 to 3 feet tall. Larger plants often have potbound root systems and can fall over even in the lightest wind. If they're given water and fertilizer, 2-foot-tall papayas will quickly grow to 8 feet and produce fruit eight to ten months after planting.

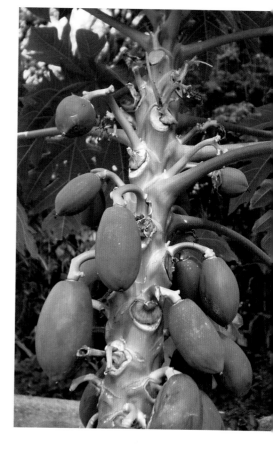

Care and Maintenance

For obvious reasons, bisexual plants do not need other plants to produce fruit. If you have only female plants, ask a neighbor or fellow gardener for male seeds to grow a male plant to obtain well-formed fruit. Papayas are odd plants in that some plants will show various levels of being a male or female plant depending on temperature, day length, and the amount of available water in the soil. Some plants can produce more than one kind of flower at the same time and some plants produce flowers that are not one of the three basic forms, but have a mixture of male and female qualities.

Generally, female plants produce very large, oblong fruit of very high quality. Fruit from bisexual plants are small to medium in size with a small interior cavity. Male plants often produce elongated fruit of little or no quality.

Apply ¼ pound of a general 8-8-8-2 fertilizer when the plants are young and increase to 1 to 2 pounds every two months as the plants get larger. A foliar or ground application including zinc and manganese should be applied at least twice per year.

Additional Information

Depending on the area of the Sunshine State where you live, bugs and diseases can either be serious or simply a nuisance. It seems the farther south you go, the more problems you may encounter. One important insect pest is the papaya fruit fly; you'll know it's present if you see yellow areas on the fruit itself and premature fruit drop. The easiest way to avoid the effects of this pest is simply to place a paper bag over the fruit and wait until the fruit matures. Papaya webworms look like a large spider web on an emerging stem or among the flowers. These can simply be removed with a hard stream of water. The papaya whitefly can cause premature fruit drop and often turns the very large leaves yellow. Whitefly of any kind is often an indicator of stress. Keep a watchful eye on water and fertilizer levels and whiteflies should not be a serious problem. The same is true for the papaya two-spotted mite. Stress is usually the culprit so keep the water and fertilizer levels up. Spider mites are indicated when the leaves turn yellow and there are "spider webs" on the bottom sides of the leaves and among the new leaf growth. A hard stream of water will help keep them under control.

A serious disease is the papaya ring spot disease. The leaves turn yellow, the veins become clear, and the fruit get little "C"-shaped spots. There isn't much you can do to prevent this disease except to remove any plant that exhibits these characteristics. If you are growing papayas from seed, try to get seed from the larger, oval-shaped fruit rather than the 'Solo' pear-shaped fruit, which seem to be susceptible. Powdery mildew can be a problem but it's usually during the late spring to early summer months when nighttime temperatures range from 60° to 65°F. Remove any yellowed leaves when possible and wait until nighttime temperatures get above 70°F. The last disease to discuss is apical necrosis, which is identified by the drooping of new growth and a downward "cupping" of the leaves. There are no known cures for this one so remove the diseased plants and try a different location. Good varieties for Florida include 'Sunrise Solo', 'Red Lady', and 'Maradol'.

> *I know I can grow papayas from seeds but can I take cuttings, too?*
Papaya plants can also be grown from cuttings, which should be hardened off for a few days before being propped up with the tip touching moist, fertile soil until roots form. Semi-hardwood cuttings planted during the summer root rapidly and should fruit the following year.

PASSION FRUIT

Passion fruit are the edible podlike fruits of the passion flower vine. The fruit itself is either purple or yellow at maturity with a delightful juice inside and lots of seeds. There are two main types of passion fruit; both have evergreen leaves and both make nice vines to cover a pergola or fence. One passion flower is purple and is egg-sized with a rumpled skin. The other, the yellow passion flower, can have fruit the size of a large orange and has a shiny, smooth exterior and a "pulpy" rind. The yellow form is the preferred variety for eating fresh off the vine. Its flavor has a musky, guava-like taste.

Where to Plant

Passion flower vines can easily reach 40 feet long so give them plenty of room. They need full sun or the vines may grow but not produce flowers and fruit. Any average soil will do, but if compost-enriched soil is available you will have more fruit than you can eat. Passion flowers also enjoy a good layer of mulch to moderate variances in soil temperatures.

How to Plant

Plant container-grown plants into the garden anytime. Dig a hole twice the height and depth of the rootball and place the rootball in the hole. Backfill, alternating the soil and water to eliminate air pockets. This vine likes to be planted a bit high, so plant the rootball about 1 inch higher than the native soil line.

Care and Maintenance

Passion flower vines are virtually maintenance free provided they get plenty of sun and water. Most questions regarding their care revolve around too little sun, but the bottom line is they *cannot* get too much sun. The more sun, the better. Although they have little tendrils to attach themselves to things as they grow, it's a good idea to give them a helping hand while the vines are still young. Thread them in and out of a chain-link fence to help them get started or use "hook and loop" ties designed for outdoor use to give them a leg up. If either is impractical, strings of 50-pound. test fishing line attached to the top and bottom of the gazebo pergola make wonderful, and virtually invisible, supports on which to grow the vines. Make sure you use galvanized nails to prevent rust. Simply stretch the lines from nail to nail and train the vines around them.

Additional Information

The passion flower vine is native to Brazil and Paraguay so don't plan on growing it as a landscape plant north of the Tampa/Daytona Beach line. Given that they grow very fast and with little care, passion fruits are popular as a container-grown fruit-producing plant in colder areas of the state. Passion flowers are also important larval plants in a butterfly garden, attracting a variety of butterflies including zebra longwing and gulf fritillary butterflies.

➤ *Why do my vines flower but don't set fruit?*
This could be due to several reasons. Overcast weather could account for poor fruit set, as could poor pollenization. Often, passion flower vines need a little boron to help them flower. An annual soil drench with a water-soluble fertilizer with minor elements will help.

➤ *Why do my passion fruits drop off the vine?*
Maintaining an irregular water regimen is probably the reason. The vines enjoy damp soil during their fruiting period. Keep up a regimen to fight spider mites, too, especially when the fruits are young. With a stiff stream of water, spray the undersides of the leaves to wash the mites away.

PEACH, NECTARINE, & PLUM

Growing peaches, nectarines, and plums—commonly called "stone fruits"—in Florida has been possible only for those gardeners living in the northern areas of the state where winter temperatures can give the buds at least 400–500 hours of cold below 50°F (referred to as "chilling hours"). New varieties released only a few years ago as part of an intensive breeding program at the University of Florida have enabled gardeners everywhere in the Sunshine State to grow high-quality, good-tasting stone fruits that require only 150 chilling hours. Given that most fruit types that have a hard, stone-like seed in the middle of the fruit have the same growing habits, I will refer to "peach" with the understanding that my advice pertains to peaches, nectarines, and plums.

Where to Plant

Peaches need full sun and well-drained soil with a pH of 6.0-7.0. Planting them directly into alkaline or marl soils can be a problem leading to poor overall growth, leaf drop, and insect infestations. For that reason, in those areas of the state where the pH level is high, plant peaches in an elevated bed 2 feet tall and 10 to 12 feet wide made of good garden soil. A liberal sprinkling of granulated sulfur once a year in the spring will help lower the pH, as well. The trees can reach 10 to 12 feet tall and 12 feet wide.

How to Plant

Peaches are grown in 3- to 5-gallon plastic nursery containers and can be planted anytime. Dig a hole twice the depth and width of the rootball and place the rootball into the hole. Alternate adding water and the native soil into the hole to eliminate any air pockets. The top of the rootball should ultimately rest 1 to 2 inches above the soil line. Create a soil ring with the remaining soil and water once a day for three weeks and taper off watering as the tree becomes established.

Care and Maintenance

The secret to growing good stone fruit trees is proper pruning. The ultimate goal after several years of good growth is to have a peach or nectarine tree that is open in the middle (free of branches facing inward) with an upward growth pattern. It takes some discipline, but if good quality and quantity is your ultimate goal, some hard pruning at the beginning is essential. When the tree arrives from the nursery, it should be about 4 to 5 feet tall with several lateral branches. The first pruning cut should be a decisive cut 36 inches above the ground to remove the primary single, upright leader. This will encourage side branching, sometimes called scaffold branching. As the tree matures, continue to remove any sprouts in the center of the tree that will try to grow and keep the center wide and open, removing all branches that begin to grow towards the center of the tree. New fruit will grow on one-year-old wood so annual pruning is necessary for good fruit production. Plums, however, grow best with a strong central leader. Rather than utilize the pruning technique described for peaches and nectarines, *do not* remove the central leader but instead encourage a central branch in the center of the tree.

Additional Information

Fruits ripen in early to mid-May. Varieties of low-chill peaches that are good for Florida's climate include 'Florida Prince', 'Florida Glo', and 'UF Beauty'. A good nectarine with both good fruit and ornamental landscape characteristics is 'Sunhome'; it has dark-purple new growth. Good plum varieties for Florida include 'Gulfbeauty', 'Gulfblaze', 'Gulfruby', and 'Gulfrose'.

PEAR

Easy to grow and an enjoyable addition to any mid- to late summer fruit salad, pears should be in nearly every Central and North Florida garden. Pears grown in the Sunshine State are smaller than those found in the local markets, but their flavor is just as good. Florida pears come in two main versions: soft and hard. Some varieties are good for canning only and some are equally good for fresh eating and canning. A pear tree's growth is quite handsome and would be a welcome addition to any landscape.

Where to Plant

Pears prefer well-drained sandy loam soil but can grow in a variety of soil types with a pH of 6.0-6.5. Plant in full sun and avoid frost pockets; pears can be damaged by unseasonable frosts. Give them plenty of room in the landscape—pear trees can grow to 15 feet tall and 12 feet wide. Garden locations with good air circulation will lessen the occurrence of disease organisms and reduce cold damage. For varieties that require cross-pollination, plant no more than 30 feet apart. With a few exceptions, fruiting pear trees are best suited for North and Central Florida gardens.

How to Plant

Most pear varieties are grown as containerized nursery plants and can be planted anytime. Dig a hole twice as wide and as deep as the rootball and place the plant in the hole. Alternating soil and water, backfill the hole with the native soil making sure that the top of the rootball is 1 inch above the native soil line. Create a basin with the remaining soil and water three times a week for the first month and taper off watering as the plant becomes established. Place a 3-inch layer of mulch around the bottom of the pear tree in a 3-foot diameter to moderate soil temperatures.

Care and Maintenance

Provided the trees were placed in locations conducive to good growth—good loamy soil, proper pH, and an area with good air circulation—pear trees are virtually trouble free. Established pear trees require 1 inch of water each week. Leaf spot diseases can be prevented by periodically spraying copper fungicides during the warm summer months. Other insects, including cotton cushion scale and mealybugs, can be a problem; applications of insecticidal soap or Neem oil will control them. As a preventative, spray the tree trunk, branches, and stems thoroughly with ultrafine horticultural oil in mid- to late winter to reduce summer infestations.

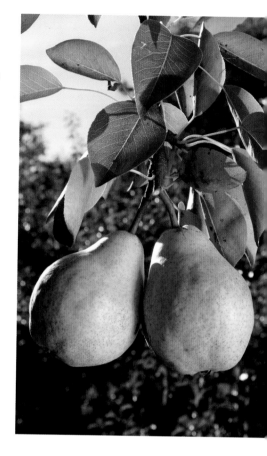

A balanced fertilizer (6-6-6, 8-8-8, or similar mixture) is recommended. About 1 pound for each year of the tree's age is usually sufficient until a maximum of 10 pounds is reached. This should be applied in two applications, during dormancy (January) and at the beginning of the rainy season (June). The fertilizer should be broadcast under the trees.

Additional Information

Good soft pear varieties for North and Central Florida include 'Floridahome'; 'Baldwin' (eating and canning); 'Hood' (yellow fruit, good for fresh eating); and 'Tenns' (fresh eating). Hard varieties include 'Carnes' (fresh eating, also called "apple pear"); 'Orient' (very large, best for cooking); and the old-time favorite 'Pineapple' (best cooking pear, very prolific).

PECAN

Although pecans will grow from Pensacola to Miami, it's North Florida where most of the Florida-grown pecans can be found. There are more than 500 registered selections of pecans throughout the world, and each has its own special characteristics. The trees themselves can often reach 70 feet tall and the "old-timers" have been known to grow more than 6 feet in diameter. Although Georgia grows the most in the United States, Florida often produces more than 10 million pounds a year. Fruit production is best in locations where the daytime temperatures are warm and the winter temperatures are moderately cool.

Where to Plant

Pecans need plenty of room to grow (at least 40 feet apart) and they need full sun. Plant them at least 30 feet away from any structure. Well-drained soil is a must and good air circulation will reduce the incidence of diseases. Pecans enjoy growing in deep sand with a clay bottom so their roots can spread out to absorb available water and nutrients. A soil pH of 5.5-6.5 is best.

How to Plant

Unlike many plants, pecans prefer to be planted in the fall to allow good root development before the onset of cooler temperatures. Pecans can be planted either bare root or as container-grown plants. The planting hole should be twice the size of the containerized rootball if you are planting nursery-grown plants. Place the top of the root zone at the same level as the native soil and alternately backfill the hole with water and soil to eliminate the risk of air pockets. Create a shallow basin around the base of the tree to hold water, and water at least three times per week until the plant is established (usually about two months). Reduce the amount of water you apply until warm weather returns. A diluted solution of white latex paint can be applied to the trunk at least 4 feet high to reduce sunscald to the bark; only one application is usually necessary. Apply 1 pound of a general fertilizer (10-10-10-3 NPKMg) to the tree after planting.

Care and Maintenance

Keep weeds away from the trunk to prevent competition for nutrients and water. Apply 1 pound of a general fertilizer (10-10-10-3 NPKMg) per 1 inch of trunk diameter in early March and again in June. Evenly spread the fertilizer over the root zone of the tree. Once the tree begins nut production (which varies by variety), increase the fertilizer amount to 2 to 4 pounds in February and June. If planted as a "whip" (a short, single leader upright stem), pecan trees can be pruned by one-third and trained to have a symmetrical scaffolding of branches. If they have been trained appropriately in the nursery, containerized trees seldom need to be pruned. Mature trees are never pruned unless it's to remove dead or diseased branches or branches that cross over each other and cause wounds.

Additional Information

Highly recommended varieties of pecans for Florida include 'Cape Fear', 'Moreland', and 'Elliott'. Other satisfactory varieties include 'Curtis', 'Sumner', 'Stuart', 'Choctaw', and 'Pawnee'.

PERSIMMON

An American native, persimmon trees have long been an important part of southern culture. Unfortunately, the flavor of the native fruits is far less appealing than the Asian selections and it is the latter that are discussed. The trees perform well in the landscape, and like carambola trees, even if they didn't produce an edible fruit they would be a nice landscape plant. Improved taste has been the primary goal of persimmon hybridization research around the world, but improved hardiness and resistance to disease are also part of the equation. If you have never tried a persimmon fruit you are in for a real treat—provided you select one that is ripe. If you taste one that isn't quite ready, I'll guarantee it will take some serious persuasion to get you to try another!

Where to Plant

Native persimmon trees can grow to 30 feet tall, although the Asian selections generally grow to only 8 to 10 feet tall. Trees will grow in full sun or dappled, high-canopy shade. They tolerate a variety of well-drained soil types although they prefer a soil in the 6.0-7.0 pH range.

How to Plant

Most persimmons are grown in 3- to 5-gallon plastic containers and can be planted anytime. Dig a hole twice as wide and as deep as the rootball of the containerized plant and place the rootball in the hole, backfilling the hole with alternating amounts of soil and water. Asian persimmons are grafted and the graft union (the swollen part of the tree trunk just above the container soil line) should be 1 to1½ inches *below* the native soil line. Use the remaining soil to create a soil berm (ring) around the rootball to act as a water reservoir. Water the tree three times a week for the first month and reduce the amount of water as the tree becomes established.

Care and Maintenance

Keep weeds and turf at least 3 feet away from the trunk of the newly planted tree to prevent competition for water and nutrients. Do not fertilize during the first year of growth. Mature trees should receive 10 pounds per year of a general 10-10-10-3 (NPKMg) four times per year.

Additional Information

Persimmons are divided into astringent and non-astringent varieties. In Florida, astringent varieties are picked, peeled, skewered, and allowed to dry. The dried fruit is sweet and delicious. Non-astringent types are the commonly grown persimmon and account for most of the trees grown in Florida. These varieties can be picked when the fruit is hard or soft, they are eaten fresh, and are often used in fruit salads with pears, raisins, citrus, and dates. Fruit size can range from 4 to 7 ounces and fruit ripen in the fall.

Good varieties of astringent types for Florida include 'Saijo', 'Tenenashi', 'Sheng', 'Ormond', and 'Giombo'. Good non-astringent types include 'Izu', 'Hana Fuyu', 'Fuyu', and 'Suruga'.

PINEAPPLE

Besides growing and eating fresh bananas, being able to go into the garden and pick a fresh pineapple is one of my favorite Florida things to do. Fresh, sweet, and delicious pineapple from the garden mixed in a fruit salad with fresh mango, papaya, and star fruit is one of life's rare pleasures.

Where to Plant

Plant pineapple plants anywhere in the garden where full sun is available and it is free of frost. Pineapples can grow in a wide variety of soils from pure sand to alkaline marl, and make great container-grown plants. Full sun, water, and regular applications of fertilizers are all you need.

How to Plant

The easiest way to grow pineapple is simply to stroll on down to the local market and buy a pineapple. Cut off the spiky top 1 inch below the top (eat the bottom fleshy part as usual) and set the top aside to air dry for two to three days. Many gardeners in frost-free zones simply plant the top into the soil, but just to be safe it's recommended that they be planted in a container first and then into the garden. Begin with a 1-gallon container (plastic or clay, it doesn't make any difference) and fill it to within 2 inches from the top with good potting soil. Once the top is ready for planting, place it into the soil so that just the green spiky top is sticking out of the soil. Place the container in part to full sun and water daily. Once adequate roots have formed from the bottom of the spiky top (generally 45 to 60 days), plant directly into the garden in frost-free zones of the state. Avoid letting the plant be rootbound; restricted root systems may not grow properly once they're planted in the ground. For those gardening where frost is commonplace, simply place the container in full sun during the warm months. When nighttime temperatures reach 55°F, bring pineapple plants indoors until warm weather returns.

Care and Maintenance

Young plants should be fertilized with 1 to 2 ounces of 6-6-

6-4 (NPKMg) every eight weeks, increasing the amount to 6 ounces as the plant grows after two years. Occasionally, root rot diseases occur on pineapples and can be deterred by not overwatering the plant and by planting them in well-drained sandy soil. Mealybugs often attack the plant where the spike meets the root top. An application made from Ivory soap (1 teaspoon to 1 quart of water) as a soil drench (don't get any *in* the spike) will do the trick. Should your pineapple grow large enough, a bamboo stake tied to the fruit stalk with stout garden twine will prevent the stalk from breaking. From the day you cut the store-bought pineapple to the time a new fruit is produced can take anywhere from two to three years. If the plant is large enough to produce a fruit but hasn't, simply place an apple in the top of the plant and cover the entire

plant with a plastic trash bag overnight. Remove the bag the next morning. The plant will produce a fruit in about three months.

Additional Information

Raccoons and opossums have the uncanny ability to seek out and eat ripening fruit the night before you plan to harvest it. Often, simply placing a paper bag over the top will work, but it's just as easy to harvest the fruit right when the bottom starts to change from green to yellow. Once harvested, the fruit will ripen on the kitchen counter in a day or two.

POMEGRANATE

If ever there was fruit that has taken over the grocery stores in every conceivable form it has to be pomegranate. It shows up in juice, jellies, wine, desserts, breads, yogurt, vitamins—you name it and there is *something* with pomegranate in it. And that's for good reasons, too. The fruits are rich in antioxidants (more than three times that of wine and green tea) and pomegranate juice contains about 40 percent of the Recommended Daily Allowance (RDA) of vitamin C. It also has Vitamin A, E, and folic acid in good quantities. The fruits can be eaten fresh and the juice can be extracted just like an orange. The orange-red flowers are quite attractive and look great in the garden. Pomegranate fruits range from 2 to 5 inches in diameter. In North and Central Florida, they mature from July to November, but may produce year-round in South Florida.

Where to Plant

Pomegranates are most often grown as shrubs from 6 to 10 feet tall but they can be trained as a tree to reach 20 feet tall. They grow as far north as Washington, DC. They need full sun to produce an adequate number of fruit and grow well in deep, well-drained soil with a soil pH of 5.5-6.5, although they are able to grow in a wide variety of soils. They even tolerate minor, short-term flooding.

How to Plant

Pomegranates are usually grown in 3- to 5-gallon containers in the nursery and can be planted into the garden anytime. Dig a hole twice as deep and as wide as the rootball and place the plant into the hole. Alternate adding soil and water until the hole is filled, making certain the top of the rootball is 1 inch higher than the native soil line to compensate for settling. With the leftover soil, create a saucer around the tree and fill the saucer three times a week with water for the first month after planting.

Care and Maintenance

One of the reasons pomegranates are so popular in the landscape is because they are so easy to grow. Fruits are borne on new growth so it's a good idea to lightly trim the end of the branches before July 1 to create buds for the next year's fruit. The showy shrubs enjoy regular (four times per year) applications of a general fertilizer (8-8-8-4, NPKMg) with micronutrients including, but not limited to, manganese, boron, zinc, and molybdenum. One cup of fertilizer for every year of a shrub's age, sprinkled widely over its root zone, works well. After the plant is two years old fertilize once in the fall and once in the spring and withhold winter and summer applications. Too much plant food can cause the fruit to drop prematurely, so be careful with the "groceries."

Pomegranates are virtually pest free. Scale insects can be controlled with a dormant oil spray in winter and mealybugs can be sprayed with insecticidal soap.

Additional Information

The variety 'Wonderful' is grown commercially in California, having been exported as cuttings from Florida. 'Purple Seed' and 'Spanish Ruby' are popular home garden selections.

THE FINAL REWARD: HARVESTING AND STORING FRUITS AND VEGETABLES

After planting the seeds, watering the plants, controlling the bugs, and pulling the weeds, you come to the final reward—harvesting. After all, picking the fruit and bringing it to the kitchen as fresh, safely grown food for the family is why you got into this project in the first place, right? Homegrown vegetables can taste *so* much better than those usually available in markets, but to be at their best, they need to be harvested at the peak time. Each vegetable has a window of opportunity for harvest. While some vegetables and fruits are quite forgiving and have a long harvest window, others can go from tender and tasty to tough and bitter virtually overnight. For instance, tomatoes can be left on the vine until they're fully ripened or picked when they're partially ripened. Other crops, such as winter squash and watermelon, are not ready until they are fully developed.

Fruits and vegetables should be picked at the proper time to assure the best quality and to have optimum vitamins and mineral content. Vegetables left in a garden and fruit left on a tree too long will often become fibrous, tough, or rotten. In the case of vegetables, harvesting at the proper stage tends to keep the plants producing. Because vegetable and fruit growth depends on many factors, including precipitation, temperature, and soil fertility, their maturation can vary from year to year. The best way to determine when a vegetable or fruit is ready to harvest is based upon the characteristics of the plant itself. These signs can often be subtle and it takes practice to become familiar with them.

There are just a few things to remember after harvesting. The fruit, even though it has been removed from the plant, is still very dynamic and will continue to change until it is processed in some way or eaten. In some plants, peas and corn for instance, the sugars within the fruit that are inherent to its sweetness change very quickly to starches. Although it's still edible, it won't be as sweet if it's left lying around. For vegetables like corn, for example, my grandmother used to tell us that the water should be boiling on the stove when the ears of corn are picked so you could run to the garden, pick some ears, and drop them in! If freezing fruits and vegetables is your plan, then prepare the containers by washing them ahead of time. The water to blanch the fruit should be boiling before harvesting. If, for some reason, processing must be delayed, cool the fruit and vegetables in ice water or crushed ice, and store in the refrigerator to preserve flavor and quality.

Storing vegetables and fruit is equally important. When possible, harvest during the cool part of the morning, and process or store the harvest as soon as possible. Leafy vegetables, such as mustard and lettuce, need high humidity to maintain their crispness (hence the overhead sprayers in the produce department at the stores). Others, such as onions, should be stored where it's dry (50 to 65 percent humidity).

Be careful when harvesting fruits and vegetables. A tiny scratch from a shovel or pruning shears can cause a fruit or vegetable to rot at a faster rate while it's in storage. It's a good idea when harvesting vegetables to use hand clippers to remove the fruit from the plant. Okra, for instance, not only is difficult to remove without a sharp cutting blade, but without it, the plant can be damaged, jeopardizing the health and future fruit production. The same approach is true for digging root crops such as potatoes. A lifting fork works best for harvesting root crops and causes less damage than a shovel. Remember, too, do not harvest while the plants are wet. Diseases like to catch a ride when they can, so harvest after the plants have dried from the morning dew or any overhead irrigation. Be careful to avoid stepping on vines or breaking stems because that could create openings through which diseases can enter a plant. Size is important when picking fruits and vegetables. Cauliflower, for example, will become bitter and "grainy" if it's allowed to grow too large. Most crops can be harvested several times if only the part that is ready is harvested.

Vegetables

If you want the vegetables you have grown to arrive on your table at the peak of perfection, the following are a few suggestions and basic rules on how and when to harvest them.

Beans, Snap. Pick snap beans when the pods are young, succulent, and are almost full size but before the seeds inside begin to bulge. Tips should be pliable. Beans should be crisp and snap easily. To dry the beans, let the bean pods mature on the vines, but be sure to harvest before they get so dry that they shatter.

Beans, Lima. Pick lima beans when the pods and seeds reach full size but before the pods turn yellow. The end of a pod should feel spongy, and the pods and seeds should be fresh and juicy. Open a few pods to check. Use only the seeds; the pods are tough and fibrous.

Beets. Beets can be eaten as greens when the leaves are 4 to 6 inches long. When they're grown for tops and beets, harvest when the beets are 1 to 1½ inches in diameter. To use only the beets, wait until they are 1½ to 3 inches in diameter. If they're allowed to get much larger, they become woody, especially in warm, dry weather. Remove all but about 1½ inches of tops on late crop beets. Wash and refrigerate immediately.

Broccoli. Gather broccoli when the buds are compact but before the buds turn yellow or open into flowers. Cut the stems off 6 to 7 inches below the flower heads. Broccoli's small, tender leaves are also nutritious. Store in the coldest section of the refrigerator.

Brussels Sprouts. Harvest when the sprouts (buds) at the base of the plant become solid. Remove the buds higher on the plant as they become firm, but do not strip leaves from the plants since they are necessary for further growth. Before the onset of warm weather, pinch out the growing point at the top of a plant to get larger sprouts. Store in the coldest section of the refrigerator.

Cabbage. Harvest cabbages when the heads becomes solid and firm. The outer leaves should possess a uniform green or purple color (depending on type). Excessive water uptake by plant roots will cause the heads to split. To prevent mature heads from splitting, twist plants one-quarter turn to break several roots. Store cabbage in a crisper drawer and use within one to two weeks.

Carrot. Harvest carrots when they are small and succulent. Do not let them get over about 1 inch in diameter. Always pull the largest carrots in the row. Remove the tops and wash them before transferring carrots to refrigerated storage.

Cauliflower. Cauliflower is ready to harvest when a head is firm or when the curds (which are immature flower heads) are full sized (6 to 8 inches) but still compact, white, and smooth. It's too mature when the head is soft or when the leaves turn yellow.

Corn, Sweet. Corn silks darken and dry out as the ears mature. As the kernels fill out toward the top, the kernel ends become more blunt instead of pointed. Pick sweet corn when it's in the milk stage, when a milky juice exudes from kernels when they're crushed with a thumbnail. Sweet corn is very susceptible to rapid sugar-to-starch conversion and is at prime eating quality for only 72 hours before becoming too mature. Cook, eat, or chill the ears immediately after harvest. It's best to harvest early in the morning or during cool weather.

Cucumber. Pick cucumbers when they're 6 to 9 inches long and still bright green and firm. Overly mature fruits are dull in color or yellowed and less crisp. Cucumbers intended for sweet pickles should be 1 ½ to 2 ½ inches long; and for dill pickles, 3 to 4 inches long. Cucumbers can be stored in the refrigerator about five days. Do not try to pickle the salad-type cucumbers.

Eggplant. Harvest eggplant when the fruits are nearly full size (approximately 6 to 8 inches in diameter) but still firm and bright in color. Older fruits become dull colored, soft, and seedy. Store eggplants in a cool and humid location.

Greens (mustard, collard, turnip, kale, Swiss chard, beet). Break off the outer leaves when they are 6 to 10 inches long and before they start to yellow. Avoid wilted or flabby leaves. Wash and chill immediately.

Kohlrabi. Harvest when the bulbs (which are really thickened stems) reach 2 to 3 inches in diameter. Store in refrigerator. If kohlrabi bulbs are allowed to get much larger than 2 to 3 inches, they become woody, especially in warm, dry weather.

Lettuce. Harvest leaf varieties when the outer, older leaves are 4 to 6 inches long; harvest heading varieties when the heads are moderately firm. Older, outer leaves may be removed from plants of either leaf or head lettuce as soon as the leaves are 4 to 6 inches long. New leaves provide a continuous harvest of tender, tasty lettuce until hot weather brings on bitter flavor and seed stalks start. Wash and store in the refrigerator.

Melon, Honeydew. Harvest honeydew when the fruit is yellowish to creamy white with a soft, velvety feel. The rind should be slightly soft at the blossom end and have a faint, pleasant aroma.

Melon, Muskmelon. Harvest muskmelons whey they are at the three-fourths to full-slip stage (ripe stage). When the stem separates readily from the fruit under moderate pressure and leaves a circular depression, the full-ripe stage has been reached. The outer rind should not have any green color. If the melons are fully ripe, store them in the refrigerator. If they are not fully ripe, store them in a cool area.

Melon, Watermelon. Harvest watermelon when the fruits are full size and have a dull surface and cream-colored ground spot.

Okra. Okra pods are ready to harvest when they're 2 to 3 inches long, about four to six days after the flower wilts. Okra stops producing if the pods are not picked, so gather them every one to two days. Chill immediately.

Onion. Onion may be harvested anytime after planting until maturity. Harvest when the tops fall over and begin to die. Dig the bulbs, brush off most of the dirt, and dry for several days. Cut off the tops and roots, and store in a cool, dry place. Harvest green onions when they are 6 to 8 inches tall.

Peas, English and Snow. If you expect to shell the peas, harvest the pods when they are shiny green and fully developed; overly mature peas are of poor quality. For edible podded varieties (snow and Chinese), harvest when the pods are fully developed (about 3 inches) but before the seeds are more than one-half developed. Deterioration occurs rapidly at high temperatures. Wash and chill immediately.

Peas, Summer. Summer peas will be ready to harvest about 55 days after sowing the seeds. Harvest the pods when they are well filled and have changed to a light straw, silver, or purple color (depending on the cultivar) because they shell easiest at this stage. The peas themselves should have a greenish appearance. Ideally, shell and use the peas the day they are harvested. If the pods are going to be held for more than a day, they should be refrigerated until they can be shelled. Shelled peas may be stored for several days prior to cooking in a covered bowl in the refrigerator. For longer storage, freeze peas; the quality is excellent when they are thawed and cooked later.

Pepper. Harvest bell peppers when they are shiny green, in their prime, and are about the size of a baseball (3 to 4 inches long) with full, well-formed lobes. Immature peppers are soft, pliable, thin fleshed, and pale. Harvest jalapeños when they are 2 to 2½ inches long. Mature peppers turn orange or red; this does not mean they are hotter. Store at 45 to 50 degrees F.

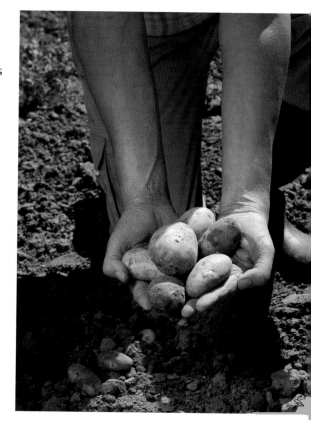

Potato, Irish and new. For Irish potatoes, a good tuber size is 2 to 3 inches in diameter, but individual preference is the rule here. You can harvest new potatoes at any size but generally do not dig them before the tubers are 1¼ to 1½ inches in diameter. Let potatoes dry several hours in the garden after digging them. But do not expose potatoes to sunlight for any length of time. Remove the soil but do not wash the potatoes before storage. Store in a cool, dry place.

Potato, Sweet. Sweet potatoes should be harvested when the vines begin to turn yellow in the fall. Lift the plant with a spading fork to avoid any bruises and broken roots. Remove any soil from the sweet potatoes but do not wash them. Allow the tubers to dry (cure) in a warm, well-ventilated place for two to three weeks. Store in a cool, dry place.

Pumpkin. Pick pumpkins when the fruit is full size, the rind is firm and glossy, and the bottom of the fruit (the portion touching the soil) is cream to orange colored. Store in a cool, dry area.

Radish. Pull radishes when they are about 1 inch in diameter. Radishes become "hot" and tough when they're left in the garden soil too long. Wash and chill immediately.

Rutabaga. Harvest rutabagas when the roots reach full size (4 to 6 inches in diameter). They'll become woody and dry if the soil is too dry. Store in the refrigerator.

Spinach. Spinach leaves are ready when they're 4 to 6 inches long. Pull out larger, whole plants or harvest older leaves to allow new growth. Wash the leaves thoroughly and store in the refrigerator.

Squash, Summer. Harvest summer squash when it is 4 to 6 inches long for yellow crookneck squash, 6 to 8 inches for yellow straight neck, and 3 to 4 inches in diameter for white scallop. A glossy color indicates tenderness.

Squash, Winter. Harvest winter squash when the fruits are full size. The rind will be firm and glossy and the bottom of the fruit (the portion touching the soil) is cream to orange colored. A thumbnail pressed into the skin will not leave a mark. A light frost will not damage mature fruit. Squash, like cucumbers, are susceptible to chilling injury; do not store at cold temperatures for more than two to three days.

Tomato. Harvest tomatoes when they're fully colored but still firm. Harvest red tomatoes for eating fresh. For canning or juicing purposes, pick tomatoes that are fully colored. If fruit cracking at the top is a problem in hot weather, pick them when they are turning pink. These tomatoes will ripen in the shade indoors. Before a frost or the onset of hot weather (depending on the season grown), pick green tomatoes and store in a *dark* place where they can ripen. Store ripe tomatoes in the refrigerator.

Turnip. Harvest turnips when the roots are 2 to 3 inches in diameter but before it's cold enough to frost. When turnips are grown for their greens, pick the leaves when they're 4 to 6 inches long. Keep topped turnips cold and humid.

Fruits

If you want the fruit you have grown to arrive on your table at the peak of perfection, use the following suggestions and basic rules on how and when to harvest them.

Avocado. Oddly enough, avocado fruits do not ripen on the tree. Usually, the fruit is picked when it is of maximum size, but that can change from year to year depending on weather conditions. Select the largest fruit and set it on a table (do not refrigerate). If the fruit softens in four to eight days the remaining fruits are ready, too. If, on the other hand, the fruit gets wrinkly or becomes rotten it's not ready; try the same test in a week or two. That's the great thing about avocados; they don't all have to be picked at the same time. Once harvested, avocados ripen in four to eight days.

Banana. The fruit at the top of the "hand" ripen first and the entire hand should be picked at that time. Hang in a cool, dark location and pick individual bananas as they ripen. Be careful! Banana sap will permanently stain clothes.

Blackberry. There are two methods to determine if blackberries are ready for harvest. First, look at the color; the berries should be deep purple or burgundy (almost, but not quite, black) and look plump. The second method is to pick a test blackberry. Grasp a berry between your thumb and finger and then gently twist. If the fruit comes off easily leaving the stalk behind, then it's ripe. Wash the berries and store them in the refrigerator.

Blueberry. Ripe blueberries can retain their freshness for as long as ten days on the bush. Multiple pickings are required to harvest blueberries because they do not ripen uniformly within clusters on the plants. Most of the common cultivars can be picked clean in two to three harvests, spaced seven to ten days apart. Use both hands to harvest by rolling the ripe fruit from a cluster into the palm of the opposite hand (do not squeeze the fruit). After a rain, wait until the bushes have dried before harvesting the berries. Handling fruit when it is wet will lead to a loss of the berries' surface wax, leading to an increase in decay. Gently wash berries and then refrigerate.

Carambola. Gently shake a carambola tree and harvest those that fall. Star fruit that is difficult to remove from a branch is not fully ripe. Star fruit trees can produce three to four crops per year.

Citrus. The best test to determine if a citrus fruit is ripe is to pick a sample fruit and taste. Readiness of fruit can change from year to year depending on a variety of climatic factors. For general harvesting guidelines see the Citrus Harvest Table on page 181.

Fig. Figs must be allowed to ripen fully on the tree before they are picked. They will not ripen if they're picked when immature. A ripe fig will be slightly soft and starting to bend at the neck. Harvest the fruit gently to avoid bruising. Fresh figs do not keep well and can be stored in the refrigerator only for two to three days.

Grape. Pick muscadine grapes by spreading a cloth beneath the vines and shaking the branches gently. Gather the ripe grapes that fall onto the cloth. Eat the grapes fresh or store unrefrigerated, but in a cool place, for up to one week.

Guava. The fruit of a guava require care when they are being picked and are ready for harvest when they begin to turn soft and have a musky fragrance to them. The picked fruit should be kept in a cool place away from the sun. To maintain quality, it is best to use the fruits soon after harvest. In addition to eating fresh guava, it can be pureéd and chilled or frozen.

Jaboticaba. When the individual jaboticaba fruits become somewhat soft, select an individual fruit and taste it for sweetness. Fruits on the tree will remain edible for several days. However, jaboticabas, once harvested, ferment quickly at ordinary temperatures. Eat the fruit within hours of harvest or wash and store in the refrigerator.

Jackfruit. Pick jackfruit when the rind is soft, emitting an aromatic scent, and when the leaf nearest the stalk turns yellow. At this stage, the flesh of the fruit is yellow-orange, shiny, and juicy. When you cut the stem of the fruit with a sharp knife, be sure

another person wears gloves to protect his hands from the spines. When harvesting from tall trees, place the fruit in a sack to prevent it from falling to the ground. Tie a rope to the stalk, snap the fruit from the tree, and slowly lower the bundle to the ground. Harvesting should be done from midmorning to late afternoon to reduce the latex flow. Remove the leftover stem and unwanted water sprouts from the trunk after picking the fruit.

Longan. During mid- to late summer, longans are harvested and eaten fresh. The best practical test is to taste the fruit, which should be quite sweet. Longans are best harvested with the entire fruit stalk, or they should at least retain a short piece of stem. Not only does plucking the fruit during harvest result in skin tears but fruit left on the fruit cluster lasts longer. When stored at room temperature, longans remain in good condition for several days. Because of their firmer rind, longan fruit is less perishable than the lychee. Preliminary tests in Florida indicate that longan fruit can be frozen and will not break down as quickly as the lychee does when it's thawed.

Loquat. Loquats can produce one or two crops of fruit a year depending on their location. When the fruit becomes plump and slightly soft, cut off the individual fruit with a knife or pruning shears for eating. Loquat fruit ripen at different times on the same plant, and it can take several weeks to complete the ripening of the entire plant. Refrigerated loquats can be stored for up to two weeks.

Lychee. Unlike many fruits, lychees should remain on the tree to ripen. Should the fruit be permitted to stay on the tree too long, however, the fruit turns darker and loses its sheen. As with longans, it's important to clip the entire fruit stem cluster rather than select individual fruits. The fruit must be allowed to ripen fully on the tree. Overly mature fruit darken in color and lose their luster. Lychees can be stored for up to five weeks in the refrigerator. They can also be frozen or dried. Lychees are highly perishable and will begin to deteriorate within three days at room temperature.

Mango. For the best flavor allow mangoes to ripen on the tree. The fruit will change to its characteristic color (depending on the variety) and will be soft to the touch. Mangoes should be removed from the tree with a sharp knife or hand pruners. When the first fruit shows color while it's on the tree, all of the fruit that size or larger may be removed; repeat when the remaining fruit changes colors. Do not store below 50°F.

Papaya. Pick papaya when most of its skin is yellow-green; any early harvesting of dark-green fruit is in vain as papaya will not ripen properly off the tree. After several days of ripening at room temperature, they will be almost fully yellow and slightly soft to the touch. Papaya can be stored in the fridge for a few days once they're fully ripe.

Passion Fruit. Pick the fruit when they change color and shrivel just slightly, or wait till they fall off the vine. Homegrown fresh passion fruit will keep for several weeks in the fridge, but fruit will gradually lose its sweetness.

Peach, Nectarine, & Plum. Ripe fruit will be slightly soft to the touch and easily removed from the branch. Fruits will ripen at different times on the same tree and it's important to check every other day or so to prevent an invasion of opossums and raccoons. Ripe peaches, nectarines, and plums can be stored in the refrigerator for up to two weeks.

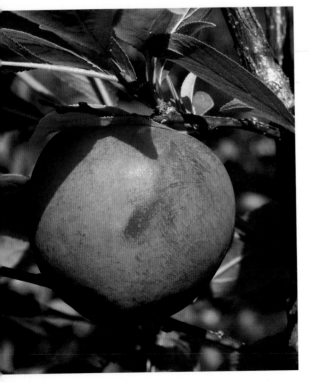

Pear. When the fruit begins to change to its characteristic color (depending on the variety) a pear is ready to pick. Pears ripen well off the tree, and by harvesting at different times over several weeks the fruit can be enjoyed for up to one month. Pears can be refrigerated but to slow the ripening process remove any apples from the same storage drawer. (Apples release ethylene gas, which promotes fruit ripening.)

Pecan. When mature nuts begin falling from a pecan tree in the autumn, that's the sign that the others in the tree are ready to be harvested, too. Gather the nuts by spreading a cloth beneath the tree and shaking the branches gently. Store the collected nuts loosely in cloth sacks in a cool, dry place after harvest. As the pecans cure, their flavor and quality will improve over time.

Persimmon. Persimmons are harvested when their color has fully developed (color varies depending on the variety), and they're somewhat soft to the touch. The fruit is removed from the tree by clipping or breaking the stems, leaving the lobes attached to the top of the fruit. Persimmons must be handled carefully to avoid damage. Rough handling causes bruising and skin discoloration.

Pineapple. Because pineapples ripen from the bottom, it's important to pick the fruit at the first signs of a color change. If you wait one more day, the raccoons and opossums will beat you to it. Pineapples ripen well at room temperatures so be sure to pick them early.

Strawberry. Strawberries should be picked when the berry is fully red (with no white spots) or with slightly green "shoulders." Diseased or damaged fruit should be removed at the same time usable berries are harvested to prevent further disease infestation.

PESTS: BUGS, DISEASES, AND WEEDS

No discussion of gardening in Florida would be complete without talking about pests. Insects will do their best to eat vegetables down to a nub, diseases are always lurking around the corner, and weeds will do their best to choke out your fruit trees or vegetables and absorb every last bit of fertilizer you applied last week. That's the bad news. The good news is that all of these are manageable. Gardeners in North Florida will have it a little easier than those in Central and South Florida. North Florida often gets cold temperatures down into the teens, and such weather will severely diminish the insect populations in the following growing season. Cold weather is a two-edged sword, however. As much as Central and South Florida gardeners would like fewer bugs and diseases, cold weather will freeze to the ground or even kill many tropical and subtropical plants, especially fruit trees. Sometimes, we have to take the good with the bad and make the best of it. Living and gardening in Florida still beats pulling the snow boots out of the closet every November.

BUGS: BELIEVE
EVERY WORD

Everything you have heard about bugs in Florida—living, breathing, biting bugs—is true. For every one you see there are twenty more hiding somewhere, just waiting to chew and suck the life out of the your precious seedlings that you babied from a seed, or that you just spent your children's allowance to purchase. They are just waiting for you slip up, giving them an invitation to stop by.

Rather than think of ways to kill them, think instead of ways to *prevent* or *deter* them. Plants are living things pretty much just like people, and they act pretty much the same way. If you don't get enough sleep, don't eat properly, and are under pressure from daily activities, then the chances are if you're exposed to a cold virus or a flu bug you will get it. On the other hand, if you eat properly, get plenty of sleep to help your body defend itself against infections, and relieve the anxiety in your life, there is a good chance that, even though you may be exposed to germs, you won't get a cold or come down with the flu.

Don't get me wrong—there are some plants (such as roses, orchids, and turfgrasses) that, despite your best efforts, *will* suffer from bugs no matter how hard you try to prevent it. For the most part, however, healthy plants will not get sick. Think about that ficus tree in your home with its constant state of hosting mealybugs and spider mites. If that tree had good air circulation, proper sunlight (instead of being stuck in the corner), and proper water (instead of water every day or worse, once a month) it would not play the role of a B&B host to mealybugs or spider mites. With the proper growing conditions, it would have the ability to defend itself. Fruit trees and vegetables are the same way; give them well-drained soil, adequate water, good nutrition (regular, small applications of fertilizer), and enough sunlight (don't try to grow fruit trees and veggies in only five hours of full sun) and they will be healthy as can be. Last summer, the eggplant in my garden was covered in mealybugs and it was not the plant's fault. It was mine; there wasn't enough water, I forgot to fertilize the plants regularly, and I didn't pick the mature fruits when I was supposed to. And as if that wasn't enough, I didn't weed for several weeks. There might as well have been a flashing "Welcome Mealybugs" sign.

> To repel cucumber beetles, squash bugs, and borers around squash plant a few seeds of nasturtiums at the same time you plant the squash seeds.

Think of it this way: bugs are not the problem, but rather a symptom of something that's gone wrong. Let's face it; given the arsenal of chemicals found in any garden center or home improvement store, bugs are easy to kill. But until the reasons *why* a plant is stressed are alleviated (water, sunlight, nutrition, and so forth), the bugs will continue to come back. Plants will tell you when they need help; just correct the problem and the bugs won't get a foothold. And who wants to blast their food with an arsenal of chemicals?

Now, there are some insects that will attack plants despite your best efforts. Take the army-worm, for instance. They are about 1½ inches long when they're mature, and they hide in the soil during the day. At night, they crawl out and chew down newly emerged vegetable seedlings. It's as if a miniature Paul Bunyan visited during the night. In this case you can't kill them but you can prevent them from doing damage. In anticipation of their arrival, place a paper towel or toilet paper roll around each tender stem and push it into the soil to prevent the caterpillar from reaching the plant.

The best thing to do is to get started on the right foot. At the garden center, select healthy plants free of bugs. Keep the garden free of weeds; weeds can act as an incubator for bugs waiting for your plants that show signs of stress. Select plants that are genetically resistant to pests. Tomatoes, for instance, that have the letters "VFN" after their name on the plant label will be stronger than those without this designation. The letters indicate that the specific variety has been bred to be resistant to certain pests (in this case, Verticillium wilt, Fusarium wilt, and nematodes). Finally, time the planting to its proper season. Vegetables placed out too soon in spring may be stressed by too much cold and could succumb to insect pressures soon after.

Biological Controls

If we're given a choice, our natural tendency is not to use chemicals. After all, one of the reasons we grow our own food is to know that they haven't been sprayed and they are completely safe to eat. That's where biological controls—the use living organisms to combat pests—come into play.

First, let me stress there are "good" bugs and "bad" bugs. (Maybe we should call the good ones something other than "bugs.") The good bugs can be killed by the same chemicals that are used to kill the bad bugs. When plants are stress free, the good bugs will stop by periodically to eat whatever bad bugs are around. Once the buffet is over, they move on. If the use of chemicals sprays is stopped, then the good guys can move in and out without danger. Note: even "organic" sprays such as rotenone, Bt, and pyrethrins kill good bugs, and they should *only be used when absolutely necessary.*

Because you want the "good" bugs to stick around, you need to make your garden appealing to them in ways other than stopping the use of chemicals. Many beneficial insects are attracted to plants other than vegetables and by including nectar plants in the vegetable garden a beneficial insect will stay around longer. (See the table of beneficial nectar plants on page 245.)

Insects can get diseases, too, and one in particular is called Bt (*Bacillus thuringiensis*); it is perfectly safe to humans but deadly to any caterpillar that ultimately turns into a butterfly or moth. Note I said *any* caterpillar. After a caterpillar eats any part of the plant that has been sprayed with Bt, it dies from a bacterial infection. In addition to being nontoxic to people, Bt is not toxic to animals and can be used safely around pets. Just beware that Bt is nondiscriminatory and will kill all caterpillars that eat it. Be careful when you use Bt in your yard and garden. If you spray it specifically on a plant that needs it, you will probably not cause harm to butterflies found elsewhere in the yard.

> A collar made of a cardboard paper towel roll cut into three lengths will frustrate cutworms. Cut the collar down the side and push it down into the ground 1 inch deep.

Plants Fighting Plants: Pesticides Derived From Plants

There are many useful insecticides that are derived from plants themselves. Pyrethrins (not be confused with synthetic pyrethroids) are derived from the flowers and seedheads of the pyrethrum daisy. Pyrethrin insecticides work by direct contact with an insect so it is essential that the "chemicals" have direct contact with the pest. Apply pyrethrins when the temperatures are at the lowest of the day and spray at two-hour intervals. Once the spray has been applied wait two hours (to give the insect time to come out of hiding) and spray again for the best control.

Rotenone is another good natural-control material. It is derived from the root of a legume (Lonchocarpus) found in South America. It is a broad-spectrum, slow-acting material that paralyzes insects. It works very well on the flea beetle, potato beetle, aphid, cucumber beetle, spider mite, whitefly, and other chewing insects.

Of all the insecticides derived from plants, Neem is the newest member in the arsenal. This broad-spectrum insecticide comes from the seeds of the Neem tree, which is native to India. Depending on the insect, Neem can act as a repellent, a growth inhibitor, or it can even paralyze some bugs. It controls a wide range of insects including, but not limited to, the Colorado potato beetle, aphid, flea beetle, whitefly, two-spotted spider mite, striped cucumber beetle, and even some nematodes.

Chemical Controls

Despite our best efforts, there may come a time when biological and manual pest controls don't work. Let's face it, given that we live in Florida Bug Central, sometimes the bugs invade in such force that we have to use the method of last resort—chemical controls. When that happens we must select chemicals that don't harm insects other than those we are trying to control. Also, we must only use those that won't have a long-lasting effect, won't build up in the environment, and will stay out of the food chain.

One chemical control is horticultural oils; they work by covering an insect pest with a fine film of highly refined oil, which suffocates it. Oils have to be used carefully in Florida; generally they are used only when the daytime temperatures are below 85°F. Otherwise, the oils cover up the breathing apparatus on the undersides of leaves and the leaves can suffocate, causing leaf burn or total leaf drop. Horticultural oils are generally used in winter, just before the new growth begins to emerge on trees and shrubs. When applied properly and in adequate volume, horticultural oils flow into every nook and cranny of the bark where eggs of insects and spider mites overwinter. Volck oil is an example of highly refined horticultural oil.

Insecticidal soaps work very well to control a wide range of insects. Both commercial forms of horticultural soaps and concoctions made from Ivory soap are equally toxic to pests. Both utilize the salts of fatty acids to interfere with an insect's growth cycle or to paralyze them on contact. Beetles are less susceptible to insecticidal soaps, meaning they can be used when ladybugs are present (although the soap is lethal to ladybug larvae). Be careful using these around beans, Chinese cabbage, young peas, and cucumbers; these vegetables can be harmed by insecticidal soaps.

Most chemicals need to be applied using some sort of equipment. If your garden isn't too large, mainly in containers for instance, use premixed chemicals that come in a one-quart spray bottle. Dusts such as Dipel® or rotenone often come in shaker cans and additional tools aren't needed. It's when you need to spray to the top of a fruit tree or spray many plants that some sort of equipment is needed. The most common is a hose end sprayer. The best type is the kind to which a chemical is added to the spray bottle beneath the hose connection. With this type, the dial at the top allows you to spray the chemical at the recommended dilution rate on the label. Here's how to do it: Pour the concentrate into the sprayer bottle, set the dial to the proper amount, and spray as directed. These sprayers usually have a fine spray for spraying at close range for foliage and a removable tip that allows you to spray to the top of small trees. The fine tip can also be rotated to let you direct the spray beneath leaf surfaces where bugs often hide. Leftover concentrate can be put back into the chemical bottle. Hose end sprayers are used when spraying large areas. One primary disadvantage of hose end sprayers is that some of the chemical may drift onto other plants simply due to the sheer volume of water being applied.

If you need more specific application of a chemical, a pump sprayer may be the best method. The inexpensive one-quart sprayer works well if you only have a few plants. But if you have more plants, then larger sized sprayers come with 1- to 3-gallon-sized steel or plastic bottles with a pump handle at the top and a spray wand. Here's how it works: Water is added to the bottle, and the chemical is added to the water. The pump handle, which screws into the top of the bottle, is pumped up and down to create pressure. The spray wand handle has a trigger, and when the trigger is pulled the chemical is dispersed. The spray wand tip can be adjusted to provide a fine or coarse spray depending on your objective. Fine sprays use less chemical but the chemical also has the tendency to drift. A coarse spray uses more chemical mix but because the droplets are larger, they tend to stay where you want them to without drifting. Try to buy one with a plastic bottle rather than a steel bottle; no matter how carefully you rinse, eventually the steel bottle will rust. There is nothing more aggravating than trying to remove rust particles from a sprayer tip when you are trying to work.

To deter aphids on squash (which can lead to mosaic on the leaves), place aluminum foil over the mulch underneath the leaves. The aphids don't like the shiny reflection and will go elsewhere to eat.

Other Controls

When our children were little we would give them a nickel for every tomato hornworm they could find. (Some met their demise under the wheels of the "Big Wheel.") Handpicking insects from plants is the easiest, and perhaps the most therapeutic, method to rid the garden of insect pests. When webworms make their nests in fruit trees, simply saw the tip of the branch off with the "tent" and throw it in the trash. Slugs are another satisfying victim. Slugs eat virtually *everything*, but they can be trapped by placing a 1- x 6-inch board on the ground of a slug-infested zone and leaving it overnight. Slugs come out only at night and before daytime comes around they will hide under the board. They can then be removed from underneath the board and thrown away. (Keep reading for more about slugs.)

When a plant produces new growth, the tender shoots are prime targets for the piercing mouthparts of aphids. Rather than spraying some sort of chemical, a sturdy stream of water is the best solution. The aphids will fall to ground and not return. Likewise, a hard stream of water applied to the undersides of leaves infested with spider mites in three- or four-day intervals will do a good job, too.

A variety of barriers will lessen if not eliminate pests. A synthetic row cover will keep birds away from vegetables and berries. Fine netting placed over vining berries and fruit-laden trees will protect the fruit from harm. A collar made from a paper towel roll and slipped over a young seedling will prevent cutworm damage. Dusts that dehydrate harmful insects will protect plants, too. Although somewhat limiting around vegetables because it disappears after irrigation or rain, diatomaceous earth added to a little liquid soap and spread around the trunk of a fruit tree will discourage pests from climbing the tree trunk.

If you're not a beer drinker, then dissolve 1 teaspoon of dried yeast in three tablespoons of water and place in the slug trap instead of beer. It will kill the slugs, all the same.

In addition to insects, slugs are tough and sneaky pests that eat both leaves and fruit. There are a number of chemicals available to kill them but the best deterrent is a slug trap. Slugs love beer of any kind, and if they happen upon a small container of beer during the night, well, they can't help themselves. Provided the trap is readily accessible (a pot pie tin works well and the tin has to be flush with the soil level) they mosey on in and drown. In the morning, check the trap for dead slugs. It won't take long to rid the garden of the nasty critters. Commercially available traps with covers that prevent the dilution of the beer from irrigation water work very well and may be worth the investment (see www .kinsmancompany.com).

NECTAR PLANTS THAT ATTRACT BENEFICIAL INSECTS

Plant	Beneficial Insect
Aster	Honeybees, green bees
Catnip	Honeybees, parasitic wasps
Cilantro	Honeybees
Cosmos	Honeybees
Dill	Aphid predators
Fennel	Hover flies
Goldenrod	Honeybees, spiders, aphid predators
Lavender	Honeybees
Marigold	Hover flies
Penta	Honeybees
Rudbeckia	Honeybees, spiders, aphid predators
Sage	Honeybees, Lace bug
Salvia	Dragonflies
Thyme	Honeybees

VEGETABLE INSECT CHART

Vegetable	Insect Name	Control	Additional Information
Bean	Aphid	Neem, insecticidal soap, malathion	Wash insects off with a strong stream of water.
	Corn ear worm	carbaryl, spinosad, Bt, Neem	
	Mexican bean beetle, bean leaf beetle, flea beetle, cucumber beetle	carbaryl, Neem	Crops mulched with straw or other organic materials appear to suffer less damage.
	Potato leaf hopper, stink bug	malathion	
	Spider mite	Neem, malathion, insecticidal soap	Wash mites off the bottoms of leaves with a strong stream of water; keep plants well watered.
	Whitefly	insecticidal soap	
Beet	Flea beetle, blister beetle	carbaryl	Time the last spray 14 days before eating if the tops are used; 3 days, if roots re used. Crops mulched with straw or other organic materials appear to suffer less damage.
Broccoli, Cauliflower, Brussels sprouts	Aphid and flea beetle	malathion, insecticidal soap	
	Cabbage looper, imported cabbageworm	Bt, spinosad, esfenvalerate	
	Harlequin Bug	malathion	
Cabbage	Aphid	malathion, insecticidal soap, Neem, rotenone, spinosad, Bt	
	Cabbage looper, imported cabbageworm, cutworm	Bt, carbaryl, spinosad, esfenvalerate, lambda-cyhalothrin	Purchase only clean transplants, and practice weed control in nearby fields that act as an overwintering sites for the imported cabbageworm. After harvesting early-season crops, crop debris should be tilled into the soil to destroy larvae and pupae that could lead to higher populations on later crops.
	Flea beetle, blister beetle	carbaryl, malathion, rotenone, spinosad, Neem, capsaicin	Crops mulched with straw or other organic materials appear to suffer less damage.
	Harlequin bug	malathion, lambda-cyhalothrin	

VEGETABLE INSECT CHART

Vegetable	Insect Name	Control	Additional Information
Cantaloupe	Aphid and thrips	malathion, insecticidal soap	
	Cucumber beetle (striped and spotted), squash bug, squash vine borer	esfenvalerate	Reflective mulches may help to repel aphids while also providing horticultural benefits. Use varieties that are less attractive to beetles or less susceptible to bacterial wilt. Crop rotation and sanitation are important. Avoid leaving cucurbit crop debris available for overwintering sites.
	Spider mites	Neem, insecticidal soap	
Carrot	Armyworm, leafminer, and leafhopper	Bt, carbaryl, cyfluthrin	Bt will not control leafhoppers.
Collards	Aphid and flea beetle	malathion, insecticidal soap	
	Cabbage looper, imported cabbageworm, cutworm	Bt, spinosad	
	Harlequin bug	malathion	
Corn, sweet	Aphid	insecticidal soap	Avoid rotenone, pyrethrum, or other broad-spectrum insecticides in corn. If an aphid outbreak occurs, insecticidal soaps can be used.
	Corn earworm, flea beetle	esfenvalerate	
	Corn earworm, European corn borer, fall armyworm	Bt, cyfluthrin, esfenvalerate, lambda-cyhalothrin, permethrin, spinosad	Practice weed control in nearby fields that act as an overwintering site for the imported cabbageworm. After harvesting early-season crops, the crop debris should be tilled into the soil to destroy larvae and pupae that could lead to higher populations on later crops.
Cucumber	Cucumber beetle (striped and spotted), squash bug	esfenvalerate,	Reflective mulches may help to repel insects while also providing horticultural benefits. Use varieties that are less attractive to the beetles or less susceptible to bacterial wilt. Crop rotation and sanitation are important. Avoid leaving cucurbit crop debris available for overwintering sites.
	Spider mite	insecticidal soap	
	Whitefly	insecticidal soap	

VEGETABLE INSECT CHART

Vegetable	Insect Name	Control	Additional Information
Eggplant	Aphid	malathion, insecticidal soap	
	Colorado potato beetle, hornworm, and corn earworm	Bt, carbaryl, spinosad, Neem	Crop rotation out of susceptible crops is the first line of defense. Mulch crops with straw or hay before adults arrive.
	Flea beetle, blister beetle	carbaryl, malathion	
	Lace bug, spider mite, white fly	malathion, insecticidal soap	
Endive	Aphid	Malathion, insecticidal soap	
	Cabbage looper, corn earworm	Bt, spinosad	Purchase only clean transplants. Practice weed control in nearby fields that act as an overwintering sites for the imported cabbageworm. After harvesting early-season crops, till crop debris into the soil to destroy larvae and pupae that could lead to higher populations on later crops.
Garlic	Onion thrips		Keep areas surrounding garden free of weeds. Release lady beetles.
	Onion maggot		Spread liberal amounts of wood ash in furrows prior to planting.
Leek	Onion thrips		Keep weedy areas surrounding garden free of weeds. Release lady beetles.
	Onion maggot		Spread liberal amounts of wood ash in furrows prior to planting.
Lettuce	Aphid	malathion, insecticidal soap	
	Cabbage looper, corn earworm	Bt, spinosad	Purchase only clean transplants, and practice weed control in nearby fields that act as an overwintering site for the imported cabbageworm. After harvesting early-season crops, the crop debris should be tilled into the soil to destroy larvae and pupae that could lead to higher populations on later crops.
	Leafhopper	malathion	
Mustard Greens	Aphid, flea beetle	malathion, insecticidal soap	
	Cabbage looper, imported cabbageworm	Bt, spinosad	Purchase only clean transplants, and control weeds in nearby fields that act as an overwintering site for the imported cabbageworm. After harvesting early-season crops, the crop debris should be tilled into the soil to destroy larvae and pupae that could lead to higher populations on later crops.

VEGETABLE INSECT CHART

Vegetable	Insect Name	Control	Additional Information
Okra	Corn earworm, European corn borer, flea beetle, stink bug	carbaryl	Control weeds in nearby fields that act as an overwintering site for the imported cabbageworm. After harvesting early-season crops, the crop debris should be tilled into the soil to destroy larvae and pupae that could lead to higher populations on later crops.
	Stink bug	malathion	
Onion	Onion thrips		Keep weedy areas surrounding garden free of weeds. Release lady beetles.
	Onion maggot		Spread liberal amounts of wood ash in furrows prior to planting.
Parsley	Aphid	insectcidal soap	Parsley is a host plant for swallowtail buterflies. Their larvae may eat a few leaves but there is usually enough for both of you to eat.
Peas	Aphid	insecticidal soap	
	Cowpea curculio	endosulfan	
Pepper	Aphid	esfenvalerate, malathion, insecticidal soap	
	European corn borer, flea beetle, tomato fruitworm, hornworm, stink bug	carbaryl, cyfluthrin, esfenvalerate, permethrin, spinosad	Purchase only clean transplants, and control weeds in nearby fields that act as an overwintering site for the imported cabbageworm. After harvesting early-season crops, the crop debris should be tilled into the soil to destroy larvae and pupae that could lead to higher populations on later crops. Crops mulched with straw or other organic materials appear to suffer less damage.
Potato	Aphid	malathion	
	European corn borer	carbaryl, esfenvalerate	Purchase only certified seed potatoes. Control weeds in nearby fields that act as an overwintering site for the imported cabbageworm. After harvesting early-season crops, the crop debris should be tilled into the soil to destroy larvae and pupae that could lead to higher populations on later crops.
	Potato leafhopper, potato flea beetle, Colorado potato beetle, blister beetle, stink bug	carbaryl, Neem	Crops mulched with straw or other organic materials appear to suffer less damage. Crop rotation out of susceptible crops is the first line of defense. Mulch crops with straw or hay before adults arrive.
	Potato tuberworm	Bt, carbaryl, esfenvalerate	

VEGETABLE INSECT CHART

Vegetable	Insect Name	Control	Additional Information
Pumpkin	Aphid	insecticidal soap	
	Cucumber beetle (striped and spotted), flea beetle, leafhopper	insecticidal soap, esfenvalerate	Crops mulched with straw or other organic materials appear to suffer less damage; reflective mulches may help to repel aphids while also providing horticultural benefits.
	Squash bug	Malathion	
	Squash vine borer		Winter squash and zucchini are particularly susceptible. Butternut squash (*C. moschata*) is resistant. Soon after the crop is harvested, plow the vine debris deeply to bury over larvae. Rotate fields.
Radish	Flea beetle, imported cabbageworm	cyfluthrin	
Rutabaga	Aphid, flea beetle	insecticidal soap	Crops mulched with straw or other organic materials appear to suffer less damage.
	Cabbage looper, imported cabbageworm	Bt, spinosad	
	Harlequin bug	Malathion	
Spinach	Aphids, leafminer	insecticidal soap	
	Corn earworm and loopers	Bt, spinosad	
Squash, Pumpkin	Aphid	insecticidal soap	
	Cucumber beetle (striped and spotted), flea beetle, leafhopper	insecticidal soap, esfenvalerate	Crops mulched with straw or other organic materials appear to suffer less damage. Reflective mulches may help to repel aphids while also providing horticultural benefits.
	Squash bug	malathion	
	Squash Vine Borer		Winter squash, pumpkin, and zucchini are particularly susceptible. Butternut squash (*C. moschata*) is resistant. Soon after crop harvest, plow the vine debris deeply to bury over larvae. Rotate fields.
Tomato	Aphid	malathion, insecticidal soap	
	Cutworm	esfenvalerate	
	Flea beetle, Colorado potato beetle	carbaryl, spinosad	Crops mulched with straw or other organic materials appear to suffer less damage. Crop rotation out of susceptible crops is the first line of defense. Mulch crops with straw or hay before adults arrive.

VEGETABLE INSECT CHART

Vegetable	Insect Name	Control	Additional Information
Tomato (con't)	Spider mite	insecticidal soap, malathion	
	Stink bug	cyfluthrin, lambda-cyhalothrin, malathion, permethrin	
	Thrips	insecticidal soap	
	Tomato fruitworm, cabbage looper, tobacco hornworm	Bt, carbaryl, cyfluthrin, esfenvalerate, lambda-cyhalothrin, permethrin, spinosad	Purchase only clean transplants, and control weeds in nearby fields that act as an overwintering site for the imported cabbageworm. After harvesting early-season crops, the crop debris should be tilled into the soil to destroy larvae and pupae that could lead to higher populations on later crops.
	Whitefly	malathion, pyrethrum, insecticidal soap	
Turnip	Aphid, flea beetle	insecticidal soap	Crops mulched with straw or other organic materials appear to suffer less damage.
	Cabbage looper, imported cabbageworm	Bt, spinosad	
	Harlequin bug	malathion	
Watermelon	Aphid	insecticidal soap	Reflective mulches may help to repel aphids while also providing horticultural benefits.
	Cucumber beetle (spotted and striped)	esfenvalerate, malathion, insecticidal soap	Reflective mulches may help to repel aphids while also providing horticultural benefits. Use varieties that are less attractive to the beetles or less susceptible to bacterial wilt. Crop rotation and sanitation are important. Avoid leaving cucurbit crop debris available for overwintering sites.
	Spider mite	insecticidal soap	
	Thrips	carbaryl, malathion, insecticidal soap	

Disclaimer: Mention or exclusion of any product is not intended to discriminate for or against any products. No endorsement is intended for the products mentioned, nor is criticism meant for products not mentioned. Please read labels before purchasing and then read them before using to ensure that target sites are properly listed.

FRUIT INSECT CHART

Fruit	Pest	Control Methods
Avocado	Lace bug	Citrus oil, insecticidal soap
Banana	Nematodes	Maintain a high level of organic matter in the soil.
Blackberry	Aphids	Carbaryl, pyrethrin, Rotenone
	Flea beetles	Rotenone
	Leaf hoppers	Malathion, pyrethrin
	Leafminers	Rotenone
	Leaf rollers	Carbaryl
	Mites	Malathion, pyrethrin
	Crown borers	Carbaryl
	Red spider mites	Insecticidal soap
	Thrips	Pyrethrin, Malathion
Blueberry	Blueberry maggot	Carbaryl, Malathion
	Obliqued-banded leaf roller	Bt
	Ants	Spinosad
Carambola	Scale	Horticultural oil
	Aphids	Horticultural oil
	Mites	Horticultural oil, Spinosad
Citrus	Rust mites, broad mites	Sulfur
	Plant bugs	Malathion
	Flower thrips	Spinosad
	Scale	Horticultural oil
	Orangedog	Bt, carbaryl
Fig	None of note	
Grape	Grape leaf skeletonizer	Bt, carbaryl
	Grape leaf folder	Bt, carbaryl
	Grape leaf roller	Bt, carbaryl, pyrethrin
	Leaf hopper	Malathion
	Aphids	Neem oil
	Mites	Neem oil, Spinosad
	Spider mites	Neem oil
	Red spider mite	Sulfur
Jaboticaba	None of note	
Jackfruit	Borers	Remove dead branches, where they lay eggs
	Scale	Horticultural oil
	Mealy bugs	Neem oil, horticultural oil

FRUIT INSECT CHART

Fruit	Pest	Control Methods
Longan	Scale	Insectcidal soap, horticultural oil
	Webworms	Bt
Loquat	Caterpillars	Bt
Lychee	Scale	Insecticidal soap, horticultural oil
	Webworms	Bt
Mango	Thrips	Imidacloprid
	Whitefly	Imidacloprid
	Caterpillars	Bt
Papaya	Caterpillars	Bt
	Scale	Malathion, horticultural oil
	Thrips	Malathion, horticultural oil
Passion Fruit	None of note	
Peach	Scale	Horticultural oil, insecticidal soap
Nectarine	Mealy bugs	Horticultural oil, insecticidal soap
Plum	Caterpillars	Bt
	Borers	Carbaryl, Lorsban Endosulfan, Thiodan
	Plum curculio	Imidan
	Scale	Imidan, horticultural oil, insecticidal soap
Pear	Scale	Insecticidal soap, horticultural oil, Neem oil
Pecan	Hickory leaf stem gall	Carbaryl, imidacloprid
	Casebearers	Carbaryl, imidacloprid
	Aphids	Insectcidal soap, horticultural oil
	Pecan weevil	Carbaryl, imidacloprid
Persimmon	Aphids	Insecticidal soap
	Caterpillars	Bt
	Mites	Rotenone, pyrethrin, Spinosad
	Scale	Insectcidal soap
	Thrips	Rotenone, pyrethrin
Pineapple	None of note	
Pomegranate	None of note	
Strawberry	Two-spotted spider mite	Spinosad
	Caterpillars	Bt

Disclaimer: Mention or exclusion of any product is not intended to discriminate for or against any products. No endorsement is intended for the products mentioned, nor is criticism meant for products not mentioned. Please read labels before purchasing and then read them before using to ensure that target sites are properly listed.

DISEASES

Most plant diseases, like animal diseases, are caused by microscopic bacteria and viruses. They are everywhere and the goal of the gardener is prevent their spread and keep them from becoming more active. Diseases are spread a number of ways. Some transmission methods are by insects carrying disease organisms around on their bodies, or by gardeners handling plants and working in the garden when the plants are wet. Some diseases attack the stem, harming a plant's vascular system. Others affect the leaves and even the roots.

Have you heard this expression: "An ounce of prevention is worth a pound of cure." I have rarely seen a *healthy* vegetable or fruit tree attacked by disease. Plants, like people, have the ability to fend off diseases if they are supplied adequate sunshine, water, and nutrition. There are a number of things you can do to prevent diseases in vegetables and fruit trees, such as:

> - Control the insect population. Insects carry diseases around with them and infest plants as they travel.
> - Good air circulation can help prevent many diseases. Planting plants close together will certainly maximize the yield but at the expense of the plant's health.
> - Fruit trees and vegetables need at least 8 hours of full sun. Anything less and a plant will be stressed, making it a prime candidate for disease infestation.
> - Make certain the soil is well drained. If the spot where you planted the garden is soggy, move the garden to a different spot or create a raised bed to provide good drainage.
> - Touch the plants as little as possible. It's not just the bugs that carry diseases with them; gardeners carry plant diseases around with them, too. The more you handle the plants, the greater the chances that you will infect them with something. Never, ever till, harvest, or pull weeds when plants are wet. Your hands and clothing may become infected and wet plants are more susceptible to diseases than dry plants.

> Water plants only when they have a chance to dry off quickly. Watering in the late afternoon or at night creates perfect conditions for pathogens to grow.

> Keep plants well fed. The amounts of fertilizer and the timing of the applications are described in the individual plant profiles.

> Do a little research to find those selections of vegetables and fruit trees that have a proven track record of disease resistance in your area.

> Crop rotation will help prevent the buildup of disease-causing organisms in the soil. Some disease-causing organisms affect one vegetable or group of vegetables, but they may not affect another. Even several vegetables of the same family, such as squash, cucumber, and cantaloupe, may be affected by the same disease. Therefore, it is not a good practice to grow plants in the same family in the same place in the garden year after year. The table gives crop groupings for rotation to control soil-borne diseases.

Group 1	Group 2	Group 3	Group 4	Group 5	Group 6
Cantaloupe	Brussels	Beet	Sweet corn	Bean	Eggplant
Cucumber	sprouts	Carrot		Cowpea	Tomato
Honeydew	Collards	Garlic		Pea	Okra
melon	Cabbage	Shallot			Pepper
Pumpkin	Cauliflower	Onion			Tomato
Squash	Lettuce	Sweet potato			
Watermelon	Mustard				
	Radish				
	Rutabaga				
	Swiss chard				
	Spinach				
	Turnip				

VEGETABLE DISEASE CHART

Vegetable	Disease Name	Description	Control	Additional Information
Bean, Snap	Anthracnose	Brown spots on leaves with pink ooze	*B.s.*, Daconil, copper sulfate	Destroy infected plants. Do not plant beans in the same location for three years. Spray at weekly intervals, and do not work in garden while it's wet.
	Bacterial blight	Water-soaked spots on leaves and pods with red margin	*B.s.*, Fixed copper	Same as Anthracnose.
	Gray mold (Botrytis)	Gray, fuzzy mold on leaves and pods	*B.s.*, Daconil	Begin spraying at 25-50 percent bloom in wet weather.
	Mosaic virus	Leaves yellow, with or without yellowing. Leaves cupped.		Remove diseased plants and replant elsewhere.
	Powdery mildew	White, powdery mold on leaves	*B.s.*, Sulfur	Plant in the garden after nighttime temperatures remain above 70°F. Water when plants have a chance to dry off before nighttime.
	Rust	Reddish brown pustules on leaves	*B.s.*, Daconil	Do not work among plants when they are wet.
Beet	Downy mildew	Various leaf spots	*B.s.*, Fixed copper	Spray every 7 days.
	Rust	Orange pustules	*B.s.*, Sulfur	
Broccoli	See Cabbage			
Brussels sprouts	See Cabbage			
Cabbage, Rutabaga	Alternaria leaf spot	Target spots in older leaves	Daconil, Maneb	Begin spraying when the disease is first seen and continue every 10 days until it's under control.
	Downy mildew	Yellowing on upper leaf surface, downy growth on lower leaf surface	*B.s.*, Daconil, Maneb	
	Bacterial soft rot	Soft, watery rot occurs, favored by hot, wet conditions; begin in center of broccoli or cabbage head	*B.s.*	Only water the soil (when possible); otherwise, prevent overwatering from overhead irrigation. Remove the central head to encourage side shoots from below.
Cantaloupe	Alternaria leaf spot	Tan spots on leaves	Daconil, Maneb, Mancozeb	Begin spraying when the disease is first seen, and continue at 7- to 10-day intervals until it's under control.
	Anthracnose	Sunken spots on fruit and tan spots on leaves	*B.s.*, Daconil, Maneb, Mancozeb	Begin spraying when the disease is first seen, and continue at 7- to 10-day intervals until it's under control.

B.s. = QST 13 strain of *Bacillus subtillis* (Natria Disease Control)

VEGETABLE DISEASE CHART

Vegetable	Disease Name	Description	Control	Additional Information
Cantaloupe (cont.)	Downy mildew	Yellow, irregular spots on leaves	B.s., Daconil, Maneb, Mancozeb	Begin spraying when the disease is first seen, and continue at 7- to 10-day intervals until it's under control.
	Bacterial wilt	Runners suddenly wilt and die	B.s., Rotenone	Apply insecticide at regular intervals to control cucumber beetles that spread disease.
	Powdery mildew	White, powdery mold on leaves	B.s., Sulfur	Apply at 10- to 14-day intervals. Do not apply when temperatures exceed 90°F.
Carrot	Alternaria blight	Numerous dark-brown spots on leaves	Daconil	Apply at 7- to 10-day intervals until it's under control.
	Cercospera leaf spot	Numerous back-to-brown spots on leaves	Daconil	
	Southern blight	White mycelial at plant top, eventual death of plant	Fixed copper, Maneb	Do not plant carrots in the same location every season.
Cauliflower	See Cabbage			
Collards, Kale, Mustard, & Turnip	Alternaria leaf spot	Brown target spots on leaves	Fixed copper, Maneb	Maintain thinned plant stand. Avoid low lying or poorly drained soils. Avoid the hot part of the growing season. Use Maneb for kale only. Begin spraying when the disease is first noticed, and repeat at 7- to 10-day intervals. Use a spreader-sticker for better fungicide coverage.
	Anthracnose	Small spots with dark-brown margins	B.s., Fixed copper, Maneb	
	Cercospera leaf spot	Tan spots with yellow halos on leaves	Fixed copper, Maneb	
	Downy mildew	Yellow spots on upper surfaces of leaves with white, downy growth on the undersides	B.s., Fixed copper, Maneb	
Corn, Sweet	Blights	Spots on leaves and drying or blighting of leaves	B.s., Daconil, Mancozeb	Apply at 7-day intervals when the disease is first seen.
	Maize dwarf mosaic	Alternating light and dark streaks on leaves; plants are stunted		Plant early in the season where Johnson grass is not growing. 'Silver Queen' is tolerant of this disease.
	Rust	Bronze elongated spots	B.s., Daconil, Mancozeb	Apply at 7-day intervals when the disease is first seen.
Cucumber	Downy mildew	Yellow, irregular spots on leaves	B.s., Daconil, Maneb, Mancozeb	Apply at 7-day intervals when the disease is first seen.
	Gummy stem blight	Dark brown spots on leaves, cracks on stems that ooze	Daconil, Maneb, Mancozeb	Apply at 7-day intervals when the disease is first seen.

B.s. = QST 13 strain of *Bacillus subtillis* (Natria Disease Control)

VEGETABLE DISEASE CHART

Vegetable	Disease Name	Description	Control	Additional Information
Cucumber (cont.)	Bacterial wilt	Runners turn brown and entire plant eventually dies.	*B.s.*, Rotenone	Apply an insecticide to control the cucumber beetle, which transmits the bacterium
	Powdery mildew	White powdery mold on upper leaf surfaces	*B.s.*, Sulfur	Apply at 7- to 10-day intervals. Do not apply when temperatures are above 90°F.
	Scab	Sunken spots on fruit	*B.s.*, Daconil	Plant resistant varieties. Apply at the first sign of the disease in 7- to 10-day intervals.
Eggplant	Leaf spots and fruit rots	Spots develop on fruits and leaves	*B.s.*, Daconil	Apply at 7- to 10-day intervals when the disease is first seen.
Kale	See Collards			
Lettuce, Endive	Bottom rot	Sunken, reddish-brown spots on leaves that are touching the soil		Apply straw to keep leaves off soil. Thin plants to recommended spacing to increase air circulation.
	Fusarium wilt	Seedlings wilt and die; mature plants exhibit tipburn, a yellowing of leaves; infected plants may be stunted		Remove diseased plants. Do not replant lettuce in the same location for at least two years.
	Leaf drop	Soft, watery decay of plant tissue		Avoid excess irrigation.
Mustard	See Collards			
Okra	Verticillium wilt	Yellow leaves; inside stem is discolored brown		Rotate crops every year.
Onion, Leek, Garlic	Downy mildew	Pale-green or purple spots on leaves	*B.s.*, Daconil, Maneb, Mancozeb	Apply when the disease first appears and repeat at 7- to 10-day intervals. Do not apply Mancozeb or Maneb to exposed bulbs. Do not apply Chlorothalonil within 7 days of harvest on dry-bulb onions or within 14 days on green onions, leeks, or shallots. Do not apply Chlorothalonil to sweet Spanish onions.
	Leaf blast (Botrytis)	White to tan streaks on leaves; leaves eventually die	*B.s.*, Daconil, Maneb, Mancozeb	Same as Downy Mildew.
	Purple blotch (Alternaria)	Purple target spots on leaves	Daconil, Maneb, Mancozeb	Same as Downy Mildew.

B.s. = QST 13 strain of *Bacillus subtillis* (Natria Disease Control)

VEGETABLE DISEASE CHART

Vegetable	Disease Name	Description	Control	Additional Information
Peas, Southern	Cercospera leaf spot	Light- to dark-brown leaf spots on leaves	Daconil	Apply at pre-bloom and at 7-day intervals.
	Rust	Brown to rust colored spots on leaves that rub off on fingers		
	Mosaic virus	Alternating light- and dark-green areas on leaves		Plant resistant varieties.
	Powdery mildew	White, powdery mold on upper leaf surfaces	Sulfur	Apply at 7- to 10-day intervals when the disease is first seen.
Pepper	Bacterial leaf spot	Black, angular spots appear on leaves and fruits; plants drop affected leaves	Fixed Copper, Maneb	Buy disease-free plants. Fixed copper will prevent spread of the disease.
	Blossom end rot	Tan, sunken areas on the bottoms and sides of fruit		Maintain adequate and consistent soil moisture.
	Cercospera leaf spot	Circular spots with gray centers on leaves	Fixed copper, Maneb	Apply at 7- to 10- day intervals when the disease is first seen.
	Anthracnose	Sunken spots on ripening fruit	Fixed copper, Maneb	Apply at 7- to 10-day intervals when the disease is first seen.
	Phytophthora	Rapid wilt and death of plant in wet areas		Plant in drier location or plant in raised beds.
	Sunscald	White, sunken areas on fruit		Healthy plants rarely get sunscald. When bacterial blight occurs and the leaves drop as a result, the fruits often get sunscald.
Potato	Scab	Brown, scruffy areas on tuber		Use disease-free seed and rotate crops.
	Seed piece decay	Seed piece decays after planting	Maneb, Mancozeb	Dust seed pieces with dust. Plant two to three days later. Allow scabs to dry before planting. Do not use treated seed pieces for food.
	Ring rot	Brown discoloration of vascular tissue of tuber		Use disease-free seed potatoes and practice crop rotation.
	Virus diseases	Curled, discolored leaves; plants may be stunted		Use disease-free seed potatoes and practice crop rotation.
Pumpkin	Gummy stem blight	Cracked, oozing stems and black ,circular spots on fruit	Daconil, Maneb	Begin spraying when the disease is first seen.
	Downy mildew	Yellow, irregular spots on leaves		Begin spraying when the disease is first seen.
	Michrodochium blight	White streaks on stems		Begin spraying when the disease is first seen.
	Scab	Sunken or raised spots on fruit		Begin spraying when the disease is first seen. Use higher rates for scab control.
	Mosaic virus	Discolored green patterns on fruit		Control is difficult. Control aphids that spread disease, use reflective mulches, and control weeds that harbor insects that carry the disease.

VEGETABLE DISEASE CHART

Vegetable	Disease Name	Description	Control	Additional Information
Rutabaga (see Cabbage)				
Spinach	Downy mildew (blue mold)	Yellow spots on leaf surfaces; gray downy mildew on undersides	*B.s.*, Basic copper sulphate	Start fungicide applications after the first sign of the disease and apply at 7- to 10-day intervals.
	White rust	Yellow spots on upper leaf surfaces and white mildew on the undersides	*B.s.*, Basic copper sulfate	Start fungicide applications after the first sign of the disease and apply at 7- to 10-day intervals.
Squash	Downy mildew	Yellow, irregular spots on leaves	*B.s.*, Daconil, Maneb, Mancozeb	Begin spraying at the first sign of disease. See label directions for spray intervals.
	Powdery mildew	White powdery mold on upper leaf surface	*B.s.*, Sulfur	Begin spray regimen at the first sign of disease. Do not apply sulfur when temperatures exceed 90°F.
	Scab	Sunken or raised spots on fruits	*B.s.*, Daconil	Begin spraying at the first sign of disease. See label directions for spray intervals.
	Blossom blight	Blossom rots and sticks to the end of young fruit; the ends of fruit often turn black		Provide good air circulation.
	Mosaic virus	Greening of fruit; leaves mottled and stunted		Difficult to control. Try controlling aphids that spread the disease, and use reflective mulches.
Sweet Potato	Black rot	Sunken black spots on surface that extends into the flesh of the root		Use certified seed and practice crop rotation.
	Scurf	Brownish-black discoloration on the surface of roots		Use certified seed.
	Cork	Small, black, corky spot in the flesh of the potato		Use certified seed.
	Soil rot	Circular sunken areas on the root; feeder roots are black		Maintain soil pH of 5.8–6.4 or less in infected areas.
	Stem rot	Leaves are yellow; stunted interior of plant is brown		Select disease-free seed.
Tomato	Bacterial spot	Small raised spots on fruit; water-soaked spots on foliage	*B.s.*, Fixed Copper, Maneb, Mancozeb	
	Blossom end rot	Sunken black area at bottoms of fruit		Maintain consistent, adequate soil moisture.
	Early blight	Brown target spots on leaves	*B.s.*, Daconil, Maneb, Mancozeb	Begin preventative spraying as soon as the plants are established. Spray at 10- to 14-day intervals.

B.s. = QST 13 strain of *Bacillus subtillis* (Natria Disease Control)

VEGETABLE DISEASE CHART

Vegetable	Disease Name	Description	Control	Additional Information
Tomato (cont.)	Anthracnose	Circular sunken spots on ripe fruit	*B.s.*, Daconil, Maneb, Mancozeb	Begin preventative spraying as soon as the plants are established in the garden. Spray at 10- to 14-day intervals.
	Septoria leaf spot	Small, circular leaf spots with gray borders	*B.s.*, Daconil, Maneb, Mancozeb	Begin preventative spraying as soon as the plants are established in the garden. Spray at 10- to 14-day intervals.
	Buckeye fruit rot	Large, circular spots on fruit, especially on the lower clusters		Stake plants to keep fruit off soil.
	Fusarium wilt	Yellowing and wilting of leaves; brown discoloration of inside of stems		Use resistant varieties.
	Gray mold (Botrytis)	Leaves turn brown from the tip back	*B.s.*, Daconil	Begin fungicide applications at the first sign of the disease.
	Late blight	Irregular water-soaked spots on leaves, especially in wet weather	Daconil, Maneb, Mancozeb	Begin preventative spraying as soon as the plants are established in the garden. Spray at 10- to 14-day intervals.
	Leaf mold	Yellow spots on upper surface; olive-green mold beneath	Daconil	Begin spraying with fungicides at the first sign of the disease.
	Pythium stem rot	Dark water rot of lower stem		Remove diseased plants.
	Verticillium wilt	Yellowing of leaves; brown discoloration inside stems		Use resistant varieties and practice crop rotation.
Turnip (see Collards)				
Watermelon	Alternaria leaf spot	Brown target spots on leaves	Daconil, Maneb, Mancozeb	Begin spraying at the first sign of the disease. See label for frequency of spray.
	Anthracnose	Brown, irregular spots on leaves; sunken spots on fruit	*B.s.*, Daconil, Maneb, Mancozeb	Begin spraying at the first sign of the disease. See label for frequency of spray.
	Cercospera leaf spot	Tiny dark-brown spots	Daconil, Maneb, Mancozeb	Begin spraying at the first sign of the disease. See label for frequency of spray.
	Downy mildew	Yellow, irregular spots on leaves	*B.s.*, Daconil, Maneb, Mancozeb	Begin spraying at the first sign of the disease. See label for frequency of spray.
	Gummy stem blight	Irregular spots; cracked stems that ooze	Daconil, Maneb, Mancozeb	Daconil
	Scab	Small, raised warts on fruit	*B.s.*, Daconil	Begin spraying at the first sign of the disease. See label directions for spray interval.
	Fusarium wilt	Yellowing and wilting of leaves; brown discoloration inside vine stems		Grow resistant varieties. Practice crop rotation.

B.s. = QST 13 strain of *Bacillus subtillis* (Natria Disease Control)

FRUIT DISEASE CHART

Fruit	Disease	Control Methods	Additional Information
Avocado	Scab	B.s., Copper sulfate	One spray should be applied at bud swell; the second during late bloom; and the third three weeks later
	Cercospora spot	B.s., Copper sulfate	Effectively control by timely applications of fungicide
	Anthracnose		Good anthracnose control depends on good control of Cercospora spot and avoiding cuts and bruises to the fruit
	Powdery mildew	B.s., Copper sulfate	If timely applications of fungicides are applied to control other common diseases, powdery mildew rarely exceeds threshold levels in the home garden
	Algal leaf spot	Copper sulfate	If timely applications of fungicides are applied to other common diseases, powdery mildew rarely exceeds threshold levels in the home garden
Banana	Panama disease		'Gros Michel', 'Apple', 'Oro Noco' are susceptible; replace with resistant cultivars 'Goldfinger' (FHIA 01), 'Mona Lisa' (FHIA 02), FHIA 18
	Black sigatoka		If 50 percent of leaf is diseased, remove entire leaf
Blackberry	Anthracnose	B.s., Fixed coppers	Plant certified, disease-free stock; prune old cane stubs after planting; prune old canes as close to the ground as soon after harvest as possible; thin weak canes; eliminate weeds to provide good air movement; avoid overhead irrigation or limit the time plants are wet from irrigation
	Leaf spot	B.s., Fixed coppers	Remove old fruiting canes after harvest; control weeds
	Crown Gall		Use certified nursery stock; inspect planting stock and do not plant new canes that show signs on canes, crowns, or roots; remove infected plants
	Rosette		Use certified nursery stock; plant disease-resistant varieties
	Orange rust	B.s.	Scout for the disease during summer and quickly remove and destroy infected plants; establish new plantings from a clean source
Blueberry	Phytothphora root rot	B.s.	Lasting control is accomplished by improving drainage
	Botrytis	B.s.	Less serious on rabbiteye varieties; flowers and flower buds should be kept as dry as possible; overhead irrigation should be avoided during bud swell and bloom; keep plants well pruned to improve air circulation
	Stem blight		Prune infected wood; remove flower buds and fruit from young plants; prune mature bushes to thin crop loads; minimize drought
	Mummy berry		Rake the soil or mulch layer beneath the plants as leaf buds swell; pick off and remove infected berries from the patch before harvest; pick up and throw away infected berries that fall to the ground

B.s. = QST 13 strain of *Bacillus subtillis* (Natria Disease Control)

FRUIT DISEASE CHART

Fruit	Disease	Control Methods	Additional Information
Carambola			No diseases that require control measures
Citrus	Greasy spot		Remove old and diseased leaves beneath tree
	Citrus scab	Copper	Lemons, Murcotts, Mineola tangelos, Temple and Page oranges are susceptible; apply copper sprays 2-3 weeks after petal fall, and again 2-3 weeks later; install drip irrigation to avoid overhead irrigation that spreads the disease
	Melanose	Copper	Remove small dead twigs; avoid overhead irrigation
	Foot rot		Remove mulch from around base of tree; remove low-hanging branches to improve air circulation
Fig	Rust	*B.s.*, Copper	Apply copper in May and June
Grape	Angular leaf spot	*B.s.*, Mancozeb	
	Black rot	Manzate, Maneb	
	Powdery mildew	*B.s.*, Sulfur	
	Bitter and black rot	Manzate, Maneb	Remove old fruits and leaves
Jaboticaba			No serious diseases that affect fruit quality
Jackfruit	Root rots		Avoid flooding
	Anthracnose	*B.s.*, Mancozeb	Prune/remove damaged limbs
	Phomopsis fruit rot		Careful handling will prevent this disease
	Phytothphora	*B.s.*	Do not plant in flood-prone sites; control weeds and cover soil with mulch; remove damaged stems
	Pink disease	Mancozeb	Remove damaged stems; encourage good air circulation
Longan	Anthracnose	*B.s.*, Copper	
	Algal spot	*B.s.*, Copper	
	Stem canker		Remove damaged wood
	Pink limb blight		Prune exposed wood
Loquat			No serious diseases
Lychee	Anthracnose	*B.s.*, Copper	
	Algal spot	Copper	
	Stem canker		Remove damaged wood
	Pink limb blight		Prune exposed wood
Mango	Anthracnose	*B.s.*, Copper sprays	Begin sprays when new growth flushes and continue until flowers open; begin again until fruits form
	Soft nose		Reduce nitrogen fertilizer applications
	Sunscald		Fruits burn in high temperatures; no cures

B.s. = QST 13 strain of *Bacillus subtillis* (Natria Disease Control)

FRUIT DISEASE CHART

Fruit	Disease	Control Methods	Additional Information
Papaya	Ring spot		No effective controls
	Necrosis		Remove affected plants; isolate papaya from other plants
	Anthracnose	B.s., Copper	Begin copper applications at fruit set
	Phytothphora	B.s., Copper	
	Corynespora leaf spot	Copper	
Passion Fruit	Grease spot		Remove diseased leaves beneath vines
	Brown spot		
	Septoria blotch		
	Bitter rot	Copper	Pick up and remove infected fruit
	Sclerotinia	B.s.	Pick up and remove infected fruit; cut out infected shoots below the lesion and destroy
Peach, Nectarine, Plum	Scab	B.s., Sulfur	Spray 4-6 weeks after full bloom
	Bacterial spot	B.s.	Not controlled by sprays, use resistant varieties; maintain good fertilizer program
	Brown rot		Prune dead wood; remove brown rot and mummies
	Rust	B.s., Copper	Not usually a problem
Pear	Black rot	Pyraclostrobin	Remove damaged/dead limbs
	Bot rot/white rot	Pyraclostrobin	Fruit should be picked up and removed from the orchard; cut out infected shoots below the lesion and destroy
	Cercospora spot		Remove infected fallen leaves
	Fireblight	B.s., Copper	Remove cankers during dormant period; prune active sores 8 in. below damage; disinfect pruners between cuts
	Flyspeck	Manzate, Mancozeb	
Pecan	Scab	B.s.	Pecans have several diseases but these rarely affect fruit production in home gardens; once trees are more than 15 ft. tall, chemical control is impractical; plant resistant varieties
Persimmon	Cercospora spot	Copper	Apply a fungicide cover spray during full bloom and again in 3-4 weeks
	Alternaria, anthracnose	B.s., Copper	Apply fungicide cover spray during full bloom and again in 3-4 weeks
Pineapple	Phytothphora, pythium	B.s.	Avoid overly wet soil; provide adequate drainage
Pomegranate	Leaf blotch	Copper	

B.s. = QST 13 strain of *Bacillus subtillis* (Natria Disease Control)

FRUIT DISEASE CHART

Fruit	Disease	Control Methods	Additional Information
Strawberry	Alternaria rot		Remove overripe berries
	Angular leaf spot	Copper	Plant certified, disease-free plants
	Anthracnose	*B.s.*	Use pathogen-free plants; varieties 'Carmine' and 'Sweet Charlie' are resistant; 'Strawberry Festival', 'Camarosa', and 'Treasure' are susceptible
	Botrytis (gray mold)	*B.s.*	Remove infected fruit and plant debris
	Leaf scorch		Reduce prolonged overhead irrigation
	Leaf spot	*B.s.*	Plant disease-free plants
	Phytothphora crown rot	*B.s.*	Plant disease-free plants
	Powdery mildew	*B.s.*	Use disease-resistant varieties; 'Strawberry Festival', 'Camarosa', and 'Winter Dawn' are quite susceptible

B.s. = QST 13 strain of *Bacillus subtillis* (Natria Disease Control)

GLOSSARY

Acclimation: Also called "hardening off." The process of subjecting young plants grown under ideal climatic conditions, such as in a greenhouse, to the fluctuating temperatures and humidity of the outdoors.

Acid soil: Soil with a pH below 7.0 on a scale of 0 to 14, with 7.0 being neutral. Most vegetables prefer soil pH in the 6.5 to 7.0 range.

Adjuvant: A substance that is added to pesticide sprays to help the chemical adhere or spread over plant surfaces. Also called "spreader sticker."

Aerobic: Any condition where oxygen is readily available. The addition of organic matter or peat to clay soils, for example, will increase the aerobic activity of the soil.

Alkaline soil: Soil with a pH above 7.0

Allelopathy: The harmful effects of one plant on another. Walnut and camphor leaves, for instance, should not be used as vegetable garden mulch because their leaves produce a harmful chemical that will prevent or dwarf another plant's growth.

Annual: A plant that grows from seed, flowers, and produces seed in one growing season. Peas and tomatoes are examples of annual plants.

Biennial: A plant that grows only leaves in the first season, and flowers and seeds in the second season. Beet, Brussels sprouts, cabbage, carrot, celery, lettuce, parsley, and Swiss chard are examples of biennial vegetables.

Blanching: 1.) The whitening of a particular plant part by excluding light. Cauliflower turns white when the leaves are tied together over the sprouting flowerhead, and endive (escarole) turns white when a board is placed over the leaves.

2.) The quick submersion of vegetables into boiling water to prevent the plant from changing sugars into starches. Peas, beans, and sweet corn are dipped into boiling water for 3 to 4 minutes prior to placing into a freezer for long-term storage.

Bolting: Going to seed. Lettuce will "bolt", or go to seed, late in its growing cycle due primarily to excessive heat. Leaves of bolting plants are usually bitter and inedible.

Broadcasting: The spreading of fertilizer, seeds, or soil amendments over a large area instead of in tight, straight rows or "drills."

Bt: An abbreviation of *Bacillus thuringiensis*, an organic bacteria harmful to any larvae (caterpillars) of moths and butterflies. Used to control armyworms, loopers, and hornworms on vegetables and fruit trees.

Bulb: Encased leaves or flowerbuds (as in an onion).

Carrot fly (or carrot maggot): A worm (that matures into a fly) that tunnels through the roots of carrots, ultimately causing the foliage to yellow and kill the entire plant. Do not plant carrots in the same location more than two years in a row and apply liberal amounts of wood ashes to the soil prior to sowing seeds as a preventative.

Central leader: The central, straight stem of a fruit tree with lateral branches that sprout from the stem's sides. Many fruit trees are pruned to create a central leader (such as plums and pears) while others (such as peaches and figs) are pruned to create a modified central leader to make it easier to pick the fruit.

Clay soil: A soil type comprised of very fine soil particles. Clay soils hold water and nutrients longer than sandy soils but can often become "waterlogged," which causes many plant diseases. Because clay holds onto nutrients for a long period, fewer fertilizer applications are required. Clay soil is characterized by a sticky, slimy feel when it's compressed in the hand.

Companion planting: The planting of plants together for symbiotic purposes. Often marigolds and nasturtiums are planted with vegetables because many gardeners think that they repel harmful pests.

Compost: Decomposed plant material that is used as mulch or as a soil amendment to improve the water- and nutrient-retention abilities of garden soil.

Crop rotation: The moving of the same type of plants from one area of a garden to another in subsequent years to deter pest infestations and to prevent the depletion of certain nutrients from the soil.

Cultivar: The end result of humans crossing positive traits of several different plants to develop a superior selection.

Cultivation: 1.) The hoeing or plowing of the soil to bring compost and nutrient-rich soil to the surface. 2.) The elimination of weeds by pulling their roots out of the ground using a pronged cultivator.

Curd: The unexpanded flower of cauliflower.

Cutworm: The larvae of an unadorned nocturnal moth that eats young seedlings at ground level or girdles older plants. Particularly susceptible vegetables include lettuce, corn, onion, and members of the Brassica family (cabbage, broccoli, and cauliflower). The worms usually hide beneath the soil surface during the daytime and emerge at night.

Damping off: The occurrence of a young seedling's stem rotting off at the soil level. To prevent dampening off, allow seedlings to slightly dry out between watering, space seeds far enough apart to ensure proper air circulation, and utilize pathogen-free soil mixes for seed germination.

Deciduous: Trees whose leaves fall off when they're no longer functional are called "deciduous." Many fruit trees (such as pear, plum, and peach) are deciduous, meaning they lose their leaves in the fall and produce new growth in the spring.

Dibble: A small hand tool with a sharp pointed end and a right-angle handle at the top. A dibble is used to plant young seedlings.

Direct sow (or direct seeding): Planting seeds directly into garden soil rather than planting them in trays or pots.

Drainage: The ability of water and nutrients to flow through the soil. Clay soils have very poor drainage because the particles are small and packed very closely together. Sandy soils have very good drainage because the individual soil particles are spaced far apart and water flows through them freely.

Drench: The liberal application of pesticides to the soil around the roots of a plant.

Dried blood: A fast-acting organic fertilizer containing 12 to 14 percent nitrogen.

Drift: Any part of a pesticide spray that travels beyond its intended target area.

Drill: A shallow furrow usually made for sowing seeds.

Drip line: 1.) An imaginary line on the soil surface below a tree canopy where the leaves shed raindrops. 2.) A term used to describe irrigation lines that emit small amounts of water, usually through emitters.

Drought: The depletion of water moisture in the soil due to lack of rainfall or inadequate irrigation.

Fertilizer: Anything that adds nutrients to the soil. Fertilizer is derived organically (such as fish emulsion, blood meal, and seaweed) or synthetically (examples include ammonia nitrate and muriate of potash). Synthetic fertilizers generally release nutrients faster than organic fertilizers. Organic fertilizers have to break down into compounds that plants can use and as a result often remain longer in the soil.

Fish meal: An organic fertilizer made of dried and pulverized fish manure. It has a nutrient content of 7-5-2 NPK (approximately).

Flat: A shallow tray used to germinate seeds that are later transplanted to the garden.

Friable: Used to describe soil that easily falls apart in your hand when released. Clay would be the opposite of friable because it is sticky and remains in a ball when released.

Fungicide: Any product that prevents, controls, or eradicates disease organisms. Copper and sulfur are examples of organic fungicides, and Maneb is a form of a non-organic or synthetic fungicide.

Garden line: A length of string secured at both ends by a peg that is inserted into the ground. It is used as a guide to plant straight rows of seeds or transplants.

Germination: Most often refers to the sprouting of a seed into a seedling.

Harden off: After seeds are germinated indoors under ideal conditions (adequate water, light, and temperature) the new seedlings have to be acclimated to the harsher conditions of the outdoors. Over a period of several days or sometimes weeks, young seedlings are exposed to varying temperatures and humidity to prepare them for planting them into the garden.

Horticulture: The science of growing plants.

Humus: Decaying plant material that is often rich and crumbly, and often added to garden soil to increase nutrition and water retention in sandy soils (and drainage in clay soils).

Hybrid: The crossbreeding of two plants with the goal being one plant that has positive characteristics of both parents. Sometimes referred to as a "selection."

Inorganic: Relating to fertilizer, whether synthetic or natural form, of mineral origin. Relating to plants, neither plant nor animal origin.

Insecticide: Any organic or synthetic product that controls or kills insects. Insecticides can be found in liquid or powered form and produced from organic sources (such as pyrethrum, rotenone, and Neem oil) or synthetic sources (such as carbaryl).

Integrated Pest Management: An environmentally sensitive approach to pest management that relies on a combination of up-to-date information on pests with a wide variety of pest control methods. IPM is used to manage pest damage with the least possible hazard to people and the environment.

Interplanting: The planting of short-day crops (such as lettuce) in the same row or hill as a long-day crop (such as broccoli) to maximize space. Radishes can be planted 12 inches apart with carrots to mark the slower-germinating carrots' location. Radishes can be harvested 30 days later, leaving the carrots to grow for another 100 days.

Irrigation: The addition of water, often with nutrients, to sustain plant growth.

Larva: The immature stage of an insect. Several insects have larval stages in their transformation from an egg to an adult, and depending on the insect, can be described as a caterpillar, maggot, or grub.

Leaching: The loss of nutrients through soil due to downward water migration. Leaching is worse in sandy soils where the individual soil particles are spaced farther apart and water (with nutrients) flows freely downward.

Leaf beetles: A large family of insects that in both the larval and adult phase of life eat leaves. Examples of leaf beetles include the Colorado potato beetle, flea beetles, cucumber beetles, and bean leaf beetles.

Leafminers: The larvae of an insect that eats the tissue between the upper and lower leaf tissue of plants that results in a "squiggly" white line on the upper surface of the leaf.

Lesion: A defined area of diseased tissue such as that caused by a leaf spot.

Lifting: The removal of a plant from the ground, as in harvesting potatoes or peanuts.

Lime: A substance containing calcium that is used in varying quantities to reduce the acidity of soils.

Limestone: A rock that is used as a source of lime (when ground into powder form) to reduce soil acidity.

Liquid feeding: The application of water-soluble fertilizers to plants.

Loam: A general term used in all types of gardening that describes a soil that is of high quality, rich in organic matter, holds onto water, and is tilled easily.

Maggot: A general term used to describe the legless form of fly larvae. Maggots are particularly harmful to vegetable root crops and to ripening tree fruit.

Manure: A general term used to describe any material from animals or plants that, when added to the soil, increases the soil fertility and tilth. Examples of green manures include a number of cover crops like alfalfa or oats. Manures from horses, chickens, and cows are commonly used in the vegetable garden once they have decomposed.

Micronutrients: Nutrients necessary for plant growth but used in extremely small quantities in comparison to macronutrients (NPKMg).

Mildew: Many vegetable plants and fruit trees are susceptible to a variety of diseases; one group is evident by a white or black powdery residue on the upper surfaces of the leaves. Powdery mildew, downy mildew, and sooty mold are included in this group.

Mites: A group of insectlike pests with eight legs and piercing mouthparts that remove plant juices from the upper and lower leaf surface, leaving a "stipple" appearance on the upper surface. Mites are usually found on the undersides of leaves and on stems.

Mold: Visible fungus spores on leaves, flowers, and stems. Examples of molds include sooty mold (black soot on upper leaf surfaces of many plants) and gray mold usually seen on flowers and fruit.

Mulch: Any product placed on top of the soil around plants to reduce weeds, reduce water evaporation, and moderate soil temperatures. Mulches can take the form of sheets of plastic, single layers of newspaper covered with straw or leaves, wood chips, or bark. In the vegetable garden, mulch is often tilled into the soil after the growing season to increase the amount of organic matter.

Neck: The upper part of a bulb where the foliage and flowers emerge.

Nitrogen: One of the big four macronutrients used by growing plants. Nitrogen is the first letter of the letters NPKMg found on a fertilizer bag. Nitrogen is primarily responsible for the production of new growth and stems.

NPKMg: The combined chemical symbols (Nitrogen, Phosphorous, Potassium, and Magnesium) used in large quantities by vegetables and fruit trees.

Nutrients: Necessary elements and compounds used in plant growth. Nutrient deficiencies are determined by analyzing soil samples and then adding fertilizers and/or composts. Macronutrients are those compounds used in large quantities of plants and include Nitrogen, Phosphorous, Potassium, and Magnesium. Micronutrients (trace elements) are essential to plant growth but are used in smaller quantities; these include sulfur, manganese, copper, calcium, zinc, boron, molybdenum, and chlorine.

Organic gardening: A gardening method that utilizes natural substances to grow plants. Forms of pest control in organic gardening include crop rotation, weed control, mulching, resistant hybrid selection, and using natural predators. Nutrition in organic gardens is added by natural products such as cover crops, fish meal, and dried blood.

Organic matter: Substances in the soil that include dead or dying plant matter. Organic matter in the soil aids in water retention, enzyme production necessary for plant growth, and feeds good fungi that help plants grow.

Peat: As in "peat moss"; decayed ancient plant material is added to clay soils to aid in drainage and to sandy soil to retain water and add organic matter to the soil. Peat is sold in small bags or large bales.

Pelletized seed: Very small seeds are sometimes covered by seed producers with an inert coating making them larger in diameter and therefore easier to distribute in the garden or in seed trays.

pH: A scale used to determine the acidity or alkalinity of garden soils. The scale ranges from 0 to 14 with zero being acid, 14 being alkaline, and 7 being neutral. Most vegetable plants and fruit trees prefer a pH of 6.5 to 7.0 with notable exceptions such as blueberry, which grows best in 4.5 to 6.0.

Phosphorous: One of the four macronutrients used by growing plants. Phosphorous is the second letter of the NPKMg found on a fertilizer bag and is utilized by plants to grow a strong root system and help cells divide. It is rarely added to Florida soils given the high quantities found naturally.

Pinching: The clipping off of the very tips of plants to encourage new growth along the remaining stems.

Planting board: A piece of flat wood, 10 to 12 inches wide, placed in the vegetable garden used in the planting of seeds and transplants. A gardener will use a planting board to kneel on to prevent soil compaction between the rows and to provide a straight edge for creating a furrow or drill.

Plug: A seedling grown in a single unit, usually in a cell-pack purchased from a garden center or nursery.

Potassium: One of the big four macronutrients used by growing plants. Potassium is the third letter of the NPKMg found on a fertilizer bag and is primarily responsible for helping a plant resist diseases. In sandy soil potassium leaches readily and should be replaced according to the results of soil test analysis.

Potbound (or rootbound): Describing the roots of a plant that have completely filled the container in which it was grown. Potbound plants rarely recover from this unacceptable condition and should be avoided when purchasing plants for the garden.

Powdery mildew: A white fungal residue that appears on the upper leaf surfaces of vegetables when nighttime temperatures are in the 60 to 65 degree range. The fungus is controllable by several organic compounds including copper and sulfur. Plants often killed by powdery mildew include cucumbers and squash.

Pyrethrum: A safe organic pesticide made from the flowers of certain species of the chrysanthemum plant.

Raised bed: An elevated garden usually made of wide boards, in an open box-shape laid on top of the ground, and filled with soil. Raised beds are often used by gardeners who have a difficult time bending to plant vegetables or pull weeds. They are also used in areas where the native soil and/or drainage are so poor that a raised bed with enhanced soil may be the only method that will produce crops.

Riddle: A wire-mesh pan used to sift soil when covering seeds. Riddles have interchangeable mesh screen sizes depending on the type of seed being covered and particle size required.

Rootstock: The roots of a particular plant with qualities that make it resistant to diseases and insects that other plants are grafted to it. Oranges such as 'Fallglo' and 'Ambersweet' are fine tasting oranges but do not have a resistance to an assortment of diseases. Pieces of the preferred orange are joined to a tougher, hardy rootstock, most commonly *Poncirus trifoliata*. The rootstock flourishes despite the harsh conditions, and the grafted part of the plant (above the graft) performs well because of the tough roots below. Many fruit trees are grafted this way.

Rose: The pierced end of a watering can from which the water is applied.

Rotenone: An organic insecticide made of the ground-up roots of a tropical legume (*Lonchocarpus*).

Rototiller: A cultivator with an engine attached that is used to till the soil prior to planting and later to cultivate between rows.

Sandy soil: Any soil which has a large percentage of sand particles. Sandy soils are common throughout Florida. They are well drained and characterized by high aerobic activity.

Secateurs (pruning shears): Hand-held pruners used to remove small branches up to ½ inch in diameter.

Seedbed: An area of soil, either indoors or outdoors, that has been prepared to accept seeds for planting.

Seed tray: A shallow pan filled with potting soil used to germinate seeds which are then transplanted into pots or directly out into the garden.

Seedling: A young plant, usually one grown from a seed.

Sidedress: The application of fertilizers to the soil in straight rows adjacent to plant stems. Sidedressing usually occurs midway through a vegetable's life span to encourage additional new growth and new fruit.

Slow release: Often refers to various fertilizers that release their nutrients over a long period of time.

Soil test: The collection of soil samples, which are then analyzed for available nutrients and levels of acidity or alkalinity (pH).

Soluble fertilizer: Any fertilizer that quickly dissolves in water.

Sooty mold: A fungi that lives on the topsides of leaves and is nourished by aphids and/or scale insects living on the undersides of leaves. Once the pests have been controlled the sooty mold sloughs off soon after.

Spade: A hand tool (usually 40 inches or so long) generally with a sharp, square metal blade used for digging holes in the garden.

Stone fruits: The name given to a group of fruits characterized by a hard "stone" protecting an inner seed. Peaches and plums are examples of stone fruits.

Straw: The dried stems of many grain crops (and other plants) bound in bales and used as mulch to moderate soil temperatures, retain soil moisture, and eliminate weeds in the garden. Straw is different from hay, the latter often containing an abundance of weed seeds. The most common straw used in Florida vegetable gardens (and the most attractive) is called coastal hay or salt marsh hay.

Succession planting: The planting of new vegetable seeds or plants into the garden after a crop has been harvested. Because vegetables mature at different rates, young plants and maturing plants will often occupy the vegetable garden at the same time.

Tendril: A small, modified leaf that can twirl around upright structures and support the entire plant. English peas are an example of a plant that has tendrils.

Thinning: The removal of seedlings that are growing too close together for optimum growth. Thinning can occur in seed trays, cell-packs, plugs, and in the garden row. Plants that are allowed to grow too close together often don't grow properly and compete with available nutrients in the soil. Thinning can be simply removing unwanted seedlings with the thumb and forefinger or by cutting them off at ground level with a sharp pair of scissors. The distances at which individual plants grow best are usually printed on the seed package.

Tiller: See rototiller.

Tilth: An old European term that describes soil 1.) with proper nutrient levels, 2.) that crumbles between the fingers, and 3.) that has good drainage. Soil with good tilth is especially good for a seedbed.

Topsoil: A term generally used for well-prepared soil with good water retention and nutrition in contrast to sub soil, which has few, if any, good properties for growing plants.

Trace elements: Often called micronutrients, most plants need a wide variety of nutrients but in very small quantities. Trace elements can be added to the soil by applying micronutrient-rich fertilizers. Trace elements include boron, manganese, copper, molybdenum, sulfur, and others.

Transplant: 1.) A young seedling that is large enough to be moved into the garden. 2.) The act of moving a plant.

Trowel: A small hand tool used to dig small holes for small plants.

True leaves: Leaves that are produced by a seedling after the first leaves have sprouted from the seed. True leaves resemble a small version of the plant's mature leaves.

Turgor: The stiffness of a plant leaf. Wilting plants have low turgor and water-rich plants have high turgor.

Viability: The capability of a seed to germinate. Many vegetable seeds retain high viability for many years if stored in an airtight container with temperatures above 34°F and below 45°F.

Virus: A microscopic organism that damages or kills plants. The most common viruses among vegetables include tobacco mosaic and cucumber mosaic virus.

Watering can: Usually a 2-gallon metal or plastic container.

with a long neck and a rose at one end used to gently apply water to plants.

Winter garden: In growing vegetables, it refers to those plants that can withstand or prefer cold temperatures to grow. See pages 36–39 for a list of plants for the winter garden.

Wireworms: The larvae stage of certain beetles that commonly attack vegetable root crops including potatoes, turnips, and carrots. Crop rotation is important in the reduction of wireworms. The application of wood ash to the furrow will deter wireworms also.

Wood chips: Chipped tree trunks and limbs suitable for walkways through the garden. The addition of wood chips to garden soil will cause nitrogen depletion as the individual pieces of wood decompose.

RESOURCES

Seeds

W. Atlee Burpee Co.
Warminster, PA 18974
- Orders   800-888-1447
- Fax   800-487-5530
- Website   www.Burpee.com

The Cook's Garden
P.O. Box 535
Londonberry, VT 05148
- Orders   800-457-9703
- Fax   800-457-9705
- Website   www.cooksgarden.com

Harris Seeds
355 Paul Road
Rochester, NY 14624 ·
- Orders   800-544-7938

Johnny's Selected Seeds
Winslow, Maine 04901
- Orders   877-564-6697

Park Seed Company
1 Parkton Ave
Greenwood, SC 29647
- Orders   800-213-0076
- Website   www.parkseed.com

Seeds of Change
P.O. Box 15700
Santé Fe, NM 87506
- Orders   888-762-7333
- Website   www.seedsofchange.com

Renee's Garden Seeds
6060 Graham Hill Rd. Suite A
Felton, CA 95018
- Orders   888-880-7228
- Website   www.reneesgarden.com

Stokes Seeds
PO Box 548
Buffalo, New York 14240-0548
- Orders   800-396-9238
- Fax   888-834-3334
- Website   www.stokeseeds.com

Tomato Growers Supply
P.O. Box 60015
Ft. Myers, FL 33906
- Orders   888-478-7333
- Fax   888-768-3476
- Website   www.tomatogrowers.com

Vermont Bean Seed Co.
334 West Stroud Road
Randolph, WI 53956
- Orders   800-349-1071
- Website   www.Vermontbean.com

Fruit

Hopkins Tropicals Nursery
25355 Shultz Grade,
Immokalee, FL 34142
- Orders   239-658-0370
- Website   www.hopkinstropicals.com

Chestnut Hills Tree Farm
15105 NW 94 Ave
Alachua, FL 32615
- Orders   800-669-2067
- Fax   386-462-4330
- Website   www.chestnuthilltreefarm.com

Pine Island Nursery
16300 SW 184 Street
Miami, FL 33187
- Orders   305-233-5501
- Fax   305-233-5610
- Website   www.tropicalfruitnursery.com

Going Bananas
24401 SW 197 Avenue
Homestead, FL 33031
- Orders   305-247-0397
- Fax   305-247-7877
- Website   www.going-bananas.com

Excalibur Fruit Trees
5200 Fearnley Road
Lake Worth, FL 33467-5650
- Orders   561-969-6988
- Fax   561-641-3028
- Website   www.excaliburfruittrees.com

INDEX

Main entries are in **boldface**.

MEET ROBERT BOWDEN

Robert Bowden is the Executive Director of the renowned Leu Gardens in Orlando, Florida. He served in the same capacity at the Atlanta Botanical Gardens and as Director of Horticulture at the Missouri Botanical Garden. A prolific media presence, Bowden's photographs and fun-filled essays have appeared in *The New York Times* and in such magazines as *Garden Design*, *Traditional Home*, and *Southern Accents*. Bowden appears regularly on a variety of nationally syndicated television shows including Discovery Channel's *Home Matters*, *Rebecca's Garden*, HGTV's *Way To Grow!*, and *Victory Garden*. Robert travels extensively in the United States and the Caribbean talking about vegetables, perennials, tropical and sub-tropical plants, flowering vines, trees, and shrubs.

When he's not on the road, speaking to groups, taking photographs, writing books, or serving as the "answer man" for all kinds of gardening, Robert can be found in his own garden in Longwood, Florida.

WINTER

_____
_____
_____
_____
_____
_____
_____
_____
_____

SPRING

_____
_____
_____
_____
_____
_____
_____
_____
_____
_____

SUMMER

_____

_____

_____

_____

_____

_____

_____

_____

_____

FALL

_____

_____

_____

_____

_____

_____

_____

_____

_____

_____